The University in Ruins

∼ *BILL READINGS*

The University in Ruins

Harvard University Press
Cambridge, Massachusetts, and London, England

Library of Congress Cataloging-in-Publication Data

Readings, Bill, 1960–
    The university in ruins / Bill Readings.
            p.   cm.
Includes bibliographical references (p.   ) and index.

ISBN 0-674-92952-7 (cloth)
ISBN 0-674-92953-5 (pbk.)
1. Education, Higher—Aims and objectives.
2. Education, Higher—United States—Aims and objectives.
3. Education, Higher—Social aspects.
4. Higher education and state.
5. Nationalism and education.
I. Title.
LB2322.2.R42   1996
378′.001—dc20   95-47290
CIP

∿ Contents

~ Foreword

Bill Readings was in the process of making the final revisions to this book when he died in the crash of American Eagle flight 4184 on October 31, 1994. I completed the revisions on which Bill was working, taking his notes and our many conversations as my guide.

Editing each other's work was once just something Bill and I did. At the time, it never seemed extraordinary; it never seemed like something that would need to be talked about, something that would mark, as it does now, the line dividing life from death. Revision and conversation—with me, with friends and colleagues, with students—were Bill's way of trying to create possibilities for thinking together.

If there is anything I could say about how this book evolved, how Bill imagined it would continue to evolve, it would have to be in terms of the many conversations that informed it and the many more that he hoped would follow from it. Dwelling in the ruins of the University was not usually a silent occasion for Bill. Talk—whether it led to agreement or disagreement, whether it was serious or silly—had everything to do with how he worked, thought, and envisioned a future for the University.

To say that conversation with Bill can never again take place is to acknowledge the painful finality of his death. And to insist on talk as a part of the very fabric of this book is perhaps a step toward acknowledging the singularity of a voice, a place, and a time which would not exist apart from the University.

Diane Elam
Montréal, 1995

✑ Acknowledgments

It is hard work to be excellent, since in each case it is hard work to find what is intermediate.

Aristotle, *Nichomachean Ethics*

The writing of this book has been made possible in the first place by grants from the Québec Fonds pour la Formation de Chercheurs et l'Aide à la Recherche and the Canadian Social Sciences and Humanities Research Council. Besides the infrastructural support that these grants have provided, they have enabled me to work in collaboration with other members, both students and faculty, of the research team "L'Université et la Culture: La Crise Identitaire d'une Institution" at the Université de Montréal, and to benefit from a number of important conversations with speakers invited by the group. The main argument of this book was developed in the course of directing a pluridisciplinary seminar at the Université de Montréal on the topic "La Culture et ses Institutions," and I am grateful to the students, faculty, and members of the community who participated. My pressing sense of the urgency of the question of the University as an institution of culture goes back even further, to the beginnings of a number of debates with former colleagues at the Université de Genève and at Syracuse University. An invitation from the graduate students of the Department of English and Comparative Literature at the State University of New York at Buffalo first made me aware that I had something that I wanted to say on the topic. Further productive opportunities to test the general argument were offered by conferences at the University of Western Ontario, the State University of New York at Stonybrook, the Commonwealth Center for Literary and Cultural Change at the University of Virginia, Trent

University, the University of California at Irvine and at San Diego, the University of Wales at Cardiff, Stirling University, and the Université de Genève. Finally, my thanks are due to Gilles Dupuis and Sean Spurvey for preparing the index.

Earlier versions of parts of the book have been published in the following journals, and are reprinted with permission: "Privatizing Culture," *Angelaki*, 2, no. 1 (1995); "The University without Culture," *New Literary History* 26, no. 3 (1995); "Dwelling in the Ruins," *Oxford Literary Review* 17, nos. 1–2 (1995); "For a Heteronomous Cultural Politics," *Oxford Literary Review*, 15, nos. 1–2 (1993); "Be Excellent: The Posthistorical University," *Alphabet City*, 3; "Identity Crisis: The University and Culture," *Association of Canadian College and University Teachers of English Newsletter*, June 1993.

I have forborne to name the individuals who have influenced this book because they are so many and because I am not sure whether I would be doing them a favor. I will, however, take the risk of mentioning by name the person who first made me aware that the University could be a place to think: Ann Wordsworth. She taught me about something that Oxford called "Critical Theory" and she did so on a short-term contract, teaching in a hut in the garden of one of the brick mansions of North Oxford. I dedicate this book to her.

Bill Readings

The University in Ruins

~ 1

Introduction

Jeremiads abound concerning the "betrayal" and "bankruptcy" of the project of liberal education.[1] Teaching, we are told, is undervalued in favor of research, while research is less and less in touch with the demands of the real world, or with the comprehension of the "common reader." Nor is this—as some academics seem to believe—just the lament of the middlebrow media, motivated by media commentators' resentment at their failure to gain access to the hallowed groves of academe. Forever deprived of the chance to sit on the Faculty Promotions Committee, such pundits, it is claimed, take out their frustrations on the University, constrained as they are to content themselves with huge salaries and comfortable working conditions. The causes of the media's sniping at the University are not individual resentments but a more general uncertainty as to the role of the University and the very nature of the standards by which it should be judged as an institution. It is no coincidence that such attacks are intensifying in North America at the same time as the structure of the academic institution is shifting.

It is not merely that the professoriat is being proletarianized as a body and the number of short-term or part-time contracts at major institutions increased (with the concomitant precipitation of a handful of highly paid stars).[2] The production of knowledge within the University is equally uncertain. An internal legitimation struggle concerning the nature of the knowledge produced in the humanities, for example, would not take on crisis proportions were it not accompanied by an external legitimation crisis. Disputes within individual disciplines as to methods and theories of research would not hit the headlines, were it not that the very notion of a research project is now a troubled one. Thus, the impulse behind this book is not simply to argue that the University needs to recognize that new theoretical advances in particle physics or literary studies render old paradigms of study and teaching obsolete. Nor is this book simply another attempt to engage with the web of conflicting and often contradictory sentiments that currently surround the University. Rather, I want to perform a structural diagnosis of contemporary shifts in the University's function as an institution, in order to argue that the wider social role of the University as an institution is now up for grabs. It is no longer clear what the place of the University is within society nor what the exact nature of that society is, and the changing institutional form of the University is something that intellectuals cannot afford to ignore.

But first, some preliminary warnings. In this book I will focus on a certain Western notion of the University, which has been widely exported and whose current mutation seems likely to continue to frame the terms of transnational discussion. If I also pay particular attention to the changes currently occurring in the North American University, this is because the process of "Americanization" cannot be understood as simply the expansion of U.S. cultural hegemony. In fact, I shall argue, "Americanization" in its current form is a synonym for globalization, a synonym that recognizes that globalization is not a neutral process in which Washington and Dakar participate equally. The obverse of this inequitable coin is that the process of expropriation by transnational capital that globalization names is something from which the United States and Canada are currently suffering, a process graphically described by the study of Flint, Michigan, in the film *Roger and Me*. The film's director, Michael Moore, traces the profound impoverishment of the once-rich town of Flint, as a result of the flight of capital to more profitable areas—despite the fact that General Motors was in relatively good economic health at the time of the plant closings. The resulting devastation of Flint (after failed attempts to make it into a tourist destination by opening the "Autoworld" theme park) means that the majority of new jobs available there today are in minimum-wage service industries. "Americanization" today names less a process of national imperialism than the generalized imposition of the rule of the cash-nexus in place of the notion of national identity as determinant of all aspects of investment in social life. "Americanization," that is, implies the end of national culture.

The current shift in the role of the University is, above all, determined by the decline of the national cultural mission that has up to now provided its *raison d'être*, and I will argue that the prospect of the European Union places the universities of Europe under a similar horizon, both in the states of the European Union and in Eastern Europe, where projects such as those of George Soros sketch a similar separation of the University from the idea of the nation-state.[3] In short, the University is becoming a different kind of institution, one that is no longer linked to the destiny of the nation-state by virtue of its role as producer, protector, and inculcator of an idea of national culture. The process of economic globalization brings with it the relative decline of the nation-state as the prime instance of the reproduction of capital around the world. For its part, the University is becoming a transnational bureaucratic corporation, either tied to transnational instances of government such as the European Union or functioning independently, by analogy with a transnational corporation. The recent publication by UNESCO of Alfonso Borrero Cabal's *The University as an Institution Today* provides a good example of the terms in which this move towards the status of a bureaucratic corporation may occur.[4] Borrero Cabal focuses upon the *administrator* rather than the professor as the central figure of the University, and figures the University's tasks in terms of a generalized logic of "accountability" in which the University must pursue "excellence" in all aspects of its functioning. The current crisis of the University in the West proceeds from a fundamental shift in its social role and internal systems, one which means that the centrality of the traditional humanistic disciplines to the life of the University is no longer assured.

In making such a wide-ranging diagnosis, I am, of course, going to tend to ignore the process of uneven and combined development, the different speeds at which the discourse of "excellence" replaces the ideology of (national) culture in various institutions and various countries. For instance, in a move that might seem to head in the opposite direction to that suggested by my argument about the nation-state, the British conservative party is currently attempting to install a uniform "national curriculum." The proposed educational "reforms" in Britain are not, however, inconsistent with what I will be arguing. This is a book about the spinning off of *tertiary* education from the nation-state, and such a move will probably accentuate the structural differences between secondary education and universities, especially as concerns their link to the state. Furthermore, the fact that an institution as ancient as New College, Oxford, should have begun to attach an announcement of its dedication to "excellence" to all public announcements such as job advertisements seems to me more indicative of long-term trends in higher education.

Just as this book will focus on a certain "Americanization" that moves the University further away from direct ties to the nation-state, it will also tend to privilege the humanities in its attempt to understand what is going on in the contemporary University. This emphasis likewise needs a few words of preliminary explanation. In choosing to focus on the notion of "culture" as I do, I may give the impression that the humanities are the essence of the University, the place where the University's sociopolitical mission is accomplished. This would be unfortunate for at least two important reasons. First, I do not believe the natural sciences to be positivist projects for the neutral accumulation of knowledge, which are therefore in principle sheltered from sociopolitical troubles. As I shall argue, the *decline* of the nation-state—and I do believe that despite resurgent nationalisms the nation-state is declining—and the end of the Cold War are having a significant effect on the funding and organization of the natural sciences. Secondly, the separation between the humanities and the sciences is not as absolute as the University's own disciplinary walls may lead one to believe. The natural sciences take their often extremely powerful place in the University *by analogy* with the humanities. This is particularly the case when it comes to the sources of the narratives in terms of which pedagogy is understood. For example, when I asked a recipient of the Nobel Prize for physics to describe what he understood to be the goal of

4

undergraduate education in physics, he replied that it was to introduce students to "the culture of physics."[5] His drawing on C. P. Snow seems to me both very canny and fair, given that the contested status of knowledge in physics—the fact that undergraduates learn things that they will later discard if they pursue their studies—requires a model of knowledge as a *conversation* among a community rather than as a simple accumulation of facts. It is in terms of a model of the institutionalization of knowledge of which the humanities—and especially departments of philosophy and national literature—have been the historical guardians that the institutional fact of the natural sciences in the University has to be understood. In this sense, the general thrust of my argument that the notion of culture as the legitimating idea of the modern University has reached the end of its usefulness may be understood to apply to the natural sciences as well as to the humanities, although it is in the humanities that the delegitimation of culture is most directly perceived as a threat.[6]

As someone who teaches in a humanities department (although one that bears almost no resemblance to the department in which I was "trained"), I have written this book out of a deep ambivalence about an institution: it is an attempt to think my way out of an impasse between militant radicalism and cynical despair. I am still inclined to introduce sentences that begin "In a *real* University . . ." into discussions with my colleagues, even though they know, and I know that they know, that no such institution has ever existed. This would not be a problem were it not that such appeals to the true nature of the institution no longer seem to me to be honest: it is no longer the case, that is, that we can conceive the University within the historical horizon of its self-realization. The University, I will claim, no longer participates in the historical project for humanity that was the legacy of the Enlightenment: the historical project of culture. Such a claim also raises some significant questions of its own: Is this a new age dawning for the University as a project, or does it mark the twilight of the University's critical and social function? And if it is the twilight, then what does that mean?

Some might want to call this moment to which I am referring the "postmodernity" of the University. After all, one of the most discussed books on postmodernity is Jean-François Lyotard's *The Postmodern Condition,* a study of the implications of the questions posed to the legitimation of knowledge by postmodernity. Lyotard's book is explicitly framed as a report on the University for the government of Québec, a report which doubtless was something of a disappointment to its patrons, despite its later success. Lyotard argues that it is written "at this very Postmodern moment that finds the University nearing what may be its end."[7] The question of the postmodern is a question posed *to* the University as much as in the University. Yet since the postmodern has by and large ceased to function as a question and has become another alibi in the name of which intellectuals denounce the world for failing to live up to their expectations, I prefer to drop the term. The danger is apparent: it is so easy to slip into speaking of the "postmodern University" as if it were an imaginable institution, a newer, more critical institution, which is to say, *an even more modern* University than the modern University. I would prefer to call the contemporary University "posthistorical" rather than "postmodern" in order to insist upon the sense that the institution has outlived itself, is now a survivor of the era in which it defined itself in terms of the project of the *historical* development, affirmation, and inculcation of national culture.

What I think becomes apparent here is that to speak of the University and the state is also to tell a story about the emergence of the notion of culture. I shall argue that the University and the state as we know them are essentially *modern* institutions, and that the emergence of the concept of culture should be understood as a particular way of dealing with the tensions between these two institutions of modernity. However, before anyone gets the wrong idea, this is not because I am simply going to bash the University. I work in a University—sometimes I feel I live in it. It is far too easy simply to critique the University, and there is hardly anything new in doing so. After all, the specificity of the modern University that the German Idealists founded was its status as the site of critique. As Fichte put it, the University exists not to teach information but to inculcate the exercise of critical judgment.[8] In this sense, it might seem that all critiques of the modern University are

6

internal policy documents that do not affect the deep structure of the institutionalization of thought.

It is also worth mentioning right from the beginning that when I speak of the "modern" University I am referring to the German model, widely copied, that Humboldt instituted at the University of Berlin and that still served for the postwar expansion of tertiary education in the West. I would argue that we are now in the twilight of this model, as the University becomes posthistorical. In this context, Allan Bloom's *The Closing of the American Mind* seems to me to be more in touch with reality than the liberal nostrums of Jaroslav Pelikan in his *The Idea of the University*, which recalls us to a lost mission of liberal education.[9] Bloom's conservative jeremiad at least recognizes that the autonomy of knowledge as an end in itself is threatened, because there is no longer a *subject* that might incarnate this principle, hence Bloom's repeated ridiculing of much of what goes on in the University as unintelligible and irrelevant to any student (read young-white-male-American student). Pelikan, on the other hand, prefaces his work with a Newman-esque pun that suggests that *The Idea of the University* might well have been retitled *Apologia pro vita sua*. This pun arouses my suspicion because I am inclined to agree with Bloom's conclusion that the story of what he calls "the adventure of a liberal education" no longer has a hero.[10] Neither a student hero to embark upon it, nor a professor hero as its end.

Some sense of how this came about can be grasped from reading a text such as Jacques Barzun's *The American University: How It Runs, Where It Is Going*.[11] This work, which dates from 1968, has recently been reprinted by the University of Chicago Press, a remarkable feat for a text that claims a contemporary relevance in the 1990s and yet which was self-consciously out of date at the time of its first publication. Barzun remarks in a May 1968 postscript to the January 1968 preface (an ironic locus if ever there were one)[12] that he sees "no reason to change or add to the substance" of a text completed six weeks prior to the student "outbreak of April 23 [1968] that disrupted the work of Columbia University" (xxxvi). This insouciance might seem strange in a work centered on the question of how an administrator is to act. Yet it is less paradoxical once we realize that the narrative upon which Barzun is engaged is that of the production of the enlightened and liberal administrator as the new hero of the story of the University. Thus Barzun explicitly proposes the formation of an autonomous stratum of non-academic administrators within the University, a "second layer": "If caught young, such men [*sic*] can become top civil-servants and be accepted as professionals without being scholars; they can enjoy a prestige of their own and share fully in the amenities that are widely believed to adorn campus life; and they can do more than any other agency, human or electronic, to render efficient the workings of the great machine" (19). The central figure of the University is no longer the professor who is both scholar and teacher but the provost to whom both these apparatchiks and the professors are answerable. The difference between Barzun and Newman is that Barzun has realized what kind of liberal individual it is that must embody the new University. The administrator will have been a student and a professor in his time, of course, but the challenge of the contemporary University is a challenge addressed to him *as administrator*.

Herein lie the origins of the idea of excellence that I discuss in the next chapter. It should be noted, though, that Barzun does not feel the need to have recourse to the notion of excellence and is able to recognize that excellence is a "shadow" (222); whereas Herbert I. London, writing an introduction to the reissue of Barzun's text twenty-five years later, bemoans the fact that "excellence" is no longer as *real* as it was in Barzun's day (222n), since there has been a "virtual abandonment of the much touted goal of excellence" (xxviii). Thus we can make the observation that Barzun appears as the John the Baptist of excellence, preparing the way for the new law ("excellence") in the language of the old ("standards"), while London appears as St. Paul, telling us that the new law will be real only if it is as strictly applied as the Old. Things have speeded up since Christ's day, since the elapsed time required for the re-postponement of messianic promise is now down from thirty-five to twenty-five years.

Yet in comparing Barzun with the contemporaries who invoke him, I want above all to remark upon a question of tone: the tone that differentiates Barzun's work (and Pelikan's) from the denunciations of

Allan Bloom or even of Herbert London in his 1993 reintroduction of Barzun's book. The remarkable difference is the loss of the mellifluent pomposity consequent upon entire self-satisfaction, and its replacement by vitriolic complaint. This is particularly clear with regard to the question of sexism. Throughout his text, Barzun refers to professors by the metonym "men." Let me take Barzun's description of the plight of the young graduate student as an example: "after the orals a dissertation has to be written—how and on what matters less than how quickly. For many topics Europe or other foreign parts are inescapable and disheartening!—Fulbright, children, wife working (or also a candidate), more library work, and in a foreign tongue—it is a nightmare" (228). Where Barzun remarks vaguely that women can indeed fulfill secretarial roles adequately in the University and perhaps even pursue graduate studies as a way of preparing themselves to bear the children of their male counterparts, Bloom and London see their University threatened by raving harpies.[13] Where Barzun sees silliness and calls it "preposterism," London sees "contamination" (xxviii). Despite the fact that books about the University marked by the enormous self-satisfaction of its (male) products are still being written (Pelikan is a case in point), it is clear that a significant shift has taken place. It is not that our times are more troubled; after all, Barzun pronounces himself untroubled by 1968. Rather, the problem that both Bloom and London labor under is that no one of us can seriously imagine him or herself as the hero of the story of the University, as the instantiation of the cultivated individual that the entire great machine works night and day to produce.

My own reluctance to assume the tone of self-satisfaction with which many of my predecessors presumably felt comfortable is not a matter of personal modesty. After all, I have not waited for the twilight of my career to write a book about the University. What counts, and what marks the tone of contemporary diatribes, is that the grand narrative of the University, centered on the production of a liberal, reasoning, subject, is no longer readily available to us. There is thus no point in my waiting. I am not going to become Jacques Barzun; the University system does not need such subjects any more. The liberal *individual* is no longer capable of metonymically embodying the *institution*. None of us can now seriously assume ourselves to be the centered subject of a narrative of University education. Feminism is exemplary here for its introduction of a radical awareness of gender difference, as are analyses that call attention to the ways in which bodies are differentially marked by race. Both are targeted by the old guard, because they remind them that no individual professor can embody the University, since that body *would still be gendered and racially marked* rather than universal.

Given this condition, I am *not*, however, advising that we give up on the University, offering in its place reasons to indulge in cynical despair. In this book I will discuss how we can reconceive the University once the story of liberal education has lost its organizing center—has lost, that is, the idea of culture as the object, as both origin and goal, of the human sciences. My sense of this is the more acute because the particular University in which I work occupies a peculiar position nowadays. This position may seem outdated to those unaware that Québec, like Northern Ireland, is an area within the territory of the G7 group of industrialized nations where nation-statehood is still a contemporary political issue of consequence rather than a vestigial outgrowth to the increasing integration of the global economy. The Université de Montréal is a flagship of Québec culture that only recently replaced the church as the primary institution with responsibility for francophone culture in North America. Working at a flagship University of a nation-state (especially a nascent one) confers enormous benefits in that our activities of teaching and research have yet to be entirely submitted to the free play of market forces; they do not yet have to justify themselves in terms of optimal performance or return on capital.

My sense of this is the stronger in that I used to work at Syracuse University, which does have the ambition of being entirely market driven, a notion that the administration called "The Pursuit of Excellence." Hence the then-Chancellor, Melvin Eggers, repeatedly characterized Syracuse as an aggressive institution that modeled itself on the corporation rather than clinging to ivy-covered walls. Interestingly, during my time at Syracuse, the University logo was changed. Instead of the academic seal with its Latin motto affixed to University letterhead and other documents, a new, explicitly "corporate" logo was developed, and the seal reserved solely for official academic documents such as degree certificates. This seems to me directly symptomatic of the reconception of the University as a corporation, one of whose functions (products?) is the granting of degrees with a cultural cachet, but whose overall nature is corporate rather than cultural.

To analyze the University solely in terms of cultural capital, however, would be to miss the point that this is now merely one field of operation. Syracuse's rhetorical rejection of symbolic capital in favor of "bottom-line" accounting (which carried through into the decision-making process of the administration and the corporate executive ethos favored by deans) unsurprisingly meant that the percentage of alumni who gave gifts to the University was considerably lower than at other comparable institutions, since everything in the lives of students encouraged them to think of themselves as consumers rather than as members of a community. For example, the "official" graduating class T-shirt for 1990 was sold to students with a significant markup and was perceived by many to whom I spoke as an attempt to squeeze further pennies from them as they left. The students at every turn are asked to buy the signs of symbolic belonging (hence University "book" stores devote a great deal of space to logo-encrusted desk items on the Disneyland model). Thus commodified, belonging to the University carries little ideological baggage and requires no reaffirmation through giving (any more than a consumer, having purchased a car, feels the need to make further periodic donations to General Motors in excess of the car loan repayments). That some students do make such gifts is an interesting symptom of an atavistic desire to believe that they did not attend a University of Excellence but instead a University of Culture. Some support for this belief could doubtless be drawn from the persistence in some corners of the machinery of individuals, groups, and practices that hark back to prior forms of organization.

Students' frequent perception of themselves and/or their parents as consumers is not merely wrongheaded, since the contemporary University is busily transforming itself from an ideological arm of the state into a bureaucratically organized and relatively autonomous consumer-oriented corporation. Even in Universities largely funded by the nation-state, the signs of this process are to be found. For instance, Jacqueline Scott, president of University College of Cape Breton in Nova Scotia, recently referred to the University as an "integrated industry."[14] She offered a remarkable rephrasing of Humboldt's articulation of teaching and research. Where Humboldt positioned the University as a fusion of process and product that both produced knowledge of culture (in research) and inculcated culture as a process of learning (in teaching), Scott's account of this double articulation has been significantly updated. She argues that the University, as a site of "human resource development," both produces jobs (through research) and provides job training (in teaching). With remarkable fluency, she preserves Humboldt's structural articulation of teaching and research while transferring it into a new field: that of the development of "human resources" for the marketplace rather than of "national culture."

This is hardly surprising as a strategy, since it is corporate bureaucratization that underlies the strong homogenization of the University as an institution in North America. University mission statements, like their publicity brochures, share two distinctive features nowadays. On the one hand, they all claim that theirs is a unique educational institution. On the other hand, they all go on to describe this uniqueness in exactly the same way. The preeminent signs under which this transformation is taking place are the appeals to the notion of "excellence" that now drop from the lips of University administrators at every turn. To understand the contemporary University, we must ask what excellence means (or does not mean).

And in that respect, on the surface this book makes a rather simple argument. It claims that since the nation-state is no longer the primary instance of the reproduction of global capitals, "culture"—as the symbolic and political counterpart to the project of integration pursued by the nation-state—has lost its purchase. The nation-state and the modern notion of culture arose together, and they are, I argue, ceasing to be essential to an increasingly transnational global economy. This shift has major implications for the University, which has historically been the primary institution of national culture in the modern nation-state. I try to assess those implications and trace their symptoms, most notably the emergence of a discourse of "excellence" in place of prior appeals to the idea of culture as the language in which the University seeks to explain itself to itself and to the world at large. Another of those symptoms is the current fierce debate on the status of the University, a debate that by and large misses the point, because it fails to think the University in a transnational framework, preferring to busy itself with either nostalgia or denunciation—most often with an admixture of the two.

I will begin trying to think differently about the University by discussing the ways in which University administrators, government officials, and even radical critics now more and more often speak of the University in terms of "excellence" instead of in terms of "culture." Chapter 2 attempts to situate and diagnose why the term "excellence" is becoming so important to policy documents in higher education. My argument is that this new interest in the pursuit of excellence indicates a change in the University's function. The University no longer has to safeguard and propagate national culture, because the nation-state is no longer the major site at which capital reproduces itself. Hence, the idea of national culture no longer functions as an external referent toward which all of the efforts of research and teaching are directed. The idea of national culture no longer provides an overarching ideological meaning for what goes on in the University, and as a result, what exactly gets taught or produced as knowledge matters less and less.

In Chapter 2 I also trace this process and insist that it would be anachronistic to think of it as an "ideology of excellence," since excellence is precisely non-ideological. What gets taught or researched matters less than the fact that it be excellently taught or researched. In saying that some things, such as the discourse of excellence, are non-ideological, I do not mean that they have no political relatedness, only that the nature of that relation is not ideologically determined. "Excellence" is like the cash-nexus in that it has no *content;* it is hence neither true nor false, neither ignorant nor self-conscious. It may be unjust, but we cannot seek its injustice in terms of a regime of truth or of self-knowledge. Its rule does not carry with it an automatic political or cultural orientation, for it is not determined in relation to any identifiable instance of political power.[15] This is one of the reasons why the success of a left-wing criticism (with which I am personally in sympathy) is turning out to fit so well with institutional protocols, be it in the classroom or in the career profile.[16] It is not that radical critics are "sell-outs," or that their critiques are "insufficiently radical" and hence recoverable by the institution. Rather, the problem is that the stakes of the University's functioning are no longer essentially ideological, because they are no longer tied to the self-reproduction of the nation-state.

Where Chapter 2 diagnoses the discourse of excellence, Chapter 3 attempts to frame that discourse in terms of the movement of globalization in which it participates. Here I argue that the discourse of excellence gains purchase precisely from the fact that the link between the University and the nation-state no longer holds in an era of globalization. The University thus shifts from being an ideological apparatus of the nation-state to being a relatively independent bureaucratic system. The economics of globalization mean that the University is no longer called upon to train citizen subjects, while the politics of the end of the Cold War mean that the University is no longer called upon to uphold national prestige by producing and legitimating national culture. The University is thus analogous to a number of other institutions—such as national airline carriers—that face massive reductions in foreseeable funding from increasingly weakened states, which are no longer the privileged sites of investment of popular will.

In order to understand the implications of this shift, the middle part of this book engages in a historical investigation of the role that the modern University has sought to assign to itself. The history of previous ways of understanding the function of the University can be roughly summarized by saying that the modern University has had three ideas: the Kantian concept of reason, the Humboldtian idea of culture, and now the techno-bureaucratic notion of excellence. The historical narrative that I propose (reason—culture—excellence) is not simply a sequential one, however. There are earlier references to excellence that precede recent accounts; likewise, there continue to be references to reason and culture. What I want to emphasize throughout this book is that the debate on the University is made up of divergent and non-contemporaneous discourses, even if one discourse dominates over the others at certain moments.

To begin with, then, I argue in Chapter 4 that Kant defines the modernity of the University. The University becomes modern when all its activities are organized in view of a single regulatory idea, which

Kant claims must be the concept of reason. Reason, on the one hand, provides the *ratio* for all the disciplines; it is their organizing principle. On the other hand, reason has its own faculty, which Kant names "philosophy" but which we would now be more likely simply to call the "humanities." In his thinking on the University, Kant also begins to pose the problem of how reason and the state, how knowledge and power, might be unified. Importantly, as I will show, he does this by producing the figure of the subject who is capable of rational thought and republican politics.

Chapter 5 continues to trace the development of the modern University, discussing the German Idealists, from Schiller to Humboldt. Significantly, they assign a more explicitly political role to the structure determined by Kant, and they do this by replacing the notion of reason with that of culture. Like reason, culture serves a particularly *unifying* function for the University. For the German Idealists, culture is the sum of all knowledge that is studied, as well as the cultivation and development of one's character as a result of that study. In this context, Humboldt's project for the foundation of the University of Berlin is decisive for the centering of the University around the idea of culture, which ties the University to the nation-state. That this should happen in Germany is, of course, implicit with the emergence of German nationhood. Under the rubric of culture, the University is assigned the dual task of research and teaching, respectively the production and inculcation of national self-knowledge. As such, it becomes the institution charged with watching over the spiritual life of the people of the rational state, reconciling ethnic tradition and statist rationality. The University, in other words, is identified as the institution that will give reason to the common life of the people, while preserving their traditions and avoiding the bloody, destructive example of the French Revolution. This, I argue, is the decisive role accorded to the modern University until the present.

Chapter 6 looks at the way in which the British and Americans give a particularly *literary* turn to the German Idealists' notion of culture. In the late nineteenth and early twentieth centuries, the English, notably Newman and Arnold, carried forward the work of Humboldt and Schlegel by placing literature instead of philosophy as the central discipline of the University and hence also of national culture. Discussing the examples of Arnold, Leavis, and the New Critics, I trace the implicit linkage between the way "literature" gets institutionalized as a University discipline in explicitly national terms and an organic vision of the possibility of a unified national culture. The study of a tradition of national literature comes to be the primary mode of teaching students what it is to be French, or English, or German. In the case of the United States, this process is regulated in terms of the study of a *canon* rather than a tradition, in exemplary republican fashion. The canon matters in the United States because the determination of the canon is taken to be the result of an exercise of republican will. The autonomous *choice* of a canon, rather than submission to the blind weight of tradition, parallels the choice of a government rather than submission to hereditary monarchy. The role of literary study in the formation of national subjects is consequently what explains the massive institutional weight accumulated by literature departments, especially through their traditional control of the University-wide "composition course" requirement in many American universities. The current growth of a separatist movement in composition, concerned to demand its own distinct disciplinary dignity, is symptomatic of the loosening of the link that ties the study of national literature to the formation of national citizen-subjects. The terms of literacy are no longer determined in explicit reference to national culture.

Chapter 7 looks at the parallel disciplinary rise of Cultural Studies and at the American "culture wars" from the historical perspective of the previous chapters, so as to understand what is at stake in the notion of "culture" over which we are currently battling. The German Idealists attributed the guardianship of culture to philosophy, although in the nineteenth and twentieth centuries it has come increasingly to be housed in departments of national literature. We are now seeing a decline in national literary studies and the increasing emergence of "Cultural Studies" as the strongest disciplinary model in the humanities in the Anglo-American University. In this context, the radical claims of Cultural Studies display rather more continuity than might be expected with the redemptive claim that underpinned the literary model of culture, however much they oppose its institutional forms. I argue that the institutional success of Cultural Studies in the 1990s is owing to the fact that it preserves the structure of the literary argument, while recognizing that literature can no longer work—throwing out the baby and keeping the bathwater, as it were. Cultural Studies does not propose culture as a regulatory ideal for research and teaching, so much as seek to preserve the structure of an argument for redemption through culture, while recognizing the inability of culture to function any longer as such an idea. To put it in the cruelest terms—terms that apply only to the attempt to make Cultural Studies into a hegemonic institutional project and not to any specific work calling itself "Cultural Studies"— Cultural Studies presents a vision of culture that is appropriate for the age of excellence.

And even like "excellence" itself, "culture" no longer has a specific content. Everything, given a chance, can be or become culture. Cultural Studies thus arrives on the scene along with a certain exhaustion. The very fecundity and multiplicity of work in Cultural Studies is enabled by the fact that culture no longer functions as a specific referent to any one thing or set of things—which is why Cultural Studies can be so popular while refusing general theoretical definition. Cultural Studies, in its current incarnation as an institutional project for the 1990s, proceeds from a certain sense that no more *knowledge* can be produced, since there is nothing to be said about culture that is not itself cultural, and vice versa. Everything is culturally determined, as it were, and culture ceases to mean anything *as such*.

I will also refer to this process as "dereferentialization." By this I mean to suggest that what is crucial about terms like "culture" and "excellence" (and even "University" at times) is that they no longer have specific referents; they no longer refer to a specific set of things or ideas. In using the term "dereferentialization," however, I do not want simply to introduce another bulky piece of jargon into our vocabulary; rather my design is to give a name to what I will argue is a crucial shift in thinking that has dramatic consequences for the University. In these terms, we can say that the rise of Cultural Studies becomes possible only when culture is dereferentialized and ceases to be the principle of study in the University. In the age of Cultural Studies, culture becomes merely one object among others for the system to deal with. This polemical argument does not denounce the history of work in Cultural Studies so much as criticize attempts—however well-meaning—to make Cultural Studies into the discipline that will save the University by giving it back its lost truth.

The subsequent Chapter 8 seeks to imagine the University "after" culture and introduces the concluding part of the book by sketching the general terms in which the institutional question of the University can be posed in the age of excellence, once the historical project of culture has ground to a halt. I attempt to provide the terms of an institutional pragmatism that can make an argument for the tactical use of the space of the University, while recognizing that space as a historical anachronism. In so doing, I discuss the specific debates in which the University is currently engaged and the general terms in which an appeal can be made to the activity of thought. Significantly, this concerns the question of how the University is to be evaluated, and it argues for the need for a philosophical separation of the notions of *accountability* and *accounting.* I argue that it is imperative that the University respond to the demand for accountability, while at the same time refusing to conduct the debate over the nature of its responsibility solely in terms of the language of accounting (whose currency is excellence). To raise the issue of value precisely as a *question* is to refuse the automatic identification of globalization and capitalism. I want to argue that accountants are not the only people capable of understanding the horizon of contemporary society, nor even the most adept at the task.

Chapter 9 discusses how the questions of value that I am raising—and that are of such concern to the University today—become apparent in the wake of the student revolts of the late 1960s, for which "1968" stands as a synecdoche. Those uprisings open up an incredulity about the University as an institution, a committed unbelief that is helpful in trying to imagine what it would mean to be in the University without being able to believe in the University, in either its actual or its ideal form. What I find most interesting about the documents of the student revolt, as presented by Cohn-Bendit and others, is their remarkable *lack* of idealism, their tendency to deny the terms in which they have subsequently tended to be understood. In a reflection upon 1968, I seek the terms within which we can think the University in the absence of a public sphere and outside the framework of a society that aggregates individuals as consumers.

How to understand the contemporary situation of the University without recourse either to nostalgia for national culture or to the discourse of consumerism is the burden of my three final chapters, which deal respectively with questions of pedagogy, of institutions, and of community. Chapter 10 focuses on the pragmatic scene of teaching and stresses that pedagogy cannot be understood in isolation from the institutional context of education. Much of the current furor over teaching has to do with a simple contradiction between the time it takes to teach and an administrative logic that privileges the efficient transmission of information. I argue that the aim of pedagogy should not be to produce autonomous subjects who are supposedly made free by the information they learn, which is the Enlightenment narrative. Rather, by relinquishing the claim to join authority and autonomy, the scene of teaching can be better understood as a network of obligations. Arguing that teaching is a question of justice not a search for truth, Chapter 10 tries to evoke what remains persistently troubling in the business of thinking together. As such, the transgressive force of teaching does not lie so much in matters of content as in the way pedagogy can hold open the temporality of questioning so as to resist being characterized as a transaction that can be concluded, either with the giving of grades or the granting of degrees.

Chapters 11 and 12 examine the terms in which the University as a space for such a structurally incomplete practice of thought can conceive itself. I argue first that it is imperative to accept that the University cannot be understood as the natural or historically necessary receptacle for such activities, that we need to recognize the University as a *ruined* institution, one that has lost its *historical raison d'être*. At the same time, the University has, in its modern form, shared modernity's paradoxical attraction to the idea of the ruin, which means that considerable vigilance is required in disentangling this ruined status from a tradition of metaphysics that seeks to re-unify those ruins, either practically or aesthetically.

The institutional pragmatism that I call for in place of either Enlightenment faith or Romantic nostalgia leads to an investigation in Chapter 12 of the way in which we can rethink the modernist claim that the University provides a model of the rational community, a microcosm of the pure form of the public sphere. This claim for an ideal community in the University still exerts its power, despite its glaring inaccuracy—evident to anyone who has ever sat on a faculty committee. I argue that we should recognize that the loss of the University's cultural function opens up a space in which it is possible to think the notion of community otherwise, without recourse to notions of unity, consensus, and communication. At this point, the University becomes no longer a model of the ideal society but rather a place where the impossibility of such models can be thought—practically thought, rather than thought under ideal conditions. Here the University loses its privileged status as the model of society and does not regain it by becoming the model of the absence of models. Rather, the University becomes one site among others where *the question of being-together is raised*, raised with an urgency that proceeds from the absence of the institutional forms (such as the nation-state), which have historically served to mask that question for the past three centuries or so.

~ 2

The Idea of Excellence

The significance of making a distinction between the modern University as ideological arm of the nation-state and the contemporary University as bureaucratic corporation is that it allows one to observe an important phenomenon. "Excellence" is rapidly becoming the watchword of the University, and to understand the University as a contemporary institution requires some reflection on what the appeal to excellence may, or may not, mean.

A few months after I first gave a talk on the significance of the concept of excellence, Canada's principal weekly news magazine, *Maclean's*, brought out its third annual special issue on the Canadian universities, parallel to the kind of ranking produced by *U.S. News and World Report*. The November 15, 1993, issue of *Maclean's*, which purported to rank all the universities in Canada according to various criteria, was entitled, to my surprise, *A Measure of Excellence.*[1] Now what this suggests to me is that excellence is not simply the equivalent of "total quality management" (TQM). It is not just something imported *into* the University from business in the attempt to run the University *as if* it were a business. Such importations assume, after all, that the University is not really a business, is only like a business in some respects.

When Ford Motors enters into a "partnership" with The Ohio State University to develop "total quality management in all areas of life on campus," this partnership is based on the assumption that "the mission[s] of the university and the corporation are not that different," as

Janet Pichette, vice-president for business and administration at Ohio State, phrases it.[2] Not "that different" perhaps, but not identical either. The University is on the way to becoming a corporation, but it has yet to apply TQM to all aspects of its experience, although the capacity of Ohio State's president E. Gordon Gee to refer to "the university and the customers it serves" is a sign that Ohio State is well on the way. The invocation of "quality" is the means of that transformation, since "quality" can apply to "all areas of life on campus" indifferently, and can tie them together on a single evaluative scale. As the campus newspaper, the *Ohio State Lantern,* reports it: "Quality is the ultimate issue for the university and the customers it serves, Gee said, referring to faculty, students, their parents, and alumni."[3] The need felt by the author of this article to clarify the question of to whom the president was referring in speaking of the University's "customers" is a touching sign of an almost archaic vision of education, one that imagines that some confusion might still arise on the issue.

Hence we might suggest a clarification for President Gee: quality is not the ultimate issue, but excellence soon will be, because it is the recognition that the University is not just *like* a corporation; it *is* a corporation. Students in the University of Excellence are not *like* customers; they *are* customers. For excellence implies a quantum leap: the notion of excellence develops *within* the University, as the idea around which the University centers itself and through which it becomes comprehensible to the outside world (in the case of *Maclean's,* the middle and upper classes of Canada).

Generally, we hear a lot of talk from University administrators about excellence, because it has become the unifying principle of the contemporary University. C. P. Snow's "Two Cultures" have become "Two Excellences," the humanistic and the scientific.[4] As an integrating principle, excellence has the singular advantage of being entirely meaningless, or to put it more precisely, non-referential. Here is one example of the way in which excellence undermines linguistic reference, in a letter to faculty and staff from a dean of engineering (William Sirignano) complaining about his dismissal by the chancellor of the University of California at Irvine (Laurel Wilkening), reported in the campus newspaper:

"The Office of the President and the central administration at the UCI campus are too embroiled in crisis management, self-service and controversy to be a great force for *excellence* in academic programs," Sirignano wrote in the Mar. 22 memo. He encouraged the new dean, department chairs and faculty to "create those pressures for *excellence* for the school" . . . The transition in leadership "will be a challenge to the pursuit of *excellence* and upward mobility for the School of Engineering," he said. "It's not going to be easy to recruit an *excellent* dean in this time of fiscal crisis."[5]

In a situation of extreme stress, and in order to oppose the University president, the dean appeals to the language of excellence with a regularity that is the more remarkable in that it goes unremarked by the staff writer covering the incident.[6] Indeed, the staff writer has selected those phrases that include the word "excellence" as being those that most precisely sum up what the letter is about. Excellence appears here as uncontestable ground, the rhetorical arm most likely to gain general assent. To return to the example of the Ford–Ohio State partnership, a significant number of academics, I would guess, could see through the imposition from the outside of "total quality management," could resist the ideology implicit in the notion of quality and argue that the University was not as analogous to a business as Ford claimed. But Sirignano is an academic, writing to an academic, for an audience of academics. And his appeal to excellence is not hedged or mitigated, is not felt to require explanation. Quite the contrary. The need for excellence is what we all agree on. And we all agree upon it because it is not an ideology, in the sense that it has no external referent or internal content.

Today, all departments of the University can be urged to strive for excellence, since the general applicability of the notion is in direct relation to its emptiness. Thus, for instance, the Office of Research and University Graduate Studies at Indiana University at Bloomington explains that in its Summer Faculty Fellowship program "Excellence of the proposed scholarship is the major criterion employed in the evaluation procedure."[7] This statement is, of course, entirely meaningless, yet the assumption is that the invocation of excellence overcomes the problem of the question of value across disciplines, since excellence is the common denominator of good research in all fields. Even if this were so, it would mean that excellence could not be invoked as a "criterion," because excellence is not a fixed standard of judgment but a qualifier whose meaning is fixed in relation to something else. An excellent boat is not excellent by the same *criteria* as an excellent plane. So to say that excellence is a criterion is to say absolutely nothing other than that the committee will not reveal the criteria used to judge applications.

Nor is the employment of the term "excellence" limited to academic disciplines within the University. For instance, Jonathan Culler has informed me that the Cornell University Parking Services recently received an award for "excellence in parking." What this meant was that they had achieved a remarkable level of efficiency in *restricting* motor vehicle access. As he pointed out, excellence could just as well have meant making people's lives easier by increasing the number of parking spaces available to faculty. The issue here is not the merits of either option but the fact that excellence can function equally well as an evaluative criterion on either side of the issue of what constitutes "excellence in parking," because excellence has no content to call its own. Whether it is a matter of increasing the number of cars on campus (in the interests of employee efficiency—fewer minutes wasted in walking) or decreasing the number of cars (in the interests of the environment) is indifferent; the efforts of parking officials can be described in terms of excellence in both instances.[8] Its very lack of reference allows excellence to function as a principle of translatability between radically different idioms: parking services and research grants can each be excellent, and their excellence is not dependent on any specific qualities or effects that they share.

This is clearly what is going on in the case of the *Maclean's* article, where excellence is the common currency of ranking. Categories as diverse as the make-up of the student body, class size, finances, and library holdings can all be brought together on a single scale of excellence. Such rankings are not entered into blindly or cavalierly. With a scrupulousness of which the academic community could be proud, the magazine devotes two whole pages to discussing how it produced its ratings. Thus, the student body is measured in terms of incoming grades (the higher the better), grade point average during study (the higher the better), the number of "out of province" students (more is better), and graduation rates within standard time limits (achieving normalization is a good thing). Class size and quality are measured in terms of the student-teacher ratio (which should be low) and the ratio of tenured faculty to part-timers or graduate teaching assistants (which should be high). Faculty are evaluated in terms of the number with Ph.D.'s, the number of award winners, and the number and quantity of federal grants obtained, all of which are taken to be signs of merit. The category "finances" judges the fiscal health of a University in terms of the proportions of the operating budget available for current expenses, student services, and scholarships. Library holdings are analyzed in terms of volumes per student and the percentage of the university budget devoted to the library, as well as the percentage of the library budget dedicated to new acquisitions. A final category, "reputation," combines the number of alumni who give to the University with the results of a "survey of senior university officials and chief executive officers of major corporations across Canada" (40). The result is a "measure of excellence" arrived at by combining the figures at a ratio of 20 percent for students, 18 percent for class size, 20 percent for faculty, 10 percent for finances, 12 percent for libraries, and 20 percent for "reputation."

A number of things are obvious about this exercise, most immediately the arbitrary quality of the weighting of factors and the dubiousness of such quantitative indicators of quality. Along with questioning the relative weight accorded to each of the categories, we can ask a number of fundamental questions about what constitutes "quality" in education. Are grades the only measure of student achievement? Why is efficiency privileged, so that it is automatically assumed that graduating "on time" is a good thing? How long does it take to become "educated"? The survey assumes that the best teacher is one who possesses the highest university degree and the most grants, the teacher who is the most faithful reproduction of the system. But what says that makes a good professor? Is the best University necessarily the richest one? What is the relation to knowledge implied by focusing on the library as the place where it is stocked? Is quantity the best measure of

the significance of library holdings? Is knowledge simply to be repro-
duced from the warehouse, or is it something to be produced in teaching? Why should senior university officials and the CEOs of major
corporations be the best judges of "reputation"? What do they have in
common, and isn't this compatibility worrying? Does not the category
of "reputation" raise prejudice to the level of an index of value? How
were individuals chosen? Why is the "reputational survey" included in
ranking designed to establish reputation?

Most of these questions are philosophical, in that they are systemically incapable of producing cognitive certainty or definitive answers.
Such questions will necessarily give rise to further debate, for they are
radically at odds with the logic of quantification. Criticism of the categories used (and the way upon which they are decided) has indeed
been leveled at *Maclean's,* as it has at the *U.S. News and World Report*'s
equivalent survey. This is perhaps why *Maclean's* includes a further
three-page article entitled "The Battle for the Facts," which portrays
the heroic struggle of the journalists to find the truth despite the attempts of some universities to hide it. This essay also details the res-
ervations expressed by a number of universities, for example the complaint of the president of Manitoba's Brandon University that "Many
of the individual strengths of universities are not picked up in this
ranking by *Maclean's*" (46). Once again, the president argues only with
the particular criteria, not with the logic of excellence and the ranking
that it permits. And when the authors of the article remark that "The
debate sheds a telling light on the deep unease over accountability,"
they do not refer to a critique of the logic of accounting. Far from it.
Any questioning of such performance indicators is positioned as a resistance to public accountability, a refusal to be questioned according
to the logic of contemporary capitalism, which requires "clear measures
to establish university performance" (48).

Given this situation, to question criteria is necessary, yet a more
general point needs to be made concerning the general compliance of
universities with the logic of accounting. The University and *Maclean's*
appear to speak the same language, as it were: the language of excellence. Yet the question of what it means to "speak the same language"
is a tricky one in Canada. This survey is going on in a country that is

bilingual, where the different universities quite literally speak different languages. And behind the fact that the criteria are heavily biased in favor of anglophone institutions lies the fundamental assumption that there is a single standard, a measure of excellence, in terms of which universities can be judged. And it is excellence that allows the combination on a single scale of such utterly heterogeneous features as finances and the make-up of the student body. A measure of the flexibility of excellence is that it allows the inclusion of reputation as one category among others in a ranking which is in fact definitive of reputation. The metalepsis that allows reputation to be 20 percent of itself is permitted by the intense flexibility of excellence; it allows a category mistake to masquerade as scientific objectivity.

Most of all, excellence serves as the unit of currency within a closed field. The survey allows the a priori exclusion of all referential issues, that is, any questions about what excellence in the University might *be,* what the term might *mean.* Excellence is, and the survey is quite explicit about this, a means of relative ranking among the elements of an *entirely closed system:* "For the universities, meanwhile, the survey affords an opportunity for each to clarify its own vision—and to measure itself against its peers" (40). Excellence is clearly a purely internal unit of value that effectively brackets all questions of reference or function, thus creating an internal market. Henceforth, the question of the University is only the question of relative value-for-money, the question posed to a student who is situated entirely as a *consumer,* rather than as someone who wants to think. (I shall return to the question of what it means to "think" later in this book.)

The image of students browsing through catalogues, with the world all before them, there to choose, is a remarkably widespread one that has attracted little comment. While I would not want to imply that students should not get the chance to choose, I do think it is worth reflecting on what this image assumes. Most obviously, it assumes the ability to pay. The question of access to tertiary education is bracketed. Tertiary education is perceived simply as another consumer durable, so that affordability or value-for-money becomes one category among others influencing an individual choice. Think of magazine consumer reports about which car to buy. Price is one factor among others, and the effect of the integration of heterogeneous categories of ranking into a single "excellence quotient" becomes apparent. Choosing a particular university over another is presented as not all that much different from weighing the costs and benefits of a Honda Civic against those of a Lincoln Continental in a given year or period.

In its October 3, 1994, issue, *U.S. News and World Report* even takes advantage of this potential parallel between the car industry and the University.[9] An article straightforwardly entitled "How to Pay for College" is followed by a series of tables that rate the "most efficient schools" and the "best values," comparing "sticker prices" (advertised tuition) to "discount tuition" (actual tuition once scholarships and grants are factored in). Student and parent consumers are reminded that just as when they buy a car, especially in the years of the U.S. auto industry's scramble for customers, the first price quoted is not what they are expected to pay. *U.S. News and World Report* reminds its readers that there are similar hidden discounts in university education, and that wise consumers—who now span all the income brackets (the logic of consumerism no longer only influences the "less-well-off")—should pay attention to value-for-money. Fuel efficiency, whether calculated in miles per gallon or spending per student, is a growing concern when measuring excellence.[10]

However much such a vision might scare us, or however much some of us might think we can resist the logic of consumerism when it comes to tertiary education, everyone still seems to be for excellence.[11] It functions not merely as the standard of external evaluation but also as the unit of value in terms of which the University describes itself to itself, in terms of which the University achieves the self-consciousness that is supposed to guarantee intellectual autonomy in modernity. Given that, who could be against excellence? Thus, for example, the Faculty of Graduate Studies of the Université de Montréal describes itself as follows:

> Created in 1972, the Faculty of Graduate Studies [*Faculté des études supérieures*] has been entrusted with the mission of maintaining and promoting standards of excellence at the level of master's and doctoral studies; of coordinating teaching and standardizing [*normalisation*] programmes of graduate study; of stimulating the development and coordination of research in liaison with the research departments of the

University; of favoring the creation of interdisciplinary or multidisciplinary programs.[12]

Note here the intersection of excellence with "integration and standardization" and the appeal to the "interdisciplinary." The French "normalisation" gives a strong sense of what is at stake in "standardization"—especially to those familiar with the work of Michel Foucault. Is it surprising that corporations resemble Universities, health-care facilities, and international organizations, which all resemble corporations? Foucault's *Discipline and Punish* explores the eighteenth- and nineteenth-century reorganization of the mechanisms of state power, especially the judicial system, around the surveillance and normalization of delinquents in place of their exemplary punishment by torture and execution. Criminals are treated rather than destroyed, but this apparent liberalization is also a mode of domination that is the more terrible in that it leaves no room whatsoever for transgression. Crime is no longer an act of freedom, a remainder that society cannot handle but must expel. Rather, crime comes to be considered as a pathological deviation from social norms that must be cured. Foucault's chapter on "Panopticism" ends with ringing rhetorical questions:

> The practice of placing individuals under "observation" is a natural extension of a justice imbued with disciplinary methods and examination procedures. Is it surprising that the cellular prison, with its regular chronologies, forced labour, its authorities of surveillance and registration, its experts in normality, who continue and multiply the functions of the judge, should have become the modern instrument of penalty? Is it surprising that prisons resemble factories, schools, barracks, hospitals, which all resemble prisons?[13]

The notion of excellence, functioning less to permit visual observation than to permit exhaustive accounting, works to tie the University into a similar net of bureaucratic institutions. "Excellence," that is, functions to allow the University to understand itself solely in terms of the structure of corporate administration. Hence, as I mentioned briefly in Chapter 1, Alfonso Borrero Cabal, writing the report *The University as an Institution Today* for UNESCO, consciously structures his vision of the University in terms of administration: "Part I—the Introduction—deals with administration in terms of the internal institutional organization and the external or outward-projecting idea of service . . . Part II deals with the first meaning of administration: the organization and internal functioning of the university . . . Part III deals with the external sense of administration, that of service to society."[14] This primarily administrative approach is explicitly situated as a result of the University's need to "become part of the international scene" (19). Globalization requires that "greater attention is given to administration" in order to permit the integration of the market in knowledge, which Borrero Cabal situates directly in relation to the need for "development." With the end of the Cold War, as Marco Antonio Rodrigues Dias remarks in his preface, "the main problem in the world is 'underdevelopment'" (xv). What this actually means is that the language in which global discussions are to be conducted is not that of cultural conflict but of economic management. And the language of economic management structures Borrero Cabal's analysis of the university around the globe. Hence for example he argues: "Planning, execution, evaluation: the natural actions of responsible persons and institutions. They make up the three important stages that complete the cycle of the administrative process. In logical order, planning precedes execution and evaluation, but all planning has to start with evaluation" (192).

The idea that the sequential processes of business management are the "natural actions" of "responsible persons" may come as a surprise to some of us. What kind of "responsibility" is this? Clearly not that of a parent to a child, for example. The only responsibility at stake here is the responsibility to provide managerial accounts for large corporations, something that becomes clearer when Borrero Cabal begins to flesh out what he means by planning: "Since 'strategic planning,' . . . 'administration by objectives,' . . . and systems of 'total quality' are frequently discussed, it is natural to adopt these means of planning, which are as old as humanity even though they were not formalized until the end of the 18th century" (197).

Once again, the "natural" is invoked. Borrero Cabal cites a number of authorities in order to suggest that early hunter-gatherers were, in fact, engaged in reflection on total quality management, an argument that reminds one of the fine scorn Marx pours upon Ricardo:

Even Ricardo has his Robinson Crusoe Stories. Ricardo makes his primitive fisherman and primitive hunter into owners of commodities who immediately exchange their fish and game in proportion to the labour-time which is materialized in these exchange-values. On this occasion he slips into the anachronism of allowing the primitive fisherman and hunter to calculate the value of their implements in accordance with the annuity tables used on the London Stock Exchange in 1817.[15]

Borrero Cabal's recourse to anachronism is, of course, the product of a desire to make the exclusive rule of business management not seem discontinuous with the prior role of the University. Although he does admit that economic criteria and cultural development are at odds, he simply notes the fact and then passes on to give more outlines for the management of University administration by analogy with a large corporation. Hence he admits that he has omitted "the all-essential ingredient of culture" from his analysis of the relation between "the university and the work world," saying that: "Consequently it is often felt that economic criteria take precedence over the cultural development of people and nations. This reduces professional work to quantitative purposes: the profession is not conceived of as 'the cultural and moral elevation of people and nations' (Garcia Corrido 1992), but reduced to what is necessary but not sufficient, that is, tangible output and per capita income" (161).

Having acknowledged the conflict between a strictly economic rationale and the traditional cultural mission, Borrero Cabal goes on to provide a strictly economic description of the functioning of the University in terms of cost and benefit. He does make occasional remarks that we should not forget about culture but seems unsure where it should fit in. Hence, and not surprisingly, he is more at ease with the invocation of excellence. He approvingly quotes the Director General of UNESCO: "Federico Mayor (1991) gives the following qualifying terms: It is impossible to guarantee the quality of education without having the aim of excellence resting on the domain of research, teaching, preparation, and learning. . . . The search for excellence reaffirms its pertinence and closely links it to quality" (212). The aim of excellence serves to synthesize research, teaching, preparation, and learning, all the activities of the University, if we add administration (and one of Borrero Cabal's only concrete recommendations is that university administration should be made a program of study). What is remarkable is how Borrero Cabal could suggest that these are "qualifying terms" in order to understand what "institutional quality" in the University might be. Excellence is invoked here, as always, to say precisely nothing at all: it deflects attention from the questions of what quality and pertinence might be, who actually are the judges of a relevant or a good University, and by what authority they become those judges.

What Borrero Cabal suggests for the University is a process of constant self-evaluation, in relation to "performance indicators," which allow us to judge "quality, excellence, effectiveness and pertinence" (212). All of these terms are, he acknowledges, "taken from economic jargon" (213), and permit the University's self-evaluation to be a matter of accounting, both internally and externally. In short, for Borrero Cabal, accountability is strictly a matter of accounting: "In synthesis, if the concept of accountability is accepted as part of the academic lexicon, it is equivalent to the capacity that the university has for accounting for its roles, mission, and functions to itself, and for accounting to society how they are translated into efficient service" (213). Note the use of "translation" in this passage; although "accounting" may exceed bookkeeping in the sense that it is not merely a matter of money, it is the principle of cost and benefit that acts as a principle of translation. Cost-benefit analysis structures not only the University's internal bookkeeping but also its academic performance (in terms of goal achievement) and the social bond with the University at large. The social responsibility of the University, its accountability to society, is solely a matter of services rendered for a fee. Accountability is a synonym for accounting in "the academic lexicon."

In this context, excellence responds very well to the needs of technological capitalism in the production and processing of information, in that it allows for the increasing integration of all activities into a generalized market, while permitting a large degree of flexibility and innovation at the local level. Excellence is thus the integrating principle that allows "diversity" (the other watchword of the University prospectus) to be tolerated without threatening the unity of the system.

The point is not that no one knows what excellence is but that *ev-*

eryone has his or her own idea of what it is. And once excellence has been generally accepted as an organizing principle, there is no need to argue about differing definitions. Everyone is excellent, in their own way, and everyone has more of a stake in being left alone to be excellent than in intervening in the administrative process. There is a clear parallel here to the condition of the political subject under contemporary capitalism. Excellence draws only one boundary: the boundary that protects the unrestricted power of the bureaucracy. And if a particular department's kind of excellence fails to conform, then that department can be eliminated without apparent risk to the system. This has been, for example, the fate of many classics departments. It is beginning to happen to philosophy.

The reasons for the decline of classics are of course complex, but they seem to me to have to do with the fact that the study of classics traditionally presupposes a subject of culture: the subject that links the Greeks to nineteenth-century Germany, and legitimates the nation-state as the modern, rational, reconstruction of the transparent communicational community of the ancient *polis*. That fiction of communicational transparency is apparent from the erroneous assumptions of nineteenth-century historians (still apparent in mass-cultural representations) that ancient Greece was a world of total whiteness (dazzling marble buildings, statues, and people), a pure and transparent origin. That the ideological role of this subject is no longer pertinent is itself a primary symptom of the decline of culture as the regulatory idea of the nation-state. Hence classical texts will continue to be read, but the assumptions that necessitated a department of classics for this purpose (the need to prove that Pericles and Bismarck were the same kind of men) no longer hold, so there is no longer a need to employ a massive institutional apparatus designed to make ancient Greeks into ideal Etonians or Young Americans *avant la lettre*.[16]

This disciplinary shift is most evident in the United States, where the University has always had an ambiguous relation to the state. This is because American civil society is structured by the trope of the promise or contract rather than on the basis of a single national ethnicity. Hence where Fichte's university project, as we shall see, offers to realize the essence of a *Volk* by revealing its hidden nature in the form of the nation-state, the American University offers to deliver on the promise of a rational civil society—as in the visionary conclusion to T. H. Huxley's address on the inauguration of Johns Hopkins University. It is worth quoting at some length the extended opposition between past and future, between essence and promise, that characterizes Huxley's account of the specificity of American society and the American University, in order to see exactly how he can speak of America as a yet-to-be-fulfilled promise even on the hundredth anniversary of the Declaration of Independence:

> I constantly hear Americans speak of the charm which our old mother country has for them . . . But anticipation has no less charm than retrospect, and to an Englishman landing on your shores for the first time, travelling for hundreds of miles through strings of great and well-ordered cities, seeing your enormous actual, and almost infinite potential, wealth in all commodities, and in the energy and ability which turn wealth to account, there is something sublime in the vista of the future. Do not suppose that I am pandering to what is commonly understood by national pride . . . Size is not grandeur, and territory does not make a nation. The great issue, about which hangs a true sublimity, and the terror of overhanging fate, is what are you going to do with all of these things? What is to be the end to which these are to be the means? You are making a novel experiment in politics on the greatest scale which the world has yet seen.[17]

Huxley himself, as Rector of Aberdeen, played an important role in the development of the Scottish University in the later nineteenth century, its independence from the Oxbridge model being marked by an openness to the natural sciences and medicine as disciplines and by the fact that it was not controlled by the Anglican church. These two features make the Scottish University more clearly "modern," which is to say, closer to the American model.[18] And Huxley's speech picks out the crucial feature that will define the modernity of Johns Hopkins: the fact that the United States as a nation has no intrinsic cultural *content*. That is to say, the American national idea is understood by Huxley as a promise, a scientific experiment. And the role of the American University is not to bring to light the content of its culture, to realize a national meaning; it is rather to deliver on a national *promise*, a contract.[19] As I shall explain later on, this promissory structure is what makes the canon debate a particularly American phenomenon, since the establishment of cultural content is not the realization of an immanent cultural essence but an act of republican will: the paradoxical contractual *choice* of a tradition. Thus the *form* of the European idea of culture is preserved in the humanities in the United States, but the cultural form has no inherent content. The content of the canon is grounded upon the moment of a social contract rather than the continuity of a historical tradition, and therefore is always open to revision.

This contractual vision of society is what allows Harvard to offer itself "in the service of the nation" or New York University to call itself a "private university in the public service." What such service might mean is not singularly determined by a unitary cultural center. The idea of the nation is always already an abstraction in America, resting on promise rather than on tradition. Excellence can thus most easily gain ground in the United States; it is more open to the futurity of the promise than is "culture," and the question of cultural content was already bracketed in the American University in the late nineteenth century, as Ronald Judy points out. The contemporary advent of excellence may therefore be understood to represent the abandonment of the vestigial appeal to the *form* of culture as the mode of self-realization of a republican people who are citizens of a nation-state—the relinquishing of the University's role as a model of even the contractual social bond in favor of the structure of an autonomous bureaucratic corporation.

Along the same lines, one can understand the point that I have already made concerning the status of "globalization" as a kind of "Americanization." Global "Americanization" today (unlike during the period of the Cold War, Korea, and Vietnam) does not mean American national predominance but a global realization of the contentlessness of the American national idea, which shares the emptiness of the cash-nexus and of excellence. Despite the enormous energy expended in attempts to isolate and define an "Americanness" in American Studies programs, one might read these efforts as nothing more than an attempt to mask the fundamental anxiety that it in some sense *means nothing* to be American, that "American culture" is becoming increasingly a structural oxymoron. I take it as significant of such a trend that an institution as prestigious and as central to an idea of American culture as the University of Pennsylvania should have recently decided to disband its American Studies program. That universities in the United States have been the quickest to abandon the trappings of justification by reference to national culture should hardly be surprising in a nation defined by a suspicion of state intervention in symbolic life, as expressed in the separation of church and state.

The United States, however, is by no means alone in this movement. The British turn to "performance indicators" should also be understood as a step on the road toward the discourse of excellence that is replacing the appeal to culture in the North American University.[20] The performance indicator is, of course, a measure of excellence, an invented standard that claims to be capable of rating all departments in all British universities on a five-point scale. The rating can then be used to determine the size of the central government grant allocated to the department in question. Since this process is designed to introduce a competitive market into the academic world, investment follows success, so the government intervenes to accentuate differentials in perceived quality rather than to reduce them. Thus more money is given to the high-scoring university departments, while the poor ones, rather than being developed, are starved of cash (under the Thatcher regime, this was of course understood as an encouragement to such departments to pull themselves up by their bootstraps). The long-term trend is to permit the concentration of resources in centers of high performance and to encourage the disappearance of departments, and even perhaps of universities, perceived as "weaker."

Hence, for instance, the University of Oxford has been moved to envision the construction of a Humanities Research Center, despite traditional local suspicion of the very notion of the research project as something that only Germans and Americans could think of applying to the humanities. Benjamin Jowett is supposed to have remarked of research, "There will be none of *that* in my college." Such changes are hailed by conservatives as "exposure to market forces," whereas what is occurring is actually the highly artificial creation of a fictional market that presumes exclusive governmental control of funding. However, the very artificiality of the process by which a version of the capitalist marketplace is mimed throws into relief the preliminary necessity of a unified and virtual accounting mechanism. This is coupled with the structural introduction of the threat of crisis to the functioning of the institution. And the result is nothing less than the double logic of excellence at work in its finest hour.

Indeed, a crisis in the University seems to be a defining feature of the "West," as is evidenced in the Italian students' movement of 1993, or the repeated French attempts at "modernization." Of course, it was the Faure plan for the modernization of the University that produced the events of 1968 in France (which I shall discuss in Chapter 9). However, such attempts at modernization have continued, and the arguments presented recently by Claude Allègre in *L'Âge des Savoirs: Pour une Renaissance de l'Université* display a striking consonance with the developments I have discussed in the United States, Canada, and Britain. Allègre was the special counselor to Lionel Jospin at the Ministry of Education from 1988 to 1992, and his book is essentially an exposé of the arguments guiding the reform of the French University, perceived as a locus of stagnation and resistance to change (an argument with which few could disagree). Interestingly, he argues that this drive to reform is "above all a resurgence of the aspirations of 68 . . . but a discreet and calm resurgence."[21] Just to whose aspirations he is referring is never spelled out, but it turns out that what 1968 meant above all was *openness*. And the twin characteristics of this new opening are, the reader will hardly be surprised to learn, integration and excellence:

> We tried to develop [reforms] by opening up a University that was folded in on itself and bringing it closer to the City.
>
> Opening up the University to the City: this is its adaptation to professional needs.
>
> Opening up the University to knowledges: this is the effort to renew research and to recognize *excellence*.
>
> Integration of the University in its City: this is the University 2000 at the heart of urban planning, it is the policy of partnership with local groups.
>
> Integration of the French University in a European ensemble: this is the meaning of European evaluation.[22]

The internal policy of the University is to be resolved in France by the appeal to excellence, which serves as the term that regroups and integrates all knowledge-related activities. This, in turn, permits the wider integration of the University as one corporate bureaucracy among others, both in the direction of the city and of the European Community. The city is no longer the "streets," nor even a vision of civic life (the Renaissance city-state that Allègre's title might lead us to expect). Rather, it is an agglomerate of professional-bureaucratic capitalist corporations whose needs are primarily centered upon the supply of a managerial-technical class. The city gives the University its commercial form of expression. And the European Community supplants the nation-state as the figure of the entity that provides the University with its political form of expression, an expression which is explicitly tied to the question of evaluation. The University will produce excellence in knowledges, and as such will link into the circuits of global capital and transnational politics without difficulty. This is because there is no cultural content to the notion of excellence, nothing specifically "French," for example, except insofar as "Frenchness" is a commodity on the global market.

Excellence exposes the pre-modern traditions of the University to the force of market capitalism. Barriers to free trade are swept away. An interesting example of this is the British government's decision to allow the polytechnics to rename themselves as universities. Oxford Polytechnic becomes Brookes University, and so on. This classic free-market maneuver guarantees that the only criterion of excellence is performativity in an expanded market. It would be an error to think that this was an *ideological* move on the part of the Conservative government, however. The decision was not primarily motivated by concern for the content of what is taught in the universities or polytechnics. Even if the tendency of polytechnics to form links with business in the interests of incorporating practical training into degrees might seem to fuel the strand of petty-bourgeois anti-intellectualism in the British Conservative party, it is also true that it was in the polytechnics that the work of the Birmingham school of Cultural Studies had had its greatest impact. Hence the sudden redenomination of polytechnics as universities is best understood as an *administrative* move: the breaking down of a barrier to circulation and to market expansion, analogous to the repeal of sumptuary laws that permitted the capitalization of the textile trade in Early Modern England.

One form of such market expansion is the development of interdisciplinary programs, which often appear as the point around which radicals and conservatives can make common cause in University reform. This is partly because interdisciplinarity has no inherent political orientation, as the example of the Chicago School shows.[23] It is also because the increased flexibility they offer is often attractive to administrators as a way of overcoming entrenched practices of demarcation, ancient privileges, and fiefdoms in the structure of universities. The benefits of interdisciplinary openness are numerous—as someone who works in an interdisciplinary department I am particularly aware of them—but they should not blind us to the institutional stakes that they involve. At present interdisciplinary programs tend to supplement existing disciplines; the time is not far off when they will be installed in order to replace clusters of disciplines.

Indeed, this is a reason to be cautious in approaching the institutional claim to interdisciplinarity staked by Cultural Studies when it replaces the old order of disciplines in the humanities with a more general field that combines history, art history, literature, media studies, sociology, and so on. In saying this, I want to join Rey Chow in questioning, from a sympathetic point of view, the unqualified acceptance both of interdisciplinary activity and of Cultural Studies that has been fairly common among academic radicals.[24] We can be interdisciplinary in the name of excellence, because excellence only preserves preexisting disciplinary boundaries insofar as they make no larger claim on the entirety of the system and pose no obstacle to its growth and integration.

To put this another way, the appeal to excellence marks the fact that there is no longer any idea of the University, or rather that the idea has now lost all content. As a non-referential unit of value entirely internal to the system, excellence marks nothing more than the moment of technology's self-reflection. All that the system requires is for activity to take place, and the empty notion of excellence refers to nothing other than the optimal input/output ratio in matters of information.[25] This is perhaps a less heroic role than we are accustomed to claim for the University, although it does resolve the question of parasitism. The University is now no more of a parasitical drain on resources than the stock exchange or the insurance companies are a drain on industrial production. Like the stock exchange, the University is a point of capital's self-knowledge, of capital's ability not just to manage risk or diversity but to extract a surplus value from that management. In the case of the University this extraction occurs as a result of speculation on differentials in information.

The implication of this shift in function is that the analysis of the University as an Ideological State Apparatus, in Althusser's terms, is no longer appropriate, since the University is no longer primarily an ideological arm of the nation-state but an autonomous bureaucratic corporation. To take another, perhaps less weighted, example we can compare the University to the National Basketball Association. Both are bureaucratic systems that govern an area of activity whose systemic functioning and external effects are not dependent on an external reference. The game of basketball has its rules, and those rules allow differences to arise that are objects of speculation. And while Philadelphia 76ers' victories have effects on their fans, and fans have effects on 76ers' victories (both as supporters and as financiers), those victories or defeats are not directly linked to the essential meaning of the city of Philadelphia. Results are not meaningless, but they arise within the system of basketball rather than in relation to an external referent.

For the University to become such a system involves a major change in the way in which it has been understood to produce institutional meaning. As I shall show later on, Schiller positioned the University of Culture as the quasi-church appropriate to the rational state, by claiming that the University would perform the same services for the state as the Church had for the feudal or absolutist monarch. However, the contemporary University of Excellence should now be understood as a bureaucratic system whose internal regulation is entirely self-interested without regard to wider ideological imperatives. Hence the stock market seeks maximum volatility in the interest of intensifying the profits attendant on the flux of capital rather than the stability of exchange that might defend strictly national interests.

40

The corollary of this is that we must analyze the University as a *bureaucratic system* rather than as the ideological apparatus that the left has traditionally considered it. As an autonomous system rather than an ideological instrument, the University should no longer be thought of as a tool that the left will be able to use for other purposes than those of the capitalist state. This explains the ease with which former West Germans have colonized the Universities of what was once the German Democratic Republic (GDR) since reunification. The Universities of the old GDR have been purged of those considered to be political apparatchiks of the Honecker regime. No parallel purges, however, have occurred in the Universities of the former Bundesrepublik, despite the fact that reunification was not supposed to be the conquest of the East by the West. The conflict, that is, is not presented as that between two ideologies (which would have necessitated purges on both sides), but as a conflict between the East, where the University used to be under ideological control, and the West, where the University was supposed to be non-ideological.

Of course, the Western universities had a massive ideological role to play during the Cold War, and much can be said about individual cases. But overall one is struck by the silence and speed of this replacement, by the fact that the counter-arguments that could be mounted in favor of the intellectual project of the former East Germany simply *cannot be heard* any longer. This is because the fall of the Wall means that the University is no longer primarily an ideological institution, and those from the West are better positioned to play the new roles required. If the posts of the purged have in many cases gone to young academics from the former West, this is not because they are primarily agents of a competing ideology, but because of bureaucratic efficiency. The young former West Germans are not necessarily more intelligent or more learned than those they replace; they are simply "cleaner," which is to say, less easily identifiable as ideological agents of their state. This is a primary symptom of the decline of the nation-state as the counter-signatory to the contract by which the modern University, the University of Culture, was founded. As my remarks on Allègre's invocation of the European Community have already suggested, the emergence of the University of Excellence in place of the University of Culture can

only be understood against the backdrop of the decline of the nation-state.

The demand for "clean hands," be it in German universities or in Italian politics, may be presented as a desire to renew the state apparatus, but I think it is better understood as the product of a general uncertainty concerning the role of the state, a call for "hands off." Complex and often contradictory, such a desire may result, as in Italy, in such paradoxical alliances as that of integrationist Fascists (the MSI) with separatists (the Northern League). Notably, this alliance occurred under the umbrella of Berlusconi's oddly transparent organization, Forza Italia, whose nationalism is the evocation of a football chant, and whose claim to govern is based on a rather dubious assertion of "business success." If I may offer a rather strange diagnosis of this apparent paradox, it is that the alliance in Italy is between those who wish for the question of community in Italy no longer to be posed: either because the Duce may return to provide an answer about "being Italian" and impose it with brutal violence (the Lega will tell people to "be regional") or because Berlusconi will reassure us that it is not a question, that the answer is as transparent and obvious as the light blue haze emanating from a television screen, or the light blue shirt on a footballer's back. Berlusconi does not offer a renewed nationalism (as his alliance with the MSI might lead us to fear) but a sanitized nationalist nostalgia that blankets and suppresses all questions concerning the nature of community.

Instead of the question of community, which was once posed both within and against the terms of nationalism, we get a generalized but meaningless nationalism that pushes aside questions. The national question, that is, is simply accepted as a generalized matter of nostalgia, be it for the evils of Fascism (Fini, the current leader of the MSI, is not a Duce, even in his dreams), or for the light blue colors of the royal house of Savoy. And the government is to get on with the matter of running the state as a business.

The nation understands itself as its own theme park, and that resolves the question of what it means to live in Italy: it is to have been Italian once. Meanwhile, the state is merely a large corporation to be entrusted to businessmen, a corporation that increasingly serves as the handmaiden to the penetration of transnational capital. The governmental structure of the nation-state is no longer the organizing center of the common existence of peoples across the planet, and the University of Excellence serves nothing other than itself, another corporation in a world of transnationally exchanged capital.

~ 3

The Decline of the Nation-State

Universities have not always been bureaucratic systems devoted to the pursuit of excellence. As we shall see, the idea of the University has in the past been accorded the kind of referential value that excellence lacks. The reasons for this are intimately bound up with the nation-state: the appeal to excellence occurs when the nation-state ceases to be the elemental unit of capitalism. At that point, instead of states striving with each other to best exemplify capitalism, capitalism swallows up the idea of the nation-state.[1]

This shift is usually referred to as globalization: the contemporary rise of those transnational corporations (TNCs) that currently control more capital than the vast majority of nation-states. Masao Miyoshi, in a brilliant brief study, makes the point that bourgeois capitals in the industrialized world "no longer wholly depend on the nation-state of their origin for protection and facilitation."[2] Former multinationals (corporations that cross national borders but still have their headquarters clearly associated with a particular nation) become TNCs when the corporation internalizes corporate loyalty, becoming "adrift and mobile, ready to settle anywhere and exploit any state including its own, as long as the affiliation serves its own interest" (736). Drawing on Leslie Sklair's analysis, Miyoshi points out that, of the largest one hundred economic units in the global economy, more than fifty are TNCs, rather than nation-states (739–740). For example, the transnational financier George Soros reported income of $1.1 billion in 1993, surpassing the gross domestic product of at least forty-two nations, although this would have made him only the thirty-seventh-most-profitable company in the United States. And as Miyoshi argues, the discourse of multiculturalism serves TNCs very well by redirecting corporate loyalty toward the corporate logo rather than the national flag of any one country.

The upshot of Miyoshi's argument is that the nation-state no longer works as a social glue; it ceases to provide the bond of community and is being replaced in this role by the TNC. Within the global economy, "National history and culture . . . are merely variants of one 'universal'—as in a giant theme park or shopping mall," to be appropriated by "tourism and other forms of commercialism" (747). Likewise, culture is entirely internalized as an element within the flow of global capital; it is no longer the idea that the accumulation of national capital claims to serve.

My point of difference with Miyoshi arises where he addresses the implication of intellectuals and academics in this process. He situates individual involvement as a moral question, noting that instead of resisting, academics seem only too happy to become "frequent fliers and globe-trotters" (750). I would argue that individual consciousness is not the issue. I think that Miyoshi's recognition of the complicity of the discourses of Cultural Studies and multiculturalism with the needs of TNCs has to be analyzed at the level of the University, where the University is understood as a bureaucratic institution developing toward the role of TNC in its own right.[3] Hence the task of thinkers in the humanities and in other disciplines can no longer be pitched at the level of individual resistance, of the heroism of thought, since the institution doesn't need another hero. There are no heroes in bureaucracy, as Kafka indicates.

Hence the status of the subject shifts with the decline of the nation-state, and this change has important implications for the University, the primary institution outside the nuclear family for the training of subjects of the modern nation-state. The emergence of the modern subject is intimately linked to the nation-state that stands as its specular guarantor. Instead of being subject *to* the arbitrary rule of a monarch, the modern citizen becomes the subject *of* a nation-state, a state whose political discourse is legitimated by recourse to the collective enunciation of a subjective "we," as in the phrase "we, the people." Hence the aim of the modern state is the revelation of the identity of a national subject, be it the universal subject of humanity (in republican democracies like revolutionary France or the United States) or the ethnic identity of the national subject as the object of rational discussion (in liberal-democratic nation-states in Europe).

This subjection of the subject to the state arises in general because the revelation of this identity requires passage through the institutions of the state: in order for an "I" to become an "I," to realize itself, it must pass through a "we." The individual citizen, that is, must become for him or herself the bearer of a meaning that is only accessible as part of a collectivity. The subject finds itself as it is mirrored to itself through the representational institutions of the state: as he or she who says, "I am an American." In Wlad Godzich's words, "those who hold state power first co-opt individuals, thereby making them other with respect to the rest of society, and then let the state as an apparatus of power determine the configuration of the social."[4] The modern University, I shall argue, was conceived by Humboldt as one of the primary apparatuses through which this production of national subjects was to take place in modernity, and the decline of the nation-state raises serious questions about the nature of the contemporary function of the University.

In this book, therefore, I want above all to do two things. First, to trace how the integration of the University as an institution under the aegis of the concept of "culture" has been linked to the question of the nation-state. Second, to ask whether there is an alternative to the discourse of excellence: At the twilight of modernity, which is also the twilight of the University as we have known it, can another way be found to think the University? This is to ask whether the University, once stripped of its cultural mission, can be something other than a bureaucratic arm of the unipolar capitalist system. But if we are to grasp the nature of this question, it is first necessary to understand the contemporary situation in which the decline of the nation-state means that the economic is no longer subjugated to the political (this means that we speak of global consumers, not of national production). Rather than being under national political control, the economy is more and more the concern of transnational entities who transfer capital in search of profit without regard to national boundaries. The erstwhile all-powerful state is reduced to becoming a bureaucratic apparatus of management. As Miyoshi has pointed out, the contemporary indicators of "statesmanship"—what all "world leaders" have in common nowadays—are domestic unpopularity and international weakness (744). The nation-state is a formation on its way to becoming as vestigial as the playing of drivers' national anthems in celebration of Grand Prix victories, victories that are, in fact, the work of transnational technological conglomerates with whom no nation could any longer compete.

Let me be clear about what I mean here when I say that the nation-state is withering. This is not the same thing as claiming that *nationalism* is no longer an issue. Nationalism, in places such as Bosnia and the former Soviet Union, is the sign of the breakdown of the nation-state (and not of its resurgence) precisely because no nation-state can be imagined that could integrate so many conflicting desires. Hence the despair of so many intellectuals in the face of such events. The kinds of nationalist movements we are currently witnessing are actually more in the service of globalization than the old nation-state. Under globalization the state does not disappear; it simply becomes more and more managerial, increasingly incapable of imposing its ideological will, which is to say, incapable of imposing its will as the *political* content of economic affairs. The state can no longer ask what constitutes "economic health," since even to presume to ask this question is a sign of economic weakness. One sign of such weakness, for instance, is the absence of an "independent" central bank. The International Monetary Fund (IMF) determines the creditworthiness of nation-states on the basis of several criteria, but an important one is the presence of a central bank that is "independent" of governmental control (such as the Federal Reserve or the Bank of England), which is to say, more amenable to IMF control.

This hollowing out of the state is a process that appears to the erstwhile national population as "depoliticization": the loss of belief in an alternative political truth that will authoritatively legitimate oppositional critique.[5] The loss of faith in salvation is actualized in the rise of the modern bureaucratic state as an essentially unipolar society. Thus, the capitalist system in its contemporary form offers people not a national identity (which was always a bad ideological bargain) but a non-ideological belonging: a corporate identity in which they participate only at the price of becoming operatives. The emergence of the unipolar or managerial state thus marks a terminal point for political thought. Rather than the political question being that of what kind of state can establish the just society and realize human destiny, the positioning of the state as the unifying horizon for all political representations indicates that social meaning lies elsewhere, in an economic sphere outside the political competence of the state.

Consumerism—which is correctly perceived as the most pressing threat to the traditional subject of university education in North America—is the economic counterpart of the hollowing out of political subjectivity that accompanies the decline of the nation-state. As such, it is a symptom of the almost complete internalization and reconsumption of the product of the system. Consumerism thus is less of an ideological falsification of well-being (bread and circuses) than a mark that no benefit exterior to the system can be imagined, no benefit that would not be subject to cost-benefit analysis (was that vacation a good buy?). Consumerism is not a political or ideological matter; it is not a matter for the nation-state. It is the sign that the individual is no longer a *political* entity, is not a subject of the nation-state. Thus, for example, a United Nations report of 1993 indicates that the world's population now includes 100 million migrants, of whom only 37 percent are refugees from persecution, war, or catastrophe. Migration, that is, is more of an *economic* than a political phenomenon. The exponential growth in the number of migrants can be grasped when we realize that this figure has doubled since 1989. The personal and cultural costs of migration are immense, yet what is clear is that the economic pressure to migration in a global market is rendering the labor force more flexible and adaptable to capital at the direct expense of the integrity of the nation-state as a cultural formation.

The terms of such a shift are clear when applied to the University. The preface to Alfonso Borrero Cabal's report for UNESCO and the International Development Research Center of Canada, *The University as an Institution Today,* notes the "increasing internationalization of higher education. According to UNESCO, in the 62 countries responsible for an estimated 95% of foreign students in the world in 1990, the number of students abroad increased from 916 thousand in 1980 to almost 1.2 million in 1990 (29%)."[6] This horizon of globalization means that the student subject is no longer the prospective national system. The benefit of this for the global capitalist market is clearly stated in a 1990 report of the UNESCO European Center for Higher Education, which calls for "an organization of teaching and certification, possibly on a modular basis, which would permit students to transfer on pre-determined conditions between institutions and courses of different levels."[7] The payoff of such an arrangement is that it "would not only serve a process of lifelong learning, but, if adopted on a community-wide basis, would be supportive of the mobility of EC citizens."[8] The international and interdisciplinary flexibility is envisaged with the goal of producing a subject who is no longer tied to the nation-state, who can readily move to meet the demands of the global market. Where the great W. E. B. Du Bois argued that "the problem of the twentieth century is the problem of the color-line," I am tempted to add that problem of the twenty-first century is that of the borderline, a problem intimately linked to that of race.[9]

I speak of the borderline because it is the non-place (in Michel Serres's term) at which the tensions of globalization are manifest. In his remarkable book *The Coming Community,* Giorgio Agamben has characterized the effect of globalization upon the production of political subjects as the emergence of a global petty bourgeoisie: "If we had once again to conceive of the fortunes of humanity in terms of class, then today we would have to say that there are no longer social classes, but just a single planetary petty bourgeoisie, in which all the old social classes are dissolved: The petty bourgeoisie has inherited the world and is the form in which humanity has survived nihilism."[10] Agamben's argument is that the planetary petty bourgeoisie has freed itself from the Fascist positioning of the petty bourgeoisie as the class that, above all others, traced the path of its potential access to bourgeois grandeur through a discourse of popular identity and nationalism (None more chauvinist than the shopkeeper). As Agamben remarks:

The planetary petty bourgeoisie has instead freed itself from these dreams [of false popular identity] and has taken over the aptitude of the proletariat to refuse any recognizable social identity. . . . They know only the improper and the inauthentic and even refuse the idea of a discourse that could be proper to them. That which constituted the truth and falsity of the peoples and generations that have followed one another on the earth—differences of language, of dialect, of ways of life, of character, of custom, and even the physical particularities of each person—has lost any meaning for them and any capacity for expression and communication. In the petty bourgeoisie, the diversities that have marked the tragicomedy of universal history are brought together and exposed in a phantasmagorical vacuousness. (62–63)

This might seem like a lament for the end of culture, a complaint that cultural specificity is being erased by a generation of global Reebok-wearers who all support the Chicago Bulls. But when Agamben goes on to argue that this means that the "absurdity of individual existence" has lost its pathos, has become an "everyday exhibition," we recognize a reader of Walter Benjamin (63). Agamben is not content simply to mourn the lost meaning of culture. Just as Benjamin is concerned to *transvalue* rather than mourn the loss of aura once the work of art is universally exhibited, so Agamben attempts to transvalue the dereferentialization of culture—transvalue, that is, the process through which culture loses any specific referent.[11] In so doing, he actually leaves the circuit of culture altogether, since "culture," I would argue, has always been positioned in modernity either as the reconstruction of a lost authenticity (in its nostalgic or romantic mode) or as a coming to terms with the loss of origin (in its ironic or high modernist mode). As Agamben puts it rather cryptically: "Selecting in the new planetary humanity those characteristics that allow for its survival, removing the thin diaphragm that separates bad mediatized advertising from the perfect exteriority that communicates only itself—this is the political task of our generation" (64).

What is at stake in Agamben's evocation of a political task is an attempt to think against globalization from within—to think the non-coincidence of globalization and capitalism, instead of assuming their sheer isomorphy. This means that we can no longer oppose an authentic, an ideal, or a national "culture" to capitalism, as if culture were the real mode of social processes and capitalism a false or anti-culture. In the 1980s the British Left sought to attack Thatcherism as a betrayal of a true national culture, a false nationalism that served the interests of global capital. They were doomed to failure from the start, because they misunderstood that the appeal of Thatcherite nationalism, what allowed it to serve the TNCs, was precisely that it was a nationalism *against the modernist idea of the nation-state.* This internal contradiction within Thatcherite nationalism was the root of both its appeal and its flexibility, so that exposing the contradiction was not enough to defeat the argument. Global fusion and national fission go hand in hand and work together to efface the linking of the nation-state and symbolic life that has constituted the idea of "national culture" since the eighteenth century. In this situation, to appeal to a notion of universal or global culture is to misrecognize that such appeals always model the universal or the global *according to the contours of the modern European nation-state,* the very instance that is being ground up by the TNCs.

The implications of this situation for the idea of the University are enormous. As Gérard Granel has argued, it is now pointless to seek the destiny of the University in its capacity to realize the essence of a nation-state or its people.[12] Heidegger's "Rectorial Address" at Freiburg will have been the last attempt to subjugate economic technology to the political will of the nation-state through an appeal to ethnic destiny.[12] As a state ideological apparatus, the University had a cultural position roughly equivalent to that of a national airline, such as Air France. If we simply schematize an instance that in practice always has a more complicated nature, we may say that the national airline is an instance of the state's attempt to realize itself by guaranteeing the hegemony of the *political* over the *economic.* Rather than being crudely subjected to the profit motive, the national airline is subsidized by the nation-state, for which it has both an internal and an external function. The external function is to assert the technological competitiveness of the state, and the internal function is to homogenize the territory of the state by ensuring ease of access to all its areas. This internal function is basically a subsidy that attempts to subject economic to political factors. Where market forces might cause ex-centric lines of trade and transportation to develop and, in effect, cause internal divisions to arise within the state, the national airline (which must fly to all areas of the state, regardless of their economic importance) produces a kind of cartographic "flattening" and attendant centralization analogous to the demographic "flattening" of the State University (which educates all its students as subjects of the state, regardless of class origins). As with the State University, the state investment in a national airline works (although not exclusively) as a massive internal subsidy to the middle and upper-middle classes. The upper classes can always charter a private plane or hire a tutor. The middle and upper-middle classes can afford the marginal supplementary cost of state air travel or higher education in a way that ensures them and their children privileged access, while buffering them against the actual cost.

The decline of the national ideology means that capital no longer needs to offer the middle classes this ideological sense of belonging and is happy to proletarianize them—which is why most professors now travel economy class. More significantly, the fate of Pan American airlines (the refusal of the U.S. government to provide sufficient state subsidy to protect America's image abroad) is indicative of the irrelevance of such a political vision of the state to the current global economic order of TNCs. Likewise, a report to the European Economic Community of 1994 recommended abolition of state subsidies to national airlines within the common market, as a measure likely to increase "efficiency" and ensure a return to "profitability" (while also doubtless resulting in the disappearance of several national carriers). A parallel withdrawal of funding is apparent in the University sector in the case of individual students, as European governments seek to introduce programs of student loans, while the U.S. government, with loan programs already in place, introduces stringent criteria of profitability rather than subsidy to its loan programs.

So how are we to think the institution of the University in which we find ourselves? It is clear that in the University we can never "find ourselves," come into our birthright; we cannot achieve the pure auto-affection that brings thought to an end in the virtual presence of an entirely self-knowing and autonomous subject. Yet such a notion of self-finding has been, throughout the modern age, the grand narrative of the function of the University. The subject of human history strives for autonomy, for the self-knowledge that will free it from the chains of the past, from its debts to a nature and to a language that are not of its own making. Thus, Kant thought we could find ourselves as entirely reasonable. The German Idealists thought we could find ourselves as an ethnic culture. The technocrats of today think we can find ourselves as "most excellent," to cite *Bill and Ted's Excellent Adventure*—a film which is an interesting attempt to understand the impossibility of historical thought once knowledge has itself become commodified as information.

The University becomes modern when it takes on responsibility for working out the relation between the subject and the state, when it offers to incarnate an idea that will both theorize and inculcate this relationship. This is its dual mission of research and teaching, and if the latter has always lagged behind the former in terms of real service performed for the state, this is hardly surprising. As I will discuss in Chapter 5, the articulation of teaching and research is worked out by the German Idealists (most notably Humboldt). However, if we are to understand the significance of the University of Excellence, to grasp what is at stake in the posthistorical move beyond culture that is occasioned by the decline of the nation-state, then we must first take a look at how the birth of the modern University and that of the nation-state are intertwined. If we are to understand what it means that contemporary students are consumers rather than national subjects, we must first trace the emergence of the modern idea of the University.

~ 4

The University within the Limits of Reason

The characteristic of the modern University is to have an idea that functions as its referent, as the end and meaning of its activities. As I mentioned earlier, in general the modern University has had three ideas. The story begins, as do so many stories about modernity, with Kant, who envisioned the University as guided by the concept of *reason.* Kant's vision is followed by Humboldt's idea of *culture,* and more recently the emphasis has been on the techno-bureaucratic notion of *excellence.* The distinguishing feature of the last on this list is that it actually lacks a referent. That is to say, the idea that functions as the University's referent—excellence—itself has no referent. The University of Excellence is the *simulacrum* of the idea of a University.

If you want a practical example, think of what a University president is supposed to do. In the Kantian University, his or her function is the purely disciplinary one of making decisive judgments in inter-faculty conflicts on the grounds of reason alone. In the University founded on culture, the president incarnates a pandisciplinary ideal of general cultural orientation, becoming the figure of the University itself (nineteenth-century University presidents such as Charles Eliot or Benjamin Jowett spring to mind here).[1] As Schleiermacher puts it, the true "idea" of a rector is that of a single individual who can stand metaphorically for the University in the eyes of the world while remaining metonymically connected to the rest of the faculty. *Primus inter pares,* such a president figures the double function of culture as the animating principle of the University: both gradual *Bildung* and revealed unity of social meaning, both metonymy and metaphor.[2] In the University of Excellence, however, a president is a bureaucratic administrator who moves effortlessly from the lecture hall, to the sports stadium, to the executive lounge. From judge, to synthesizer, to executive and fund raiser, without publicly expressing any opinions or passing any judgments whatsoever.[3]

The contemporary move toward the University of Excellence does not mean, however, that the influence of the German University model ceases to be relevant to an analysis of the University. A clue to the decisive quality of the German University model can be found if we examine the three levels at which thought is embodied according to Kant: the individual researcher, the University, and the academy at large. In a sense, the Kantian University of Reason is modeled upon the individual researcher, perhaps despite Kant's wishes. The conflict of faculties is entirely analogous to the conflict between tradition and reason, superstition and enlightenment, that supposedly goes on in the breast of every truly fervent seeker after knowledge. By contrast, in the contemporary University of Excellence, the model of the academy rules with the process we know as "professionalization," bringing about the increasing integration of functions so that research is non-referential. That is to say, the content of the research comes to matter less and less, as research is ever more indistinguishable from the mere reproduction of the system. The result is that there is an increasing convergence of research, teaching, and professional training within the system.

This is a generalization, of course, but it explains the deep pull of a book as ill-considered as Allan Bloom's *The Closing of the American Mind*. What Bloom seems to have realized, although he has little idea about it, is that culture is no longer the watchword of the University. To put it another way, the University is no longer Humboldt's, and that means it is no longer *The* University. The Germans not only founded a University and gave it a mission; they also made the University into the decisive instance of intellectual activity. All of this is in the process of changing: intellectual activity and the culture it revived are being replaced by the pursuit of excellence and performance indicators.

To understand how *culture* could emerge as the mission of Humboldt's University and how the University of Excellence could then function without it, we first need to look more carefully at the framework Kant sketched. Importantly, Kant founds the modern University on reason, and reason is what gives the University its universality in the modern sense.[4] In the medieval University, the order of disciplines (which was not that of the faculties) reflected the orders of knowledge in the seven liberal arts, divided up into the trivium (of grammar, rhetoric, and knowledge) and the quadrivium (of arithmetic, geometry, astronomy, and music). This division is Aristotelian, a principle of separation according to the nature of the matter to be studied and requiring no immanent unifying principle. Indeed, the unifying principle of the medieval University is theodicy, and thus lies elsewhere, only intervening as external censorship of the temporal by the spiritual. What distinguishes the modern University is a universal unifying principle that is *immanent* to the University. Kant ushers in the modernity of the University by naming this principle reason, which is to say that reason provides a *ratio* between the disciplines. And reason has its own discipline, that of philosophy, the lower faculty.

According to *The Conflict of the Faculties,* the three higher faculties are those that have a content: theology, law, and medicine. The lower faculty, that of philosophy (which also includes the humanities) has no content as such, apart from the free exercise of reason. In saying that it has no content, I mean that what distinguishes historical study in the faculty of philosophy from historical study in law, medicine, or religion is that it is guided by nothing other than free, rational inquiry.

The three higher faculties are thus heteronomously authorized; they draw their authority from an instance that remains an unquestionable authority for them. Theology depends on the Bible, law on the civil code, medicine on the decrees of the medical profession. The authority of the lower faculty is, however, autonomous in that philosophy depends on nothing outside itself; it legitimates itself by reason alone, by its own practice. In the event that philosophy does recognize an external authority, such as the state, it preserves this autonomy in that it does so only by virtue of a free judgment *of its own* based on reason.

Given their reliance on heteronomous authority, the three estab-

lished faculties of theology, law, and medicine are on the side of superstition in that they promulgate the blind acceptance of tradition,
which seeks to control the people not by making them use reason but
by making them accept established authority. They do not educate the
people in reason but offer them magical solutions. Thus theology
teaches people how to be saved without being good (this is what the
TV evangelist shares with the seller of indulgences). Law tells people *sophists*
how to win cases without being honest (some things never change).
Medicine teaches people how to cure diseases rather than how to live
healthily (in the age of antismoking campaigns, we no longer recognize
this distinction). Philosophy, on the other hand, replaces the practical
savoir-faire of these magicians with reason, which refuses all shortcuts.
Hence, philosophy questions the prescriptions of the legislative power
and asks fundamental questions on the basis of reason alone, interfering
with the higher faculties in order to critique their grounds.

The life of the Kantian University is therefore a perpetual conflict
between established tradition and rational inquiry. This conflict is given
a historical force and becomes a project for progress by virtue of the
fact that it is dialectical. The conflict between the tradition established
in the three higher faculties (theology, medicine, and law) and the free
inquiry of the lower faculty (philosophy) leads towards a universally
grounded rationality. Each particular inquiry, each discipline, develops
itself by interrogating its own foundations with the aid of the faculty
of philosophy. Thus, inquiry passes from mere empirical practice to
theoretical self-knowledge by means of self-criticism. Each discipline
seeks its own purity—what is essential to it. And what is essential to
philosophy is nothing other than this search for the essential itself: the
faculty of critique. In this sense, the lower faculty turns out to be the
higher, the queen of the sciences, the discipline that incarnates the pure
principle that animates the University and differentiates it from either
a technical training school (a guild) or a specialized academy (a royal
society).

Now it might seem that the autonomy of the University, founded
on the autonomy of reason gained by self-criticism, forbids any direct
social effect, any link between the University and the state. The paradox
of the social mission of the Kantian University has been noted by Der-

rida in "Mochlos; or, The Conflict of the Faculties."[5] Kant's text explicitly addresses the question of the link between the University and the state and argues that one of the functions of the University is to produce technicians for the state, that is, men of affairs. Likewise, the function of the state with regard to the University is to intervene at all times to remind these men of affairs that they must submit their use of knowledge in the service of the state to the control of the faculties, ultimately to the faculty of philosophy. So on the one hand, the state must protect the University in order to ensure the rule of reason in public life. On the other hand, philosophy must protect the University from the abuse of power by the state, in limiting the rule of established interests in the higher faculties. This unlimited right of reason to intervene is what distinguishes legitimate conflict, *concordia discors,* from illegitimate conflict (which is the arbitrary exercise of authority by the established powers of the higher faculties and the state).

Thus the problem is already posed as the modern University begins to be thought: how to unify reason and the state, knowledge and power, how to resolve the aporia of this conflict? Autonomous reason breaks down the established authority of heteronomous superstition, but how is autonomy to be institutionalized? That is, does not the *institutionalization* of reason's autonomy in a University necessarily cause it to become heteronomous to itself? How can the reason embodied in the University not come to be the object of a superstitious rather than rational respect? Philosophy promises to do this by first carrying on the activity of self-critique and then, through that critique, realizing the essence of humanity. At the same time, in order that thought be preserved against the heteronomy of fatalism, the realization of this essence must not be the product of an empirical historical process but of rational reflection.

An example of the kind of paradox that this produces comes right at the beginning of *The Conflict of the Faculties,* where Kant describes the positioning of the University among other institutional forms for the propagation of knowledge. After explaining that the division of faculties within the University is based on what he claims are purely rational grounds, he then remarks that *by pure chance* the empirical history of the Prussian people has led them to adopt these forms of organization as well. Unlike Hegel, Kant does not attempt to derive a reason of history from this fact, so as to argue that history is a rational process. Rather, he leaves us to remark the glaring coincidence. He does this because he wants to preserve the possibility that reason can install itself in history, even if he is concerned to preserve the separation between empirical history and critique. What Kant needs, then, is a third term in which reason can combine institution and autonomy, while holding pure reason and empirical history apart.

Kant seeks to do so by producing the figure of the *republican subject* who incarnates this conflict. If the regulative principle of the Kantian University is the *sapere aude* of reason, the problematic of institutionalization is circumvented in the figure of the subject, who is rational in matters of knowledge, republican in matters of power. Thus, it might seem odd that in a text designed to appease a monarch Kant speaks with enthusiasm of the "enthusiasm" generated by the French Revolution. He is clearly not interested, however, in the empirical people but in the way in which the French Revolution, as "a historical sign," signifies the possibility of a universal subject of humanity to be realized through history: "It is provisionally the duty of monarchs, [even] if they rule as autocrats, to govern in a *republican* (not democratic) way, that is, to treat the people in accordance with principles which are commensurate with the spirit of libertarian laws (as a nation with mature understanding would prescribe them for itself), although they would not be literally canvassed for their consent."[6]

The University, then, with reason as its principle, only institutionalizes reason fictionally by analogy with the enlightened despot who rules his people *as if* they were mature. Although he imposes laws autocratically (that is, heteronomously in function of an arbitrary power) the imposition of these laws must be guided by a regulative principle of reason. A heteronomous power is invoked in order to give to a people the laws that it would give itself *if it were autonomous*. The University institutionalizes reason, but although its authority to impose reason may function heteronomously (by virtue of the superstitious respect accorded to the University as the institution of reason), that authority must only function so as to affirm the principle of the autonomy of the rational subject. Thus, in a very literal sense, the Kantian

University is a *fictional* institution. Reason can only be instituted if the institution remains a fiction, functions only "as if" it were not an institution. If the institution becomes real, then reason departs. This is a more fundamental aporia than the problem of naive optimism concerning the likely activities of the state in protecting the autonomy of the University within itself. In a sense, it precedes even the difficulties of demarcation between the state and the University, between the higher and lower faculties that Derrida notes in Kant.[7]

What was required was a way to flesh out this fiction, to allow the University to take on a form that might work out the aporia between reason and institution. Historically, as Gumbrecht has pointed out, a split supervenes at this point that has to do with the way in which the state is understood to derive its legitimation.[8] Focusing on the study of literature, Gumbrecht follows Lyotard's *The Postmodern Condition* in noting that French thought becomes concerned with the idea of humanity, while the Germans focus on the notion of ethnicity. I would add that this is because post-revolutionary France legitimates the state through an appeal to the idea of the people, while for Germany prior to and after Bismarck the problem is of legitimating the German state as an ethnic unity. The University is pressed into the service of the state once the notion of universal reason is replaced by the idea of national culture as the animating principle of the University. Thus, through an appeal to culture, the state, in effect, orients the University's institutional structure and directs its social articulation, effectively controlling both research and teaching.

This shift is less apparent in the case of the French, since they are claiming to legitimate the state in terms of universal reason, and hence their University system will be placed at the service of national culture, while continuing to think its identity in terms of a battle between superstition and enlightenment. At the same time, the English did not have a state University system, and the need to imagine such a system will only arise later, for Newman and Arnold, when the pressures of empire force an articulation of nation, state, and modernity. As I shall show, the English experience is particular in that literature, rather than philosophy, is the discipline entrusted with the elaboration of national identity, and this perhaps because the alliance of church and state (and the exclusive rule of the Anglican church over the universities of Oxford and Cambridge until the partial reforms of 1854) undermines the simple opposition guiding the Enlightenment story of emancipation as the triumph of the rational state over the superstitious church. Hence Shakespeare, not the Greeks, is positioned by the English as the pre-lapsarian moment of a spontaneous immediate organic culture that the nation-state must seek to regain by means of the rational mediation of University education.

In the first place, I will argue that the German experience has been decisive, and that Humboldt's response to Schleiermacher and Fichte, a response which provided the pattern for the institution of the University of Berlin, stands as the general model for the modern state University. The United States has the dubious honor of having, since at least the foundation of Johns Hopkins, technologized the German model to the point of developing the idea of excellence. The tension of this process has been apparent in the anglophone world from the fact that the debate on culture is governed above all by the question posed to culture by technology. C. P. Snow's argument for "two cultures" is a fascinating rhetorical ploy that Leavis correctly identified as the first step in dereferentialization, in the loss of any specific referent for culture, and I shall have occasion to return to this later on.

[handwritten margin note: VALID ARG? NOT SCIENCE VS LITERATURE]

But before looking at the installation of literary culture (in opposition to technology) as the guiding light of University education, I want to trace briefly the emergence of a philosophical notion of culture in the writings of the German Idealists. This is the idea of culture on which the modern University is founded, and it is determined primarily in opposition to fragmentation. The University will function as the glue for the emerging German nation-state. The University will allow modernity to synthesize progress and unity, to direct the destructive aspect of modern innovation toward a higher social unity: the total nation-state.

～ 5

The University and the Idea of Culture

Most projects for the University of the twenty-first century bear a striking resemblance to the University projects of the nineteenth century. The reason it is necessary to reread Humboldt, Schiller, Schleiermacher, Fichte, and Kant is that the vast majority of contemporary "solutions" to the crisis of the University are, in fact, no more than restatements of Humboldt or Newman, whose apparent aptness is the product of ignorance of these founding texts on the history of the institution. So we hear a great deal about the need to value both teaching and research, or the indirect utility of pure research, as if these were new ideas. These ideas were new once, and their recurrence is something that should probably earn sufficient respect to permit a rereading to be indulged— a rereading that I have begun in the previous chapter and will continue here by looking at Kant's successors.

The achievement of the German Idealists is a truly remarkable one: to have articulated and instituted an analysis of knowledge and its social function. On the basis of an aporia in Kantian philosophy, they deduced not only the modern University but also the German nation. The dialectic of permanent knowledge and historical tradition identified by Schelling and resolved by Schiller through the mediation of aesthetic ideology brought about an articulation of the ethnic nation, the rational state, and philosophical culture, which linked speculative philosophy to the reason of history itself (for almost two centuries of imperial expansion).

Schiller's famous critique of Kant acknowledges the capacity of reason to exalt man to the level of the universal. Reason, according to
Schiller, centers the subject as autonomous, capable of reflecting upon
a world of determinations from which it is liberated as a pure point of
consciousness. For Schiller, man is indeed emancipated by reason, but
he claims that Kant's non-empirical account of reason as pure system
is characterized by arbitrary techniques of deduction, which Schelling
elsewhere refers to as merely the conditioned understanding that characterizes logic.[1] As Schiller points out, the imposition of the moral state
of pure reason can only proceed at the cost of the destruction of the
preexisting, unemancipated condition of humanity, characterized by
the interiority of "natural sentiment."[2] The antinomy of nature and
reason in Kant leaves the subject no choice: to arrive at reason is to
destroy nature, to reach maturity is to forget childhood absolutely. This
produces the famous hermeneutic circle in which the rational state is
supposed to educate humanity, but only an educated humanity can
found that state.

The problem of institutionalization in Kant's work is phrased by
Schiller as the difficulty of how one is to move from the "state of
nature" to the "state of reason" without destroying nature. The answer,
briefly, is through culture as a process of aesthetic education. Culture,
that is, allows us to move from nature to reason without destroying
nature. Thus art removes chance from nature (to allow morality) while
at the same time art does not free reason entirely from nature. This
Bildung is a process of the development of moral character that situates
beauty as an intermediate step between the chaos of nature and the
strict and arbitrary structures of pure reason. Art stands, then, between
the purely passive determination of reason by nature (man as beast)
and the utterly active determination of nature by reason (man as machine). It is important to understand, however, that the process of
aesthetic education is not conceived by Schiller as a matter of merely
looking at pictures. It is a fundamentally historical process: reason is
given organic life through historical study. Humanity does not achieve
the moral state by rejecting nature but by reinterpreting nature as a
historical process.

Thus, reason must replace belief; the state must replace the church.

However, an intermediate institution is also required. This intermediate institution must be able to embody the process of culture by which the natural character of mankind is to be prepared for the state of reason. Schleiermacher, in developing hermeneutics as a way of reworking tradition in order to raise the work of nature to the level of reason, identifies this intermediary institution as the University.[3] The reform of institutions, Schleiermacher insists, cannot simply abolish tradition and turn to the arbitrary application of reason in place of natural formations such as the medieval University. Tradition cannot be abandoned but must be worked through in order for its true meaning to be understood. What is rational in tradition, then, is not only isolated and affirmed but also given organic life in that it is *preserved* rather than simply imposed upon a void. Thus, for example, through the hermeneutic process the nation will come to embody an ethnicity that is raised to rational self-consciousness. This differs significantly from a belief that previously existing social forms will be replaced by those deduced on the basis of the abstract idea of humanity. What this means in more practical terms is that the destruction of the French Revolution (remember Mirabeau's dictum: "*pour tout reconstruire, il fallait tout démolir*") will not have been necessary for the people to reach self-consciousness and become self-determining.[4] Hence, the German model offers considerable reassurance to state power: the University exists to produce reason without revolution, without destruction.

The process of hermeneutic reworking is called culture, and it has a double articulation. On the one hand, culture names an *identity*. It is the unity of all knowledges that are the object of study; it is the object of *Wissenschaft* (scientific-philosophical study).[5] On the other hand, culture names a *process of development*, of the cultivation of character—*Bildung*. In the modern University, the two branches of this process are research and teaching, and the particularity of the Idealists was to insist that the specificity of the University comes from the fact that it is the place where the two are inseparable. The high school practices teaching without research; the academy practices research without teaching. The University is the center of the educational system, because it is where teaching and research are combined, so that in Schelling's words, the "nurseries of science" must also be "institutions of general culture."[6]

The University of Culture, instituted by Humboldt, draws its legitimacy from culture, which names the synthesis of teaching and research, process and product, history and reason, philology and criticism, historical scholarship and aesthetic experience, the institution and the individual. Thus the revelation of the idea of culture and the development of the individual are one. Object and process unite organically, and the place they unite is the University, which thus gives the people an idea of the nation-state to live up to and the nation-state a people capable of living up to that idea.

For Schleiermacher, *Wissenschaft* names the speculative science that is the unity underlying all pursuits of specific knowledges. *Wissenschaft* is the speculative search for the *unity* of knowledge that marks a cultured people. That unity of integrated knowledges was, of course, the property of the Greeks and has now been lost. This situation of the Greeks as the pure origin of a lost culture is the common narrative of German speculative philosophy. Perhaps its clearest articulation comes in Schiller's *On the Aesthetic Education of Mankind.* According to Schiller, modernity has replaced a unified culture with a fragmented civilization, which is more various (and in some senses more advanced) in its particular knowledges but also less meaningful. As Fichte puts it, in his version of a plan for the University of Berlin that lost out to Humboldt's counter-proposal, the vastness of the modern field of positive knowledges renders the extended totality of knowledge incommensurable with individual understanding.[7] Yet if the extended totality of knowledge cannot be grasped by the individual, the Idealists claim that the individual may nonetheless seek to apprehend the essential unity of knowledge, thus participating in the organic totality of living knowledge, even if overwhelmed by the sheer mass of dead material facts.

The German Idealists propose that the way to reintegrate the multiplicity of known facts into a unified cultural science is through *Bildung,* the ennoblement of character. Through *Bildung,* the nation-state can achieve scientifically the cultural unity that the Greeks once possessed naturally. The nation-state will come to re-embody the unity that the multiplication and disciplinary separation of knowledges have imposed in the intellectual sphere, that the division of labor has imposed in the social sphere. How will this happen? Here it is perhaps

65

worth noting the minor differences among the Idealists who seek to give institutional form to Schiller's notion of "aesthetic education." In order to do this, the later Idealists develop Schiller's appeal to beauty as an appeal to culture as both a transcendence (the guiding unity of pure science that is the object and the ground of speculative thought or research) and a developmental process (the pedagogic *Bildung*). As Humboldt puts it, the principle of culture embodied in the University fuses the advancement of objective science (cultural knowledge) with subjective spiritual and moral training (cultivation).[8]

To this end, the University is organized by Humboldt according to the rule of speculative philosophy, which both reflects upon positive knowledges so as to find their origin and telos, and seeks to provide the metadiscourse that legitimates and organizes all knowledge. Thus, Schleiermacher contends that the faculty of philosophy is the exterior form which the interior necessity of the University takes on. As with Kant, philosophy is the purely autonomous moment when knowledge reflects upon itself. The difference is that in Schleiermacher's version the process of philosophical reflection grounds knowledge in an organic principle rather than as the simple self-coherence of an abstract system. Facts are not simply arranged by philosophical reflection according to a logical principle of non-contradiction; they are given life. Philology, the historical study of language, is the form that this organic grounding takes. In the hermeneutic process of philological research, history is reworked according to rational principles in order to reveal its unity. Schelling, in his *Lectures on the Method of Academic Studies,* even describes philology as history placed into a living totality, the process by which languages are given life.[9] Likewise, Schleiermacher reaffirms the national language as the unit of science. Science has its unity in the framework of a national language, which forms a closed totality within the wider totality of absolute knowledge. Hence science is grounded in a historical ethnicity rather than in the purely rational abstract idea of a people as a pure will.

Schleiermacher differs from Fichte in insisting that the relation between the University and the state must be entirely indirect. The state must intervene only to protect the freedom of the University. Such freedom permits the autonomous work of philosophical reflection, the working out of the inner necessity of knowledge itself that requires no external structuring, no fixed order of courses and disciplines. For Schleiermacher, the benefit for the state is not a direct one of utility. The University does not produce better servants of the state. Instead, the benefit is indirect: the University produces not servants but *subjects*. That is the point of the pedagogy of *Bildung*, which teaches knowledge acquisition as a *process* rather than the acquisition of knowledge as a product. This question recurs regularly, even now, in debates over the relative merits of large lecture courses versus seminars.[10]

Educated properly, the subject learns the rules of thought, not a content of positive knowledge, so that thought and knowledge acquisition become a freely autonomous activity, part of the subject. Regarding this distinction between the reflective process of *Bildung* appropriate to science and the merely mechanical acquisition of positive knowledges, the Idealists are in unison. Thus, for Fichte, pedagogy is pure process. The teacher does not transmit facts (which can be better learnt from books, the reading of which leaves more room for autonomous reflection) but rather does two things. First, the teacher narrativizes the search for knowledge, tells the story of the process of knowledge acquisition.[11] Second, the teacher enacts the process, sets knowledge to work. What is thus taught is not facts but critique—the formal art of the use of mental powers, the process of judgment.

The time of *Bildung* effectively expresses the idea of absolute science, since it is both a single moment and an eternity. In this respect, the philosophy of *Bildung* expresses its continuing debt to Kantian rationalism and distinguishes itself from any merely empirical notions of development or maturation.[12] As Schleiermacher points out, the time of University is in fact but a single moment, the moment of the awakening of the idea of knowledge, when the subject is both conscious of reason and conscious of itself as rational.[13] This single moment is also an eternity, since, as Fichte insists, the rational ordering of knowledge allows the infinite multiplication of time: "The art of ordering . . . insofar as it takes no step in vain, multiplies time to the infinite and extends the short span of a single human existence to the dimensions of an eternity."[14] Such an eternity is, of course, the temporality that is no longer available to Barzun, whose University of the 1960s is prey to time and motion consultants. The speculative philosophical reflection outlined by Fichte does not lose itself in an endless sea of facts. Rather, reflection grasps the meaning of facts, allowing memory to work systematically according to fundamental principles and not as mere aggregation.

This theory concerning the transmission of knowledge is, in the first place, a theory concerning the time of pedagogy, the *chronotope* within which the order of knowledge can be established as a spatial system. For knowledge to become an autonomous object that can be thought organically, it must be possible for teaching to be both a process of production and of reproduction *at the same time*. It is above all the time of teaching that allows the German Idealists to propose the University as the model for an institution in which the present could fuse past tradition and future ambition into a unified field of culture. This model does, however, have some variations. Most important, Humboldt's version of the University project differs from Fichte's in that it prescribes a much looser level of state control over the means by which this fusion is to be achieved. Humboldt's project prescribes a form less directly modeled after that of the state as the "regulated meshing of different forces melded into an organic unity and totality for the promotion of a common goal."[15] Where Fichte's University aspires in its structure to the condition of the state (with plans for funding provided in detail), Humboldt's appears as a productive supplement to the state apparatus, endowed with a liberal margin of tolerance, as an institution in dialogue with the state. Hence Humboldt sets firm limits to the terms of the power that the state holds over the University: "As far as external relations [of the University] with the state are concerned, and as for the action of the latter in this area, the state must only protect the spiritual resources of the University (in both their power and diversity) and its freedom of action, by means of the individuals which it appoints to the University."[16]

The plan outlined by Humboldt for the University of Berlin synthesized the fundamental reorganization of the discourse on knowledge by which the University took on an indirect or cultural function for the state: that of the simultaneous search for its objective cultural meaning as a historical entity and the subjective moral training of its subjects as potential bearers of that identity. The extent of this reorganization can be grasped if we remember Humboldt's observation that the autonomous work of philosophical reflection must be preserved from the Scylla of mere leisure (utter absence of direction) and the Charybdis of practical utility (total subservience to the direction of the state).[17] Knowledge must be neither totally undetermined nor empirically determined in its application. Rather, it must be determined in reference to the indeterminate ideal of absolute knowledge. This ideal thus entirely restructures the medieval opposition between the active life and the contemplative life, which here become respectively mere utility and mere leisure. The University's social mission is not to be understood in terms of either thought or action. The University is not just a site for contemplation that is then to be transformed into action. The University, that is, is not simply an instrument of state policy; rather, the University must embody thought as action, as striving for an ideal. This is its bond with the state, for state and University are the two sides of a single coin. The University seeks to embody thought as action toward an ideal; the state must seek to realize action as thought, the idea of the nation. The state protects the action of the University; the University safeguards the thought of the state. And each strives to realize the idea of national culture.

Such an idea of the University with culture as its animating principle has defined both the University's shape as a modern institution and its relationship to the nation-state.[18] This may seem like the triumph of Humboldt's more liberal proposal over Fichte's more conservative vision. And indeed, Humboldt does not simply identify reason with "order," as Fichte does. Yet although Humboldt's version of reason was more speculative and universal, and his vision of the nation less ethnically rooted than Fichte's, the development of the University was actually to follow the Fichtean path, defining the process of cultivation in primarily *ethnic* terms. To continue our history, the instrument by which ethnicity was to be linked to culture—especially in the anglophone world—is the invention of the notion of *national literature.* Hence, as I shall describe in the next chapter, the national literature department gradually comes to replace the philosophy department as the center of the humanities, and a fortiori, as the spiritual center of the University.

~ 6

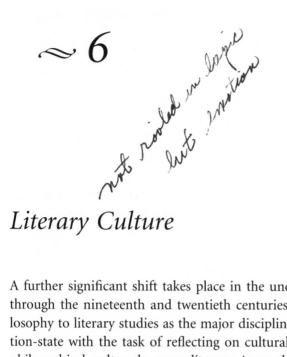

Literary Culture

A further significant shift takes place in the understanding of culture through the nineteenth and twentieth centuries: the move from philosophy to literary studies as the major discipline entrusted by the nation-state with the task of reflecting on cultural identity. From being philosophical, culture becomes literary. As we shall see, it is the invention of the category of literature that causes the split C. P. Snow noted between scientific and literary culture. For the literary is opposed to the scientific in a way philosophy is not, and this is particularly pronounced in English-speaking nations.

Of course, the role of the literary had been clearly acknowledged by Schlegel, who claims in his *Lectures on the History of Literature* that it is literature rather than philosophy that binds together a people into a nation, since philosophy tends to be both less nationally rooted (because the question of language is not posed) and more elitist:

> There is nothing so necessary . . . to the whole intellectual existence of a nation, as the possession of a plentiful store of those national recollections and associations, which are lost in a great measure during the dark ages of infant society, but which it forms the great object of the poetical art to perpetuate and adorn . . . when a people are exalted in their feelings and ennobled in their own estimation, by the consciousness that they have been illustrious in ages that are gone by . . . in a word, that they have *a national poetry* of their own, we are willing to acknowledge that

their pride is reasonable, and they are raised in our eyes by the same circumstances which give them elevation in their own.[1]

Although it would be possible to look at the rise of national literature in Germany, and others have certainly done so,[2] I want to argue that a notion of national literature has had particularly pronounced effects on the University in English-speaking nations. I will trace these effects in some detail in this chapter.

First of all, however, it is hard to realize that the category of literature has a rather recent history. It emerges in the seventeenth and eighteenth centuries, and "literature" is the primary (although not exclusive) name of the anglophone cultural project. This is something of which Goethe kept reminding Eckermann.[3] Aristotle's *Poetics,* for example, does not have a theory of literature; indeed, Aristotle doesn't even have a concept of literature as a unifying notion that would tie together different practices of writing. Aristotle sees *poesis* as a process of making with words that is essentially artisanal. That is to say, the technology of mimesis is not a general science but is specific to each activity. Hence a dramatist and a prose writer have no more in common than do a weaver and a sailmaker. Both work with cloth, but their arts are structurally heterogeneous. It is this kind of thinking that runs through the system of medieval guilds and governs the various fields of what we might be inclined to group as cultural production. Indeed, it is fundamentally anachronistic to speak of medieval art at all, if by art we mean some kind of romantic notion of an essential activity of the soul that might set the glassblower and cooper apart, while linking the activity of the itinerant stonemason with that of the manuscript copyist and that of the trainee painter trying to learn the correct combination of colors to make the blue of the Madonna's cloak.

This is not to say that there is no idea of a general science in ancient and medieval times. Plato clearly has one, and he dedicates the *Gorgias* and the *Ion* to the question. These two dialogues contrast Socrates the philosopher with Gorgias the rhetorician and Ion the rhapsode. The two practice arts of language that we might be inclined to call "literary" today. Ion specializes in dramatic readings and commentary on texts (a kind of effusive performance that we might now assign to belletristic literary criticism), while Gorgias is a public orator who argues in the courts and the *polis.*

Socrates is concerned to prove that philosophy, not the language arts of oratory or rhapsody, constitutes the only true general science. It is on this basis that he banishes poets from the republic, not because they engage in mimesis (after all, he thinks that the world is merely the mimesis of Forms) but because they perform an act of *lèse-majesté* in promulgating linguistic mimesis as a potential general science, in the place of philosophy. The Socratic philosopher shares with the orator and the rhapsode the pretension to talk about everything, from cookery to medicine. The first, however, does so on philosophical terms, the others in terms that we might want to call more or less "literary" (though we would be wrong to give in to this temptation). The difference between the two has to do with the metonymic chain of signifiers in which the rhapsode or rhetor practices—he follows along without understanding. The philosopher, by contrast, does not imitate at the level of the signifier but performs a metaphoric leap to the level of the signified. He understands the meaning of other arts but does not practice them. Hence philosophy is an autonomous general art (which is to say, a science), while the language arts are not arts at all, since they are heteronomous or dependent, mere imitations of other arts, incapable of self-understanding. For Aristotle, then, there is no general art whatsoever, while for Plato there is no general *literary* art, since philosophy is the only true general science, and the language arts offer merely a false generality.

The eventual emergence of literature as a unifying term is thus Plato's fault, like so much else, since it occurs as an explicit revaluation of Platonic criticisms. And the notion of literature emerges when writing is analyzed in terms that leave public oratory behind, a rephrasing of textual production that is intimately linked to the rise of the bourgeois public sphere. Whatever people may have said, Sir Philip Sidney is not quite talking about literature in terms of a general art of *imitation* when in *The Defence of Poetry* he calls for "speaking pictures." Sidney's account of mimetic practice is still Aristotelian, a matter of making (*poiein*) according to the rules of rhetoric rather than of illusion. Mimesis does not seek to delude an individual into taking an imitation as real but seeks rhetorically to persuade a public. Painting and poetry share the task of providing the objects around which communities of understanding form and sustain themselves. It is important to remember, then, that when Sidney calls the poem a "speaking picture" he thinks of it as functioning like a rhetorical exemplum rather than as an illustration of an absolute law.[4]

This is very different from the way in which exemplary illustrations from literature function in modernity. Each example illustrates a universal law, each speaking picture holds down a unique place within the extended and non-contradictory museal or canonical space of rational historical understanding. To call this space—which is also the space of the *Norton Anthology*—museal is to refer to the way in which the ground plan of the modern museum is already a linear map of a particular account of a history of art, offering a unified account of linear development and a generalized system of classification. Only when it is inscribed within this kind of epistemological space can literature become a University discipline.

The institutionalization of literature as bearer of the cultural task of the University has been described in the case of Germany by Peter Uwe Hohendahl, in Britain by Chris Baldick and Franklin Court, in the United States by Gerald Graff, and in Spain by Wlad Godzich and Nicholas Spadaccini.[5] Philippe Lacoue-Labarthe, in *La Fiction du politique,* has situated the "national aestheticism" of the National Socialist movement in Germany as the convulsive symptom of this link between national identity and organic culture.[6] As these examples indicate, the history of the entrusting of literature with a social mission is extant and written in the best English. For the Anglo-American University, it is generally called the function of criticism and bears first of all the name of Matthew Arnold. The specificity of the English response owes much to the fusion of church and state, which makes it impossible to oppose the discourse of an objective cultural knowledge, a state *Wissenschaft,* to the church as bearer of cultural unity. Instead, it is in opposition to *technology,* to "science" in the English sense, that the idea of culture is understood. The growth of technology through the nineteenth century switches the question of social unification. Fragmentation is no longer the result of a specific problem of German nationhood but appears as the general threat posed by industrialization. Literature then replaces philosophy as the means of preserving an ethnic identity and uniting it with an idea of historical progress that appears dangerously trans-national.

In the Anglo-American University, the founding split is between scientific and literary culture. While the German Idealists circumvented the Kantian problem of the split between religion and reason by focusing on the *Bildung* of the student as a process of empirical maturation, thinkers like Newman and Jowett instead gave us the liberal individual: the gentleman. As Newman puts it, "It is common to speak of '*liberal* knowledge,' of the '*liberal* arts and studies,' and of a '*liberal* education,' as the especial characteristic or property of a University and a gentleman."[7] For the English, hermeneutic philology could not unite science and letters; rather the identification of culture with letters was a response to the technology of industrialization. I say "the English" here, and I should perhaps say more precisely "Oxford and Cambridge," since the matter was organized rather differently at the University of London and in Scotland. The Scottish universities differed from the ancient universities of England in being more centralized and less financially endowed, giving vested interests less room to oppose reform. These features combined with the wider role of the more practically oriented dissenting academies to prepare the way for a more favorable reception of Huxley's campaign for the development of natural sciences and medicine. As Huxley put it, "for the purpose of attaining real culture, an exclusively scientific education is at least as effectual as an exclusively literary education."[8] Nonetheless, at Oxford and Cambridge, the idea of culture was linked above all to the domain of letters.

Significantly, Oxford is the model for Newman's *Idea of a University*. And it is Newman's text that probably still holds the most resonance for English speakers when they think of the institution of the University. Newman's text also displays considerable parallels with the thought of the German Idealists, which I discussed in Chapter 5. Like the German Idealists, Newman explicitly positions knowledge as an organic whole. The object of University study is not particular knowledge but what he calls "intellectual culture," which exceeds the sum of its me-chanically acquired parts.[9] The general notion of culture appears as the organic synthesis that acts as both the totality and the essence of par-ticular knowledges, "without which there is no whole, and no center" (134). Within this basic framework, Newman positions liberal educa-tion in opposition to practical knowledge and the principle of utility. As the title of one of the Discourses has it, liberal education positions knowledge as its own end, against the mechanical specter of technology: "You see, then, here are two methods of Education; the end of the one is to be philosophical, of the other to be mechanical" (112). The in-direct pursuit of the liberal or philosophical education seeks general understanding and a sense of the unity of knowledge rather than par-ticular useful knowledges. Liberal education is therefore proper to the University "as a place of education, [rather] than of instruction." The end of knowledge is not external to the University but is the immanent principle of "intellectual culture." Thus, as for Fichte and Humboldt, the University is a community: "an assemblage of learned men" (101) whose communication is dedicated to their internal pursuit of intel-lectual culture. And intellectual culture applies both to the production of knowledge ("the attainment of truth" that is "the common end" of the various disciplines) and the teaching of individuals ("the influence which they [the disciplines] exercise upon those whose education con-sists in the study of them") (99–100).

Newman's difference from the Germans, however, lies in his posi-tioning of the "truth" (which is the unity of the sciences) as *theological.* For Newman, the unity of knowledges is not itself a form of knowledge, an object of philosophical *science,* and therefore does not take the form of a project of research. The English and Irish University in Newman's world is still directly linked to the church (be it Protestant or Catholic); this link has not been replaced by the link to the state. Therefore, there is no mention of the research project, since divine truth occupies the place of the productive unity of revealed knowledge that is taken by *Wissenschaft* in the German model. This is why culture is figured in the life of a gentleman rather than as an idea. As Carnochan judiciously observes, whereas for Matthew Arnold, who was influenced by the Ger-man Idealists, the teaching of and research into secular culture was an instrument for social redemption, for Newman the teaching of secular culture is a palliative preparation for a sinful world, a world whose redemption is a matter of religious faith rather than scientific knowledge.[10] It follows, then, that for Newman philosophy is not a general *science* but a subjective attitude, "a habit, a personal possession, and an inward endowment" (113). Hence Newman can make the startling proposal that a University as a mere community without an idea of knowledge—"the University which did nothing"—would be better than a University "which exacted of its members an acquaintance with every science under the sun" (145).[11]

Although Newman qualifies "intellectual culture" as philosophical, it is not philosophy that is the discipline of such culture. Philosophy is a subjective quality of "perfection or virtue of the intellect" rather than a course of study (125). Training in the philosophical exercise of "Thought or Reason ... upon Knowledge" will actually occur in the disciplinary study of *literature* (139). Newman approvingly quotes Copleston on "the cultivation of literature" as the means to achieve the "common link" between the various aspects of life and knowledge, as the very model of the general understanding that characterizes the liberal education (169). Plato's *Ion* has been reversed, and it is literature that can train the cast of mind required to understand all other sciences and professions. Thus, along with the sciences, literature is "the other main constituent portion of the subject-matter of Liberal Education" (227). The physical sciences may be studied for the knowledge of the life-world they give us, but the living unity of knowledge, the understanding of the place of knowledge in the world, will find its formulation in literature.

While the "Nine Discourses on the Idea of a University" dedicate several pages to this subject, it is most explicitly formulated in the companion essay "Literature: A Lecture in the School of Philosophy and Letters," which Newman delivered in 1858. In this lecture, as in the lectures on English Catholic literature he delivered from 1854 to 1858, Newman explicitly positions literature as the site of the development of both an idea of the nation and the study of literature as the means of training national subjects. Literature is both the agent and the expression of the organic unity of a national culture, the synthetic power of culture in action. As Newman remarks, "by great authors the many are drawn up into a unity, national character is fixed, a people speaks, the past and the future, the East and the West are brought into communication with each other" (193).

What literature does at the level of the *Volk,* fusing the people into a single national voice, literary training does for the individual, since "the growth of a nation is like that of an individual" (310). Explicitly national, literature thus replaces philosophical science in uniting the dual sense of culture as both product and process, as general object and individual cultivation. Now literature is nothing less than the nationality of a language, since the "distinctive character" that identifies literary classics is "nationality" of a language, as opposed to the "tame and spiritless" product of a language "corrupted by the admixture of foreign elements" (328). This overt link between literature and the achievement of national self-consciousness is the grounds of a straightforward imperialism. Newman knows national culture to be an explicitly Western invention: "In the language of savages you can hardly express any idea or act of the intellect at all: is the tongue of the Hottentot or Esquimaux to be made the measure of the genius of Plato, Pindar, Tacitus, St. Jerome, Dante, or Cervantes?" (287).

In the "Discourses" Newman quotes his contemporary Davidson approvingly on the subject of linguistic culture, which he considers to be the product of the disinterested study of language, of the "faculty . . . of speaking good sense in English, without fee or reward, in common conversation." Newman cites Davidson contrasting the benefits of English literature to a remarkable picture of non-Western peoples as effectively mute, except when engaging in communication concerning specific tasks. We are exhorted to "look into the huts of savages, and see, for there is nothing to listen to, the dismal blank of their stupid hours of silence; their professional avocations of war and hunting are over; and, having nothing to do, they have nothing to say" (171–172). If literature is the language of national culture, the written proof of a spiritual activity beyond the mechanical operations of material life, then the liberal education in intellectual culture, through the study of national literature, will produce the cultivated gentleman whose knowledge has no mechanical or direct utility, merely a spiritual link to the vitality of his national language as literature.

Such is the context in which Arnold in *Culture and Anarchy* proposes culture as an organic whole against the mechanical and external effects of industrial civilization.[12] Arnold, as I have remarked, transforms the cultivation of a gentleman into a quasi-religion of secular culture in its own right. The same rhetoric that opposed unity to fragmentation for the German Idealists recurs, but here literary criticism has the task of combining the Hebraic rigor of religious "light" with the Hellenic grace of poetic "sweetness," uniting knowledge and meaning in what Arnold in "The Function of Criticism at the Present Time" calls a "national glow."[13] The poles of the debate that Gerald Graff sketches in the institutionalization of literary studies—between historical research and criticism, between scholarship and aesthetic experience, between theory and literature—are already marked out.[14]

The importance of the technological specter in this debate can be grasped when one realizes that for Arnold, as for Eliot and Leavis after him, Shakespeare occupies the position that the German Idealists ascribed to the Greeks: that of immediately representing an organic community to itself in a living language. Where Schlegel praised the Greeks as the pure origin of literature, as the people who created literature *ex nihilo* without any historical antecedent tradition, the English appeal to Shakespeare as the unlettered figure who provides an autochthonous origin.[15] Unlettered in Greek and with little Latin, Shakespeare is claimed by Dryden not to have written with anything in mind: "Those who accuse him to have wanted learning, give him the greater commendation: he was naturally learn'd; he needed not the spectacles of Books to read Nature; he look'd inwards, and found her there."[16]

Dryden presides over the development of the notion of literary appreciation: of texts as produced for an appreciating subject (of aesthetics) rather than as essentially made according to rules of craft (poesis, rhetoric). And it is at this point that a general notion of literature, rather than a series of heterogeneous rule-bound language practices, can emerge as it does with Dryden. I have described in detail elsewhere the emergence in Dryden's writing of a notion of literary reading as a way to overcome the tension between rule and appreciation by means of siting literary criticism in the paradoxical space of the preface as secondary precursor to a primary text.[17] And it is no coincidence that Dryden is the first author cited by the *Oxford English Dictionary* as using the verb "cultivate" to refer to learning. The English invoke literature in order to make knowledge a cultural matter. Crucially, Dryden and Johnson appeal to Shakespeare as the founding moment of a literary culture, an appeal that will be repeated and enshrined in the curriculum.

The nineteenth century shifts the Drydenic question of the subject of culture from the context of the opposition of ancients to moderns, in the process explicitly addressing the opposition of nature to culture, in which terms Shakespeare is positioned as nothing less than *the natural origin of culture*. As such, he stands as the instance in which the nation-state finds its origin, as the welding of an ethnic nature with a rational state, a point at which an ethnic nature spontaneously expresses itself as a *national* culture. Arnold picks up the tradition of Romantic bardolatry and aligns it with the German Idealist reading of Ancient Greece as the moment of immediacy and self-presence in social unity, the moment of the spontaneous natural origin of culture, the lost origin to which a critical culture must seek to return by means of hermeneutic reworking through the rational institutions of the nation-state, such as the research University.

Shakespearean drama thus becomes for England what Greek philosophy was for Germany: the lost origin of authentic community to be rebuilt by means of rational communication between national subjects—a rational communication mediated through the institutions of the state. Even the roundness of the Globe Theatre underpins a vision of an organically unified society much as in the German Idealist version of the political life of the Athenian city-state, where citizens (but not women or slaves) engaged in debate in a circular space in which each communicated immediately with all. Similarly, the archaeological errors that led to Ancient Greece being understood as a place of pure whiteness (because the paint had faded from statues and buildings) are paralleled by the kind of fiction that fixed Shakespeare's birthday on St. George's Day (April 23). Shakespeare is recorded as having died on

79

April 23, so it was decided in the interest of a certain circularity (the distinguishing trait of autochthonous origin), that he should have been born on that day as well.

This fiction of Shakespeare as the spontaneous and natural origin of an English culture is what causes F. R. Leavis to propose in "The Idea of a University" that all study in the University should be centered in the study of literature. What is more, in Leavis's mind all study of literature should be centered in the seventeenth century, because the seventeenth century is the moment when a "dissociation of sensibility," in Eliot's phrase, supervenes to split literature and communicational or vehicular language. Culture, that is, is severed from society. This split is the moment of the post-Shakespearean fall. Culture continues to name the lost ideal of organic wholeness, while society is henceforth a merely mechanical process of civilization.[18] The function of criticism is, according to Leavis, to heal that split, to reunite mass civilization and the organic community of the *Volk,* the fragmentary world of specialized pursuits and the idea of a cultural whole. Leavis then proposes a dialectic between culture and civilization that maps out this task for society, for language, and for the University.[19]

I will first turn to what Leavis has to say about society in this regard. In "Mass Civilization and Minority Culture," he argues that there is an opposition between culture (the lost organic unity of a people that was current in Shakespeare's time) and civilization (the age of the mass machine or "technologico-Benthamite civilization"). According to Leavis, we can neither return to the former nor survive in the latter. Neither nostalgia nor modernization will save us. Instead, a minority culture must supervene as the dialectical resolution of the opposition, embodying the principle of the lost unity of culture in order to resist and reform mass civilization through the practice of criticism. The same structure goes for language, where the literary tradition is opposed to the merely communicational language of advertising that has replaced it. In *Nor Shall My Sword,* Leavis takes his argument a bit further by proposing the task of criticism as the reanimation of language. The language of poetry has died, but it can be restored to life through criticism. Not merely *literary* criticism, however; for literary criticism can only select the vital elements of the national tradition (hence Leavis's insistence on discrimination and his relentless practice of citation). Such literary criticism acts as midwife to the writing and reading of critical poetry (such as that of T. S. Eliot), thus forging a new synthesis from among those elements of tradition.[20]

Leavis complains in "The Idea of a University" that in the field of knowledge the unified culture represented by the ancient universities of the United Kingdom, universities located in the heart of cities, has been replaced by the mechanical specializations of American campus universities, in which knowledge is a profession, an autonomous and esoteric pursuit with no immediate connection to culture as a whole. This opposition, Leavis argues, can be overcome by situating the study of English literature as the center of the University, as the animating principle that will give academic study a lived significance and a historical continuity through attention to language. Therefore, high culture, in Leavis's view, preserves the finest idiom as both a vertical separation from mass civilization and a horizontal historical continuity with a pre-industrial age. Aesthetic discrimination ensures the vertical separation, historical scholarship the horizontal continuity. Mere antiquarian erudition ignores the former in favor of such questions as Lady Macbeth's fertility, and it is therefore not critical.[21] But criticism must be given historical continuity if it is not to fall into the trap of pandering to the present tastes of the masses, if it is to avoid being contaminated by democratic populism (the fate to which Leavis sees Arnold Bennet condemned).

In short, Leavis opposes culture to a fragmentation that is no longer the result of a specific problem of German nationhood; rather, fragmentation appears as the general threat posed by industrialization. In the face of this, literature replaces philosophy as the means of preserving an ethnic identity and uniting it with an idea of technological progress that appears dangerously transnational. For both Leavis and Arnold, the idea of literary culture could synthesize the pre-industrial organic community and the technology of mass communication so as to establish a culture that would be *transparent to itself.* And as Lacoue-Labarthe has shown, such was the aim of Nazi national aestheticism.[22] Not just the aim of providing a *Volk* with Volkswagens but providing a nation as the technological expression of the organic community that marks the *Volk*. In these terms, the opposition of the organic to the technological is overcome. Culture turns technology into the mode of self-knowledge of a people, and it also turns the organicism of the lost community into a living principle of identity rather than a closed system, opening the community toward self-knowledge as a project rather than shutting it back into self-satisfaction. As a result, the village and technology are made into one as "organic culture."

I do not say this in order to accuse Leavis or Arnold of fascism. I do want to say, however, that the University of Culture is ineluctably caught up in this organicism, which is also at the heart of Nazism's thought of the state as organic machine. This is something that Wolf Lepenies has noted in "The Direction of the Disciplines: The Future of the Universities," where he points out that, whatever the activities of certain moral individuals, the University system of research and teaching continued to function without significant interruption in Germany under the Third Reich.[23] Lepenies concludes that the capacity of the University structure to adapt itself to Nazism should give us pause. In *Between Science and Literature* he diagnoses the problem in terms of C. P. Snow's distinction between the two cultures of the arts and the hard sciences.[24] The split between the two, according to Lepenies, is better understood as a split between reflection on questions of value and reflection on questions of practical application. Hence the arts may present models of the social orientation of knowledge, means of reflection upon its cultural implications, but such reflections are constitutively cut off from any practical effect. Meanwhile, the sciences pursue technological rationality on its own terms, untroubled by the need to reflect upon the social effects of the knowledges they produce or manipulate, since such thinking is supposed to take place elsewhere. Lepenies proposes the "third culture" of the social sciences as a means of providing a dialectical synthesis between questions of value and questions of practice, as a means of synthesizing practical utility and social orientation. For Lepenies, the social sciences will replace literature and philosophy as the master disciplines of a new University of Culture.

This is, as it were, the last gasp for culture: an attempt to preserve the idea of culture against the Nazi catastrophe by stripping it of the residue of organicism and entrusting social science, rather than criticism or speculation, with the task of unifying knowledges in the University. It has obvious parallels with the proposals Habermas makes in his own essay "The Idea of the University," in which communicative rationality replaces the idea of culture as the instance entrusted with the task of unifying knowledges.[25] Habermas explicitly returns to Schleiermacher's insistence that communication is the first law of the University, in order to argue "that in the last analysis it is the communicative forms of scientific and scholarly argumentation that hold university learning processes in their various functions together."[26] The structure of the German Idealist's argument is preserved, although cultural synthesis is not guaranteed by the revelation of an idea but achieved through a practice of communication. Culture is not directed toward the absolute but toward consensus. Community is grounded not in organic identity but in rational communication.

This version of community, in turn, figures in the canon debate in the United States, since it is what grounds Stanley Fish's call for "business as usual" under the aegis of an interpretative community. Similar to Habermas, Fish appeals to a horizon of rational institutional consensus rather than a cultural identity. He describes the profession as a deliberative institution that is autonomous and self-regulating, an argument that works only at the price of a certain circularity: the interpretative community determines what counts as university discourse, but the identity of that community is itself only constituted by such acts of determination. In order to preserve the illusion that the determinations arrived at by the interpretative community are the object of free or rational discussion, in order for his argument not to appear a blank defense of the status quo, Fish has to presume that such "interpretative communities" are capable of submitting their own traditions and protocols to analysis in the light of the appearance of new types of phrases in University discourse.

Such an assumption is, in fact, more possible in the United States than elsewhere. In the United States the idea of literary culture has been, appropriately in a republican democracy, historically structured by the notion of the *canon* rather than of the *tradition*. What is more, in the United States the canon has also stressed value rather than ethnicity—although racism is always one of the discourses protected by the discourse of value. However, a nation that throws off the shackles of tradition through revolution must make its literary tradition appear to be the object of a democratic choice rather than the sheer burden of heredity. After all, in the United States, the New Criticism that gave literary studies their institutional form was less overtly elitist than Leavis and the *Scrutiny* group.

Like Leavis in England, though, the New Critics had an enormous impact on the educational system. On both sides of the Atlantic, the radical claim for the benefits of literary scholarship was accompanied by a massive attention to the training of secondary school teachers, who went out from the University entrusted with a sense of their mission to uphold literary culture. However, whereas Leavis's textbooks addressed the question of the English literary tradition and had titles like *The Great Tradition* (for the novel) and *Revaluation* and *New Bearings in English Poetry* (for the lyric), the New Critics wrote textbooks with titles like *Understanding Poetry*. Whereas Leavis offered his disciples a tradition, the New Critics offered a way of reading. Of course, their way of reading tended to privilege a certain poetic mode (the short modernist lyric) but their claim was that they privileged the autonomous artwork, the poem that knew itself as a poem, regardless of cultural content. Leavis's parallel focus on self-conscious artistry ("maturity") and attention to form tended to lead him to praise the poem that knew itself as an *English* poem.

The New Critics decidedly argued against historical scholarship and positioned the artwork as essentially autonomous, capable of evoking a response without extraneous information to guide interpretation. Yet while Leavis and the New Critics differ on many issues, there is more common ground here than might first appear, since Leavis's description of historical continuity rests on the assumption that literature is self-evidently *there* as an available tradition. The New Criticism gives rise to arguments about the canon precisely because the canon is, in fact, the surreptitious smuggling of *historical* continuity into the study of supposedly discrete and autonomous artworks. This is why the Norton Anthologies of English and American Literature have been such big sellers. The point is that, as a republican immigrant democracy, the United States is founded not in tradition but in the will of the people, is more like France than Germany. But the tradition is, in effect, what the will of the American people decides it is—hence the existence of the canon. The establishment of a literary canon is thus necessary in order for the New Criticism to be able to make claims about culture as a whole, in order for criticism as practiced in the University to claim to objectify and to subjectively ingrain a national cultural identity.

The idea of the canon serves, in short, to overcome the tension between historical ethnicity and republican will, since it is claimed that in establishing the canon the American people chose their own historical ethnicity in a free exercise of rational will. Hence the canon debate is a specifically American crisis, and, let me add, a salutary one. What we are experiencing today in departments of literature in the United States is not so much a revision of the canon as a crisis in the *function* of the canon. This is perhaps the clearest sign of the breakdown of the idea of the nation-state, since the canon can no longer serve to authoritatively integrate popular will and an ethnic fiction under the rubric of culture.

The intensity of curricular battles about the canon in literary studies in the United States today is also remarkable. It is remarkable not least because it has been clearly demonstrated that the canon is an ethnocentric and non-representative basis on which to ground the kinds of claims that have been historically made for literature. Even Alvin Kernan acknowledges this. It is also clear that, once these limitations have been realized, coverage of the entirety of a discrete field of literature is no longer possible. Nor indeed was it ever actually achieved by any student in any curricular structure. Nonetheless, the teaching of literature without reference to a canonical structure seems very hard to imagine, so that curricula continue to be structured, and jobs advertised, in reference to historical fields that are no longer held to be valid by many active researchers.

I have already suggested some of the reasons why the canon is so central to literary studies in the United States. Now I want to remark upon the fact that the field of literature as such is currently structured in institutional terms that are neither practical nor ethically defensible. Such a paradoxical situation does not arise because of external political pressures on the field of literary study but from a problem regarding the status of knowledge that is inherent to the disciplinary problematic of the contemporary University. Once the link between literary study and the formation of the model citizen has been broken, then literature emerges as one field of knowledge among others. The canon therefore gradually comes to function as the arbitrary delimitation of a field of knowledge (an archive) rather than as the vessel that houses the vital principle of the national spirit.

Some critics, such as John Guillory, have even mounted a defense of the canon as just such an arbitrary archive.[27] As such, in the University of Excellence, knowledge tends to disappear, to be replaced as a goal by facility in the processing of information: something should be known, yet it becomes less and less urgent that we know what it is that should be known. Hence, while canon revisionists argue that the *Norton Anthology of English Literature* is too short, requires supplementing, my suspicion is that it is actually too long for future purposes—and probably much too long. New texts will continue to be added and attention will be paid to neglected writers. But that attention will not be the same, since the whole does not add up any longer to an organic vision of national literature, nor does anything within the system of knowledge require that it should. The function of the literary canon requires a secular religion of literature. However, the light no longer burns as brightly in the Holy of Holies of that religion: the nation-state, home of the idea of national culture.

This is basically what is going on in E. D. Hirsch's *Cultural Literacy*. Hirsch presents cultural identity as if it were not historical tradition but simply an aggregate of necessary facts, a formulation that incidentally favors the production of standardized tests in cultural identity (SATs and GREs in literature).[28] For the contents of the textbook do not give access, as they were once supposed to, to a culture of knowledge (a way of thinking and talking, a way of *being*). *Understanding Poetry* is replaced by nothing at all, which is to say, it is replaced by an imagined version of Hirsch's *Cultural Literacy:* culture as "what every American should know," ready to take its place on the self-help shelves in the local drug and bookstore.

Lest I begin to sound like Matthew Arnold, let me make it clear that I am not lamenting some decline. I am merely noting that the possibility of Hirsch's fixed list of facts represents the replacement of a highly suspect organicist notion of culture by a set of *information,* exactly the mechanical or technological specter of mere lifeless facts against which the idea of culture was supposed to protect. Whatever Hirsch may think he is doing, the defining feature of such information, the appeal of his project, is nothing other than the efficiency with which it can be administered to students. To put this another way, the question that such a list seeks to answer is a purely *functional* one. It does not offer to form a national subject; it will produce a minimally programmed unit.

This is a long way from the claim of Edgar Robinson, president of Stanford in 1928. Robinson called upon his students "to build carefully and to prepare thoughtfully for [their] work as citizen[s]."[29] By contrast, the administration of knowledge means nothing more than that it is helpful to future employers for students to know a very few things, although the development of information technology makes the number of those things ever smaller. The futility of the "Great Books" and core curriculum arguments, which Carnochan ably delineates in *The Battleground of the Curriculum,* is precisely that they depend upon there being a national culture (ethnic or republican) within which subjects are to take a place, a place that will be the determining feature of their lives. It is no accident that at this point a number of transdisciplinary movements arise that pose the question of identity otherwise: Women's Studies, Lesbian and Gay Studies, Postcolonial Studies, and Cultural Studies. Such movements signal the end of the reign of literary culture as the organizing discipline of the University's cultural mission, for they loosen the tie between the subject and the nation-state.[30]

The emergence of critical practices that question the status of the literary and pay attention to popular culture is not the cause of the decline of literature but its effect. Such practices become possible once the link between the nation-state and its virtual subjects, the link that the University's idea of culture (be it philosophical or literary) has historically served to forge, is no longer the primary ground of a generalized subjectivity. Cultural Studies, that is, arise when culture ceases to be the immanent principle in terms of which knowledge within the University is organized, and instead becomes one object among others. Women's Studies, Gay and Lesbian Studies, and Postcolonial Studies arise when the abstract notion of "citizen" ceases to be an adequate and exhaustive description of the subject, when the apparent blankness and universality of the subject of the state is able to be perceived as the repository of privileged markers of maleness, heterosexuality, and whiteness.

~ 7

Culture Wars and Cultural Studies

Each of the new inter- or trans-disciplinary movements in the humanities and social sciences seems to pose a threat to the cultural canon, to engage in revision of the canon that has been traditionally entrusted to the guardianship of national literature departments. And much of the furor over such movements has occurred in English Departments. Altering the curriculum in English Departments, however, is not the sole or even the primary effect of the rise of Women's Studies, Lesbian and Gay Studies, African-American Studies, or Cultural Studies. They mark instead the incommensurability between reason and history as modes of legitimation for the modern state, once the notion of cultural identity can no longer serve to bridge the abyss. In an entirely welcome sense, they signal the end of "culture" as a regulatory ideal that could unite community and communication so as to allow the analogy between the University and the modern state to function.

Thus far I have argued that the decline of the nation-state as the primary instance of capitalism's self-reproduction has effectively voided the social mission of the modern University. That mission used to be the production of national subjects under the guise of research into and inculcation of culture, culture that has been thought, since Humboldt, in terms inseparable from national identity. The strong idea of culture arises with the nation-state, and we now face its disappearance as the locus of social meaning. Once the notion of national identity loses its political relevance, the notion of culture becomes effectively unthinkable. The admission that there is nothing to be said about culture *as such* is evident in the institutional rise of Cultural Studies in the 1990s.

It seems to me that this scenario presents a series of options. Either we seek to defend and restore the social mission of the University by simply reaffirming a national cultural identity that has manifestly lost its purchase (the conservative position), or we attempt to reinvent cultural identity so as to adapt it to changing circumstances (the multicultural position). A third option is to abandon the notion that the social mission of the University is ineluctably linked to the project of realizing a national cultural identity, which is tantamount to ceasing to think the social articulation of research and teaching in terms of a *mission*. This is a considerably more difficult proposition to accept for both the right and the left, since it means relinquishing our claim to be intellectuals and giving up the claim of service to the state, even when that would involve a critical reimagination of the state, a counter-state behind which academics have masked their accumulation of symbolic capital for centuries.[1]

A number of factors incline me to think that the third option, which I will develop in Chapter 11, is the framework within which the future of the University as an institution will be sketched out. But first it is important to understand that to ask the question of the University, and specifically of the humanities, in this context is to run a considerable risk. In the 1970s we were (at least, I was) inclined to believe that a mixture of Marxism, psychoanalysis, and semiotics might prove sufficiently volatile to fuel Molotov cocktails. The combination is now sufficiently stabilized to be available over the counter from your local humanities and social sciences departments under a variety of brand names or under the generic label "Cultural Studies." We have to recognize that the grounds on which we used to make large claims for the humanities have been undermined. Unless, that is, we want to end up like the British, who could not resist Thatcherite cuts because they could find no better argument for the humanities than vague appeals to "human richness" in a world in which leisure has already become the primary site of capitalist penetration (as Disney and the Olympics attest).

Current developments in the humanities in the West seem to be centered on two major phenomena. On the one hand, there is the decline in the power of the University over the public sphere, with the concomitant elimination of the intellectual as a public figure. Perhaps surprisingly, I shall argue that this is not necessarily bad news.[2] On the other hand, there is the recent rise of the quasi-discipline of Cultural Studies within the University, which promises to install a new paradigm for the humanities that will either unite the traditional disciplines (this is Antony Easthope's argument) or replace them (this is Cary Nelson's argument) as the living center of intellectual inquiry, restoring the social mission of the University.[3] Perhaps surprisingly, I shall argue that this is not necessarily good news. It seems to me that the idea of Cultural Studies arises at the point when the notion of culture ceases to mean anything vital for the University as a whole. The human sciences can do what they like with culture, can do Cultural Studies, because culture no longer matters as an *idea* for the institution.

I will focus on Cultural Studies, not because it is more important than Women's Studies, African-American Studies, or Lesbian and Gay Studies, but because it is the most essentially academic of these various trans-disciplinary movements. By this I mean that the denunciation of the University as an institution within Cultural Studies is a problem not merely *for* the University but *of* the University. The call to move beyond the University outside academicism is not a response to an act of repression *by* the University; it is a response to the repressed *of* the University itself. To put it another way, the lesbian and gay, African-American, and feminist movements are different in that neither their genesis nor their goals are essentially linked to the University (though the recent emergence of Queer Theory can, I think, be seen as an attempt to academicize Gay and Lesbian Studies in just this way).[4]

Cultural Studies arises, however, *in* the University out of the predicament of those who are excluded from within, who can neither stay nor leave. And the cry of Cultural Studies that the University must be left behind has proved a particularly fruitful way of staying in the University. This is not an attack on practitioners of Cultural Studies for privately seeking the crown of laurel that they publicly refuse in print (the judgment of individual motivations is irrelevant to analysis of the system); it is merely the observation that the wish to get out of the confines of academe is a wish structurally situated within those confines. Thus, Cultural Studies must be understood to arise when culture ceases to be the animating principle of the University and, as I said earlier, becomes instead an object of study among others, a discipline rather than a metadisciplinary idea.

Now, in speaking of the emergence of Cultural Studies as a transdisciplinary movement we have to be very careful. The British genealogy lies with Raymond Williams and Richard Hoggart, continuing through the Birmingham Centre for Cultural Studies, founded by Hoggart and later directed by Stuart Hall. In the North American sphere, there is the model of "American Studies" and the rise of programs in Communications (always a burning issue in a republican democracy) as further factors. This is not to mention the intellectual genealogy, with its admixture of "left Leavisism," Gramsci on subaltern cultures, Foucault on institutions and the body, and feminism. I do not have the space here to give an exhaustive history of the rise of Cultural Studies; I will simply signal that the best short account of its history is Larry Grossberg's essay "Formations of Cultural Studies: An American in Birmingham" in *Relocating Cultural Studies.*[5] What I want to focus on here are two moments in the development of Cultural Studies.

The first moment occurs in the late 1950s and 1960s, when Williams, like E. P. Thompson, situates culture as a supplement to class analysis, and in resistance to the negative diagnoses of the working class given by more theoretical Europeans such as the Frankfurt School.[6] To speak of working class culture was to refuse to locate the existing working class and its traditions solely as a step on the way to the realization of the proletariat as subject of history, to refuse to treat the workers as primarily a theoretical problem. Williams's insistence that culture is ordinary was a refusal to ignore the actual working classes in favor of the liberated proletarians who were to be their successors after the revolution.[7] The persistence of archaic cultural forms (such as the guild structure of the British Trade Union movement) that interests both Williams and Thompson is a sign that what they like about the British labor movement is that it has never been capable of a purely *political* theory, as Williams notes in *Politics and Letters:* "I think I would say that the market and democracy are more prominent themes in the sociological tradition in Europe than in the English tradition with which I was concerned, whereas the English tradition was more specifically concerned with industry. It was the very rapid and brutal experience of industrialization in England which was most directly reflected in social thought here."[8]

Both Williams and Thompson spent a great deal of time explaining the social and historical reasons for this relative under-theorization of the British labor movement. First of all, the British proletariat is not the product of a theorization of the effects of industrial society by a Communist Party, is not born like Athena from the head of Zeus with the Communist Party as midwife. The English proletariat had never theorized itself in a modernist way, had never understood itself in the first place as an instance in the general theory of capitalism. In part, this is because the workers' movement in England was the site in which Marx and Engels worked out the materialist dialectic. So that this movement already had to understand itself otherwise, while waiting for the theory of the dialectic to be deduced from it. The proletariat was "proliterate" in advance of its own political theorization. It is for this reason that we should perhaps speak of a "labor movement" rather than a proletariat—a movement that had to make do with its traditions in the absence of a global theory of the condition of the working class in England. And when Engels proposed such a theory it was already too late. The workers were a step ahead of the theorists. Hence the persistence of guild structures in British unions and the weakness of the Trade Union Commission (TUC) relative to central trade union organizations in Europe.

This does not mean for Williams and Thompson that the British labor movement is not modern, simply that its formation did not follow the Enlightenment pattern in which local superstition is replaced by universal theory. British cultural criticism, along with the workers' movement, confronts two issues that mark its difference from the European Marxist critique: a notion of tradition and the experience of the effects of industrialization on this tradition. Here lies a link to Eliot and Leavis in the appeal to the notion of culture in place of historical materialist science. Williams, as a member of a linguistic minority, as

a Welshman, knew enough to mistrust the verticality of Marxist critique, which always claims to occur from a *central* point of wide pur-
view. Both Williams and Thompson knew that such critical verticality
went along with Marxist mistrust of the actual practices of the working
class, a mistrust of which Williams often complained. Significantly,
Williams refused to condemn the workers as "ignorant masses" who
needed the theorization of the Party, and he did not want to speak of
a "dying culture" along with the Frankfurt School.[9] This has nothing
to do with workerism. Williams did not go in for Stakhanovite eulogies.
Quite simply, he resisted the reduction of the workers to mere instances
in a historical process or a theoretical argument.

He did talk, however, of the "self-realization of the capacity of a
class." But what counts is that, as for Thompson, class-consciousness
is not simply a matter of realizing where one stands in a theoretical
analysis of a system; it is "not just instrumental decision making, within
an imposed system, but from the bottom up, as a way of deciding what
came first in the society, what mattered in it, what needs and values
we live by and want to live by."[10] There is in this remark a certain
refusal to accept that social class is determined by position in relation
to the mode of production. Even if this sounds naive, what I want to
underline is that in Williams's writing the word "culture" indicates a
limit to the determination of social meaning in terms of the history of
class struggle, a supplement that traverses social groupings in many
different fashions. The class struggle is always already a cultural struggle, and Williams refuses to understand culture as the ideological effect
of the class struggle as motor of history. Which means that the working
class is not significant solely insofar as it is in historical step with the
Communist Party's program for the liberation of the proletariat. In
other words, Williams is refusing to make the culture of the working
class into a mere unspoken referent in the Party's discourse about the
nature and goals of society.

The second feature of the appeal to culture in Williams's and
Thompson's writings is a resistance to the Arnoldian identification of
culture with high culture, an insistence that culture is a whole way of
life—an organicism with a widened franchise, which Williams himself
called "left Leavisism."[11] This feature of Williams's writing is perhaps

most evident in his seminal *Culture and Society,* which proposes a leftist counter-history of the literary-cultural tradition of modern Britain. The structure and mode of Leavis's argument are preserved but the "living culture" that is opposed to the dead hand of industrial civilization is a more open one in its organicism, is less restricted in the class perspective from which it surveys the possibility of a whole society. Hence, wholeness does not mean subjugation or happy impoverishment for the workers, with the total erasure of class mobility or conflict, as it tends to for Leavis. The perspective from which society becomes visible as an organic whole shifts. Where Leavis assumes that it is the caring member of the ruling classes who can see the organic interlinking of society, can value the ruddy-cheeked peasant in his place, Williams and Thompson insist upon the appearance of a vision of social wholeness among popular groups in their everyday struggles.[12] The true culture of Britain is not simply that of a better ruling class but that of a whole people, and the industrial civilization to which it is opposed is clearly marked by Williams as specifically capitalistic in its immorality rather than as simply immorally ugly.

However, the continuity of this vision of culture with the literary culture championed by Leavis and others is apparent, although Williams's Welsh origins are crucial to a widening of the approach in that he makes a less straightforward claim of national legitimacy than does Leavis. In Williams's description in "Culture Is Ordinary" of a journey into the country of his childhood, taking the bus along a Welsh valley, he refers to the expansion of culture as "the necessary changes . . . writing themselves into the land, and where the language changes but the voice is the same."[13] This vision of the interaction of symbolic life and landscape is deeply marked by the literary tradition of English Romanticism—an enlarged and less paternalist Wordsworthian vision (and it would be a crude oversimplification to link it to a less idyllic German tradition). However, such a vision also depends upon an acceptance of literary culture as the site where the link forged between a people and its land becomes visible or is expressed. The problems of such a notion of topo-graphy, of land-writing, become apparent once we historically relativize the emergence of literature as the poetry of landscape, and note its links to tourism: be it in the Lake Country created by Wordsworth, Hardy's Wessex, Joyce's Dublin, or even potentially the Welsh Borders of Williams's own novels.[14]

To link literature to tourism in this way is perhaps impious. Wordsworth himself fought the building of a Lakeland railway whose market he was largely responsible for creating. It is not, however, historically inaccurate. If literature took on the task of charging landscape with meaning, the availability of that meaning for economic exploitation is a more pressing reality today than ever before, to the point where it seems naive to think of tourism as a purely secondary or parasitic function. For instance, the tourist authorities of Venice now offer grants to writers to repeat Thomas Mann's boost to local industry. The cultural meaning that a certain literariness sought to inscribe in the land is—given the economic development of transportation since the beginning of the nineteenth century—no longer available primarily to an aesthetic subject whose isolation might give rise to the illusion of disinterestedness. The capitalization of the meaningful landscape as the object of tourist exchange undermines not only the exclusiveness of high cultural literariness but also the claim that a left-wing cultural resistance might be inscribed in the landscape. This vision of popular culture as a widened or transvalued version of traditional "literariness" is no longer an alternative to the capitalist system; it is always already potentially available for tourist exploitation.

To return to the question of the emergence of Cultural Studies, then, I think Grossberg has put his finger on the issue that ties together the two aspects of Williams's and Thompson's appeal to "culture": *participation*. What unites the attack on cultural exclusion and the resistance to theoretical verticality is the question of participation.[15] In this account, the preference for culture over class comes from a desire that social analysis should not imply total separation (pure critical verticality), which is also a desire not to critique the working class from the transcendent position of the proletariat with which the intellectual identifies. The widening of organicism is produced by an argument for the working class as participating in culture in general. Thus, the critic must participate in the culture that is analyzed, and the object of analysis must participate in culture as a whole.

The second moment in the history of Cultural Studies to which I want to pay attention comes more recently, around 1990 when several books appeared that seem to mark the acquisition of professional disciplinarity for Cultural Studies: Antony Easthope's *Literary into Cultural Studies;* Larry Grossberg, Cary Nelson, and Paula Treichler's *Cultural Studies;* Graeme Turner's *British Cultural Studies: An Introduction;* and Patrick Brantlinger's *Crusoe's Footprints.*[16] At about the same time, Routledge also started a journal entitled *Cultural Studies.* A phenomenology of the forms of Cultural Studies as displayed or analyzed in these volumes would come up with a number of more or less common practical and theoretical elements characteristic of work in Cultural Studies. Cultural Studies tend to be suspicious of the exclusionary force of certain boundaries: female/male, north/south, center/margin, high culture/low culture, western/other, heterosexual/homosexual. Authority for this suspicion comes primarily from Williams, Foucault, Gramsci, and Hall, to a lesser extent from Haraway, Bourdieu, and Barthes. Now what is remarkable about Cultural Studies as a discipline is how little it has by way of what might be called theoretical articulation, how little it needs to determine its object. Which does not mean that a lot of theorizing doesn't go on its name, only that such efforts are not undertaken in a way that secures the relation of an observer to a determinate set of phenomena or an autonomous object. Thus, no full description of the phenomenology of Cultural Studies is possible from within the consciousness of a practitioner. We cannot provide an account of what it is to do Cultural Studies that is theoretically self-consistent.

In saying this, I want to make it clear that I am not accusing those who practice Cultural Studies of not paying attention to theoretical questions. Quite the contrary is the case, and individual essays calling themselves "work in Cultural Studies" usually display a high coefficient of self-consciousness concerning the theoretical grounding of their methodology. A problem arises, however, when we seek to understand what it might mean to "theorize Cultural Studies," when we ask what the rubric names and what are the essential presuppositions of the new discipline.

When an attempt to theorize Cultural Studies in general is made, as by Antony Easthope for instance, the result is interestingly problematic.

In place of the "old paradigm" of literary studies Easthope offers a "new paradigm" of Cultural Studies, which appears in order to replace the entire swath of disciplines in the humanities and social sciences as a generalized "study of signifying practice."[17] Easthope's book is interestingly symptomatic in that while it can note and list problems in the traditional practices of literary study, the same systematic definition is not proposed for the new paradigm. Hence the new paradigm is characterized above all by resistance to all attempts to limit its field of reference—such as distinctions between high and popular culture, between factual texts (which require historical or sociological study) and fictional ones (which can be read as literary).[18] All manifestations of culture are signifying practice, and all signifying practices are manifestations of culture. This circularity is founded upon Easthope's description of culture as a "decentered totality" of textualities, the analysis of which requires "a methodology appropriate to the concept of a decentered totality, one whose terms relate to each other though not on the basis of a foundational coherence" (119).

Culture, for Easthope, is thus an ensemble of texts without a center. It is basically everything that happens with the proviso that "everything" is understood as inflected by questions of textuality, is understood as signifying practice. If everything is signifying practice, then the study of signifying practice is the study of anything at all; rather than a specific discipline, Cultural Studies would appear to be the refusal of all disciplinary specificity. In short, Easthope does not suggest that Cultural Studies explains things in terms of anything *in particular*. History is important, but it is itself a part of the signifying practices, not a framework within which they are to be understood.

Easthope, to be fair, does present the "terms for a new paradigm," which are "institution; sign system; ideology; gender; subject position; the other" (129). The rather Borgesian metalepsis of the final term in this list is symptomatic of the problem of defining culture, which I have just noted. Easthope's list is exhaustive because anything that is not included in it can come under the term of "the other." Or might do, were "the other" not like all the rest of the terms on the list: merely a *theme*. That is to say, despite Easthope's claim that his choice is not merely casual, these terms are not articulated against one another to form a theory. They are instead "imbricated" or overlapping, and "others could be easily added to them if required" (130). This final admission reveals the extent to which Easthope's analysis *assumes* rather than defines culture (when it defines culture, the definition is the circular appeal to "signifying practice"). The ensemble of terms is not a theoretical definition, since "crucially no term is originary or foundational, sited as final anchoring point for the others" (137).

The problem with this is not one of argumentation but one of effect. Culture finally becomes an object of study in direct proportion to the abandonment of the attempt to provide a determining explanation of culture. Cultural forms of signifying practice proceed from culture, and culture is the ensemble of signifying practices. In this sense, there is a direct ratio between the intensity of apocalyptic claims for the institutional potential of Cultural Studies and their absence of explanatory power. What allows Cultural Studies to occupy the entire field of the humanities without resistance is their very *academicization of culture*, their taking culture as the object of the University's desire for knowledge, rather than as the object that the University produces. Culture ceases to mean anything *as such;* it is dereferentialized. The difficulty with Easthope's claims, then, is that they are based on the possibility of transferring the critical energy that the German Idealists assigned to philosophical culture, and that Arnold and Leavis assigned to literary culture, to the practice of Cultural Studies. If culture is everything, then the invocation of culture cannot have redemptive force, cannot lend meaning (unity and direction) to symbolic life. In effect, Easthope is offering to recenter the University around a decentered absence that will then be invoked *as if it were a center.*

Easthope's is not the only way of thinking about Cultural Studies, though. One can, for instance, provide a strongly structuralist version of Cultural Studies in which the social anthropology of particular practices is read as a *parole* whose meaning can only be understood in terms of a *langue*—as in Dick Hebdige's reading of subcultures.[19] However, this version encounters problems as well. While it does explain the recurrent usage of counting by decades in Cultural Studies (the fixing of the spatio-temporal coordinates of a particular langue, as in "70s British popular music"), such an account misses the interventionist

99

drive that is so crucial elsewhere, in what Grossberg calls the culturalist version, coming out of the early work of the Birmingham school. Thus, as the editors of *Cultural Studies* tell us, "it is probably impossible to agree on any essential definition or unique narrative of cultural studies."[20]

Exactly the same refusal of theoretical definition marks the introduction to *Relocating Cultural Studies*: "Cultural studies resists being pigeon-holed within the constantly shifting formations of the intellectual map because its concerns are not exclusively or even primarily intellectual . . . In addressing contemporary developments in theory and research, this volume does not intend to offer a definitive version of the present condition of cultural studies."[21] What strikes one about the refusal of definition is the fact that it is repeated so many times, by so many people in the "field." Thus the publishing industry gives us textbooks for the disciplinary ensemble, such as *Reading into Cultural Studies,* which overtly presents itself as providing "eleven unrelated essays" whose "common themes, common worries, common regrets" are "striking" to the editors, Martin Barker and Anne Beezer.[22] Barker and Beezer claim that Cultural Studies has come of age as a discipline, pointing to Brantlinger and Turner as chroniclers of its history, but their attempts to characterize its "project" are notably sketchy: "In short, there was a fundamental agenda in early cultural studies which set up broad oppositions between the concepts of power/ideology and culture/participation. However crude and unsatisfactory these terms may be . . . that agenda was very different from the one which we see emergent in cultural studies now" (6).

The authors are not much more specific about what is going on now, which is less a theoretical reorientation than a shift of attitude toward the object under study: "We can decipher, then, in a number of authors a deepening concern to understand the values and strengths of the sense-making strategies used by ordinary people" (8). The ambivalence of Cultural Studies' relation to the academy is apparent in the appeal to "ordinary people" as legitimation. The legitimating instance is the passage outside the academy, to the "ordinary people," but at the same time this implies that the authors of academic essays in Cultural Studies are "extraordinary people," vertical intellectuals. And as Barker and

100

Beezer themselves remark, this shift away from critique to ethnographic witness, the problematization of "decoding the operations of power and resistance" in favor of "giving voice to the meanings that are made in the here and now," has its problems since there is no "conceptual apparatus on which they can any longer be hooked" (9). They call more or less for a return to the master-code of Marxism, insisting that cultural production is still the product of specific material interests and class determinations. As my remarks with regard to the instantiating moment of Cultural Studies may have suggested, to appeal to class "as a category for understanding social relations and systems of activity" in order to reground Cultural Studies is actually to pull the rug out from under Williams's and Thompson's initial suspicion of the explanatory power of class as a theoretical concept (16).

This is not to say, however, that Cultural Studies is without (*pace* Easthope) a center of gravity. Although healthily suspicious of theorization, writers in Cultural Studies do, as I have noted, appeal to a number of "theoretical" texts. In the weighty collection edited by Grossberg, Nelson, and Treichler under the uncompromising title *Cultural Studies,* the editors do not simply refuse to define their eponymous object. They go on to situate Cultural Studies as "an interdisciplinary, transdisciplinary and sometimes counter disciplinary field that operates in the tension between its tendencies to embrace both a broad anthropological field and a more narrowly humanistic conception of culture." This definition is buttressed by the remark that "cultural studies is thus committed to the study of the entire range of a society's arts, beliefs, institutions, and communicative practices" (4). The editors then provide a final specification that such work must also aim to make a political difference.

I focus on this introduction in such detail not because it is either right or wrong, but because it is rather representative. The theme of participation recurs in the desire for academic study to make a difference, to provide an understanding of social transformation and social change such that Cultural Studies may "provide a place which makes judgment and even intervention possible" (15). However, the problem here is that nothing in the nature of this theory of culture implies an orientation to that difference. A political orientation is assumed; however, the logic in terms of which it is grounded is one of non-specificity. Rather than revealing a positive nature to culture, Cultural Studies, committed to the generalized notion of signifying practice, to the argument that everything is culture, can only oppose *exclusions* from culture—which is to say, specifications of culture. Cultural Studies finds nothing in the nature of its object culture that orients its intervention, other than the refusal of exclusion. This is why political piety is such a burning issue in Cultural Studies debates, precisely because of the anxiety of orientation that such a notion of culture induces. The attack on exclusion is, of course, in a paradoxical critical relation to the status quo.

This problem of orientation becomes particularly acute with the transfer of Cultural Studies to the United States. Since the United States does not legitimate itself as a nation-state by appeal to any particular cultural content but only in terms of a contract among its subjects, there is no automatic political orientation to the excavation and inclusion of the popular. This was not the case in Great Britain, where the study of popular culture was automatically and systematically at the same time cultural critique, since it exposed the structural gap between the ideological state apparatuses and the people they regulated. In the United States, the system is described to itself so that it can work better; it is not overthrown. For example, in the United States it is possible to believe that capitalism's project is hindered by racism and sexism, which should be done away with so as to allow the process of expropriation to work more widely. In Great Britain, such a claim would have struck at the heart of the ethnic cultural identity on which the nation-state was founded, while in the United States it represents no fundamental challenge to the state's promise to itself or to the economic system it harbors. Cultural Studies attacks the cultural hegemony of the nation-state, and the question of its politics becomes troubled when global capital engages in the same attack. The pietistic leftism of much work in Cultural Studies, like the anxieties expressed by Barker and Beezer, is intimately linked to this context—to the fear that there is no longer an automatic leftist orientation to the struggle against cultural exclusion.

What I want to argue is that the emergence of Cultural Studies must be understood as a symptom, that its fundamental stress on participation (with Williams and Thompson) initially arises from a sense that culture is no longer immanent but is something "over there." In the early 1960s, those excluded from the institutions of culture on grounds of class, race, sex, or sexual orientation try to reimagine their relation to culture. It is no surprise that this takes place most strongly in Britain.

However, the second moment at which Cultural Studies becomes, institutionally speaking, the strongest narrative for humanistic inquiry, marks the impossibility of participating in living culture. This is a crisis for the University in that *Bildung* will no longer fuse the subjective and the objective, and we need to find out another way of understanding how what we say about culture participates in culture. This project achieves critical mass in the 1990s in North America at the point when the story of exclusion does not provide an alibi, when the denunciation of exclusions becomes the only way to understand our abiding sense of nonparticipation *despite the fact that we are no longer excluded.* We are no longer excluded, not because racism, sexism, and class difference have come to an end. They manifestly have not. Rather, we are no longer excluded because, in the strong sense of the word that the Idealists gave it, *there is no longer any culture to be excluded from.* That is to say, the word "culture" no longer names a metadiscursive project with both historical extension and critical contemporaneity from which we might be excluded.

Such an argument, however, needs to be nuanced. Although particular cultural struggles need to be engaged in, particular exclusions also must be combatted. Culture is no longer the terrain on which a general critique of capitalism can be carried out. The problem of Cultural Studies is that it attempts to deliver on the redemptive claims of cultural criticism, while expanding those claims to cover everything. This is why Cultural Studies activities find their most fertile disciplinary homes in expanded departments of national literature. The global system of capital no longer requires a cultural content in terms of which to interpellate and manage subjects, as the rise of polling suggests. The statistical poll performs the work of normalization indifferently to the content of the information it discovers; its hegemony is thus *administrative* rather than *ideological.* What the poll discovers, as it were, is the "excellence" quotient of an idea, a practice, or a subject. Consensus can thus be achieved without the appeal to the synthesizing power of a metonymic subject of culture (an imaginary single general reader or viewer) as the instance that "makes sense" of symbolic life as a whole. Conformity no longer means conformity to an idea of culture. There is no "common reader" in a regime of excellence, since everyone can be excellent in their own way.

That such a situation is in no way incompatible with racism is something Spike Lee dramatizes very accurately in *Do the Right Thing,* where one of the Italian-American boys claims to be a racist despite the fact that his sporting heroes are, in fact, all African-American. Racism is not, that is, any longer a primarily cultural or political issue. The twin poles of U.S. consumer culture—rock music and organized sports— can cheerfully offer Michael Jackson and Michael Jordan. Another way of putting this would be to say that racism is no longer primarily a matter of *representation;* it is a complex *economic* issue as well as a straightforward *political* one. The discourse of national politics cannot recognize the enormous numbers of African-Americans in U.S. jails as political prisoners, and in order to understand the magnitude of this racism we cannot treat those prisoners as political subjects (they are jailed legally as individual political subjects). Instead, we have to develop an account of economic racism's complicity with the legal apparatus that can imagine a political collectivity that is not modeled upon the nation-state. The nation-state's unification of the field of political life as the representation of a self-identical popular will is structurally complicit with such injustice.

As such, the focus on representations of race and gender in Cultural Studies is a particular symptom of American academics' inability to think beyond the paradigm of *Uncle Tom's Cabin.* Liberal academics denounce the ideology of race and gender from a position in which it becomes possible to see such representations *as ideological,* without pausing to think that if the ideological has become visible, it is because the high-stakes game has moved to another table. Some will cling to the alibi of ideology and find themselves condemned to denounce every representation as insufficient, every Michael Jordan as an Uncle Tom. For in this paradigm of the Uncle Tom, the black enters representation as less than s/he should be in the first place, and then is constantly critiqued for not being "real," for not being black enough. While such a denunciation may be accurate enough, none of this will change the fact that a young African-American man is more likely to go to jail than to college. Cultural visibility is not the sole issue, as Martin Luther King knew. The U.S. government has systematically ignored the link he drew between the struggle against racism and the struggle against poverty.

This does not mean that I am arguing against the ethical imperative to denounce racism in all its forms. I am merely arguing against understanding racism as a primarily *cultural* issue, which is to say, as an ideology. As Ronald Judy points out with considerable wisdom, "as long as the approach to Afro-American studies is predicated on a response to the demand for a demonstration of either its instrumental value or cultural worth, Afro-American studies will remain firmly within 'Western' modernity's organizational model of knowledge."[23] In lending primacy to the cultural, critics miss the fact that culture *no longer matters* to the powers that be in advanced capitalism—whether those powers are transnational corporations or depoliticized, unipolar nation-states.

A good example of these problems arises around the question of marginalization. As Grossberg notes in "The Formations of Cultural Studies: An American in Birmingham," a fundamental shift in the modeling of social relations by those working in Cultural Studies occurs when, under the influence of Foucault, we move from vertical models of dominance to a more structuralist account in terms of center and periphery. Instead of speaking of power in terms of the vertical ascendancy of the rulers over the dominated (the classical model of class domination), we speak of multiple marginalized positions in relation to a hegemonic center. This allows relations of power among transverse groups (groups that include members of all social classes, such as women or homosexuals) to be mapped.

And when we speak of mapping, it is possible to understand why the analyses of Pierre Bourdieu have been so attractive to many people in Cultural Studies, since his practice of charting power relations along twin axes of power (symbolic capital and socioeconomic capital) permits the mapping of power relations in both the economic and the cultural fields. The intersection of these axes produces a center, and positions of power are calibrated in terms of closeness to this center.[24]

The general notion of "cultural capital" is one that seems more and more attractive to North American scholars in the humanities. Bourdieu is one of the more frequently cited theoretical authorities in a certain branch of Cultural Studies. I shall discuss his analysis of the events of 1968 later on, but for now I want to ask why a thinker whose analytic mode is conservative and normative (the mapping of social positions as algorithms of deviation within a closed national cultural field) should have been so attractive to those in Cultural Studies, who are normally concerned to make radical claims. This is not simply because Bourdieu's method allows for the mapping of positions that can effectively quantify social capital (although on two axes rather than on a single scale). More fundamentally, the understanding of the model of center and periphery, as if it were a chart like Bourdieu's, allows analysis of power to proceed as usual. The relation between each peripheral position and the center is read *as if it were* a vertical one. The vertical model of power has not been fundamentally altered, merely rotated through ninety degrees. Thus power can be mapped, although with more variables than before. Instead of analyzing cultural domination in terms of relations of class, we map it in terms of class, race, and gender as positions on a scale with two axes rather than one. The rather unfair trick of turning the terms of an analysis back on itself is unavoidable in the case of Bourdieu, since his analysis insists, as John Guillory reminds us in *Cultural Capital,* that there is no way out of the game of culture, which presumably means that one can only either become a more savvy player or seek to modify the rules slightly.[25]

Since Bourdieu has written a book on the University, and since he is currently very popular as a theoretical authority on culture, I want to take the time to trace the problems of his analysis of the system of cultural capital. This analysis is based on two essential assumptions. First, it is assumed that there is only one game: in order for culture to be a relatively autonomous social totality (capable of being mapped on two axes), all cultural games are part of the great game of cultural capital. Second, there is no way out: the borders of the system are strictly drawn, and within them one can chart the distribution of cultural capital in terms of ratios of differing prestige. The single, closed game is the game of national culture, whose boundaries are accepted without question in order for analysis to proceed. Herein lies the reason for the somewhat surprising fact that Guillory's *Cultural Capital*, a reading of the American University system avowedly influenced by Bourdieu, nowhere discusses Bourdieu's study of the French system, *Homo Academicus.*

Homo Academicus charts the distribution of cultural capital within the French University system. Yet cultural capital can only be mapped within a system that is taken to be strictly closed by national boundaries that are assumed to be absolute. Bourdieu acknowledges that "there is no escaping the work of constructing this object" and enumerates the "finite set of *pertinent properties*" that will function as *"effective variables"* within the system, but he never questions the national boundaries that determine the field within which he proposes to study *Homo academicus gallicus,* even while musing on the question of that field's applicability to readers from other national University systems (xv). Within those fixed national boundaries, the unequal distribution of cultural capital can be mapped in terms of relative distantiation from a center that is located at the intersection of the two axes of institutional-social prestige and intellectual-scientific prestige. As Bourdieu puts it:

> The structure of the university field is only, at any moment in time, the state of the power relations between the agents or, more precisely, between the powers they wield in their own right and above all through the institutions to which they belong; positions held in this structure are what motivate structures aiming to transform it, or to preserve it by modifying or maintaining the relative forces of the different powers, that is, in other words, the systems of equivalence established between the different kinds of capital. (128)

Hence, for Bourdieu in *Homo Academicus* the international prestige of certain French academics is counted only insofar as it registers in

France, which is very little.[26] Hence one might rephrase the slogan of Bourdieu's *Distinction* as "There is no way out of the game of [national] culture."[27]

Bourdieu proposes a system of cultural capital that is analogous to the system of monetary capital, sometimes convergent and sometimes divergent, that allows for a refinement of the theory of ideology. Ideology does not simply reflect or serve economic interests. For Bourdieu, ideology organizes cultural forms within a system that is relatively autonomous of economic determination, but nonetheless it organizes them *according to an economic logic.* This permits a sociological reading of culture as a relatively independent economy in which prestige takes the place of the money form as the unit of value. This may, as Guillory argues, excuse Bourdieu of the charge of "economism"—the claim that cultural forms are superstructural elements that reflect a determinant economic base—but it would still be accurate to call this an economistic analysis of culture.[28] Economistic in the sense that culture is here figured along the model of a restricted economy, a restriction which is based in an unacknowledged acceptance of the fixity of national borders.

Bourdieu wants to get out of the problem of relations of determination between base and superstructure by stressing the analogy between, and the potential convertibility of, monetary and cultural capital. Cultural capital is assumed to be convertible by analogy with money in two senses. First, possession of cultural capital can lead to better economic status within a national social totality. Second, at the international level, cultural capital has different national forms, but all nations have forms of cultural capital. This is the paradox raised by the prospect of comparativist analyses of cultural capital. Each nation would presumably have to possess its own currency of prestige (like money) so that there would be the possibility of conversion between them. The possibility of general analysis implies a World Culture Bank, or at least an International Prestige Fund.

Prestige and money are not, however, directly convertible, although academics have a lot to gain, both analytically and financially, from believing that they may be. They can only appear analogous when analyses are entirely restricted within *national* frontiers, where limited context cultural capital can seem more fungible, since the question of trans-latability is not posed. Were it to be posed, one would be faced with a problem: instead of describing cultural capital as the currency of a national social totality, one would have to ask "prestige *for whom?*" without having a ready-made answer, because culture would no longer be one game but many heterogeneous games. If cultural capital is some-thing that can be distributed, then class analysis of that distribution masks ethnocentrism. If all cultures are variably capitalized, what is implied is a form of convertibility, and the form of convertibility will favor a dominant definition of culture.

The illusion that ethnocentrism is not an issue arises only when the analysis of cultural capital is played out at the *national* level, where the common currency of cultural capital appears empty of ethnic specific-ity, residing only in the abstract idea of the nation. From this perspec-tive, the underside of Guillory's rephrasing of the canon debate in terms of the distribution of cultural capital appears: the desire to preserve the form of the nation-state as the fundamental unit of cultural analysis, in a world in which global fusion (Wallerstein's "geo-culture") and national fission threaten its status. What this reveals is the withering of the nation-state in the face of the transnational corporation; the nation-state is no longer the primary instance of the reproduction of capital.[29]

Hence, insofar as Bourdieu (who likes to pretend to objectivity) and Guillory make any proposals for the University on the basis of their analysis, what is proposed is not an alternative to the system but the more equal redistribution of capital *within* the system, which Guillory thematizes as increased "access" to or "accessibility" of cultural goods. Thus Guillory, at the end of his book, proposes the following "thought experiment": What if the system of culture were reorganized so as to permit maximal access to cultural capital? This is the nearest Guillory's book comes to delivering on its many exhortations for "rethinking."[30] One can immediately observe that it begs the thorny institutional ques-tions of *who* will perform this reorganization and *how*. But this is per-haps a churlish cavil. More directly, the Marxist model of distributive justice underlying this suggestion certainly implies that the "dream of consensus," which Guillory has earlier criticized, now has reared its head. Second, such a redistribution of cultural capital would be far less threatening to the system than Guillory implies. Is not Guillory's proposal heading in the very same direction as techno-bureaucratic culture in the moment when capitalism seeks to expand its consumer base? How would Guillory's redistribution differ from the Thatcherite desire to bring all subjects within the fold of the "property-owning democracy"? Could access to culture be as finely differentiated as income?

We are, I think, entitled to require a far more pointed reflection on the politics of "access" than Guillory supplies. What he does provide, however, is the following conclusion:

> In a culture of such universal access, canonical works could not be experienced as they so often are, as lifeless monuments, or as proofs of class distinction. Insofar as the debate on the canon has tended to discredit aesthetic judgment, or to express a certain embarrassment with its metaphysical pretensions and its political biases, it has quite missed the point. The point is not to make judgment disappear but to reform the conditions of its practice. If there is no way out of the game of culture, then, even when cultural capital is the only kind of capital, there may be another kind of game, with less dire consequences for the losers, an *aesthetic* game. Socializing the means of production and consumption would be the condition of an aestheticism unbound, not its overcoming. But of course, this is only a thought experiment. (340)

These closing words, after 340 dense pages, make a rather particular claim for the redemptive power of the aesthetic. It seems to suggest that we are not yet ready for Kant, that only after Marx has done his work, and the means of production and consumption have been socialized, can we really be Kantians, engaging in the free play of aesthetic judgment in a way that is harmless. Only then, Guillory contends, will the distinctions that arise from the competition of judgments no longer have socioeconomic consequences, merely cultural ones.

This apparent plea for the relative autonomy of the aesthetic turns out to be a staggering privileging of the economic base. Only when it has been put out of the way does aesthetic judgment become free to realize its own essentially harmless nature. Aestheticism is unbound because the differences it makes are no longer real, dire differences. One hears the voice of Fourierism here: let us make the nation a phalanstery, and then we will be artists. This kind of imagination relies on the possibility that culture may be a closed system, a game with fixed boundaries—those of the nation. This seems to forget the contemporary global development of capitalism as a *jeu sans frontières,* which Guillory elsewhere notes (345n11). Moreover, the argument that culture is a field of essentially harmless differences seems to me dubious, to say the least. It is not just that cultural differences have socioeconomic consequences that makes them count for something, otherwise we would all speak the same language. But to take seriously the fact that we do not all speak the same language, that the "social totality" is not defined by the analogy between an ethnicity, a nation-state, and a national language, would render exhaustive analysis in terms of cultural capital impossible.

The appeal of Bourdieu to thinkers like Guillory and to those who work more closely in Cultural Studies is that he offers an analysis of culture that can take account of its loss of any specific reference—its dereferentialization—while still being able to produce what looks like a positive knowledge about culture, by mapping the distribution of cultural capital in terms of proximity to or distance from a cultural center. I would argue that this is a misrecognition of the contemporary nature of power. Bourdieu and his followers fail to see that the center is not a real place any longer. As Foucault knew, panopticism is only one model of power (though many of his readers tend not to notice this). Culture is not a citadel to be occupied. In fact, no one sits in the center any longer. The center was once occupied by the institution of the nation-state, which embodied capital and expressed it as a culture that radiated across the field of the social. But the decline of the nation-state means that this center is actually a lure. Capital no longer flows outward from the center, rather it circulates around the circumference, behind the backs of those who keep their eyes firmly fixed on the center. Around the circumference, the global transfer of capital takes place in the hands of multi- or transnational corporations. The so-called center, the nation-state, is now merely a virtual point that organizes peripheral subjectivities within the global flow of capital; it is not a site to be occupied. Hence everyone seems to be culturally excluded, while at the same time almost everyone is included within the global flow of capital.

To sum up, the decline of the nation-state means that culture is no longer a matter of the inclusion or exclusion of a subject in relation to a cultural center, or even of degrees of inclusion. Hence the problematic of participation, since we can no longer tell a story of liberation as the passage from the margins to the center, as the entry into the gates of subjecthood. As academics know very well, the position of enunciation is peripheral: the center is silent. By this I mean that in order to speak in today's academy one is constrained to assume a position of marginality. So even conservatives have to tell the story of their own marginalization from culture in order to speak for themselves. Thus people like David Horowitz or Dinesh D'Souza claim to be assuming a heterodox position in espousing patriarchy and arguing for the supremacy of Western Culture. What can it mean that those who speak *for the center* need to claim to be marginalized?

It is very tempting to see what Gerald Graff has called the "culture wars" as a healthy sign that the debate on U.S. national culture is once again taking place where it ought to: in the University.[31] Bliss is it in this dawn to be alive, but to be tenured and approaching middle age seems very heaven! Yet is the United States a "country in romance . . . where reason seems the most to assert her rights," like Wordsworth's revolutionary France? What worries me about the American culture wars is that I hear on both sides of the debate a conflation of prescription and description in the name of national identity: the claim that U.S. national identity is, and should be, reflective of either a selective tradition or a multicultural rainbow.[32] Personally, I am for openness, but I have some suspicions about the way in which defenders of "diversity" tend to buttress their argument by reference to the real American identity as diverse. This is tantamount to reiterating that to be truly American is to be an immigrant, a liberal argument that repeats the Enlightenment trick of establishing an opposition between human culture and nature, placing the native American or indigene on the side of nature rather than culture.

For example, Becky W. Thompson and Sangeeta Tyagi argue in their introduction to *Beyond a Dream Deferred: Multicultural Education and the Politics of Excellence* that "our project . . . is no less than rethinking 'America.' "[33] Now they are clearly concerned to avoid racism, and do indeed list "native Hawaiian" alongside the other variants of "people of color" who form their contributors. The extent to which this well-meaning collection is prey to an anxiety about the status of the University that it cannot directly address can be gleaned from a look at the contributors' notes, which paradoxically stress the marginalization of the contributors in terms of their race, gender, or sexual orientation while also insisting on a concomitant validating closeness to the real.[34] Thus the institutional affiliations of contributors are provided, yet curiously in a book on education policy, the focus of the contributors' notes is, in most cases, on extracurricular activities and cultural marginalization. Perhaps lamentably, this focus is probably an intelligent response to current pressures in the academic marketplace, where the "real" or extra-academic has become a prized academic commodity.[35] The contributors' very marginalization from culture's institutions is thus the very ground of their cultural participation. Margin and center no longer serve to explain the dynamic of power.

The logic that invokes the indigene as one name for difference, placed indifferently among a list of others (for fear of exclusion), gives voice to the indigene only at the price of a self-recognition as one immigrant among others, at the price of the qualitative *homogenization* of the very differences that lists such as the following seek to note: "In keeping with our commitment to representation of those who have led the way in progressive educational change, most of the chapters are written by people of color—African-American, Latino and Latina, Asian-American, Indian, and Native Hawaiian—in addition to chapters by white women and gay and lesbian people."[36] I indicate the indigene as merely one victim of homogenization in such listings. In general, the effect of multiculturalism is necessarily to homogenize differences as equivalently deviant from a norm. This is why multiculturalism replaces national cultural policy for a global economy, whether in the sensitivity training of transnational corporations or in the federal policy of superstates such as Canada or the European Union, which are attempting to align themselves in the global economy. To put this another way, the multicultural argument can turn out to be another form of "Americanization" that rather changes the tone of the claim by the authors of the introduction to be rethinking—which is to say, *redescribing*—America.[37]

While it would be possible to engage in an extended critique of the multiculturalist position, I am for the moment more interested in diagnosis than in denunciation, in trying to understand *why* the debate on national culture in the United States has returned to the University. The so-called debate is less specifically American than it might seem. Rather than being the result of any specific betrayal, it actually draws its energies from an endemic condition of contemporary higher education—the problems raised by the absence of a cultural center.[38] It is in this void that the culture wars arise.

In saying this, however, I do not mean to suggest that those groups who have in the past been the controlling forces of a central culture have either disappeared or resorted to espousing falsehoods about their relationship to cultural power. In this regard, I think Gerald Graff is a bit too quick when, in *Beyond the Culture Wars,* he dismisses as a falsification the story of the marginalization of dead white males that animates the polemics of Allan Bloom, William Bennett, and others. What the right wing is doing has to be understood symptomatically. Graff is correct to point out that the right under Reagan and Bush did, in fact, occupy all the positions of cultural power, while at the same time bemoaning its own exclusion. This is not simply an ideological trick, an attempt to co-opt the allure of the rebel stance, as the fictional Republican candidate does in the film *Bob Roberts.* We need to ask what it means that the holders of cultural power need to portray themselves as unorthodox rebels. It seems to me that the conservative jeremiads are motivated by the fact that their authors feel the emptiness of the cultural power they hold. That is to say, they recognize the powerlessness of the cultural power they hold, and they blame left-wing academics for usurping it. They hold the center, but they know that it is merely a virtual point. The cultural right is not rebelling against its exclusion from the center but against the exclusion *of* the center, its reduction. The "culture wars" thus arise between those who hold cultural power but fear that it no longer matters and those whose exclusion from that cultural power allows them to believe that such power would matter if only they held it.

The relentless self-marginalization of both sides is a self-blinding, a refusal to recognize that the stakes in the game have changed, that the center actually *does not speak,* that the privileged position of enuncia-tion is not that of the subject who participates in culture. What appears as the self-marginalization of a subject (and is often denounced as the culture of *ressentiment* by those on the right such as D'Souza, liberals such as Robert Hughes, and left-wingers such as Sande Cohen)[39] is the symptom that the nation-state (actual or ideal) no longer exists as a cultural form in which the speaking subject might find him or herself authoritatively reflected. The claim of subjective marginalization masks the fact that with the evacuation of the nation-state as cultural form, enunciation now proceeds from what I would call *peripheral singular-ities* rather than from traditional citizen-subjects.

I use the term "singularity," drawing on Deleuze and Guattari among others, to indicate that there is no longer a subject-position available to function as the site of the conscious synthesis of sense-impressions.[40] The shift I am proposing is from the category of the subject to a notion of singularity as the way of understanding individual existence. Ac-cording to Descartes, the thinking individual becomes a subject among other subjects, by positioning him- or herself as the locus of an activity of reasoning. The capacity to reason about one's own thought (to think oneself thinking) is self-consciousness. All individuals share this capac-ity and are hence interchangeable in principle. For someone like Ha-bermas, this is why we can all agree, or at least agree to disagree; it is the ground of communicability. The subject is thus the fact of self-consciousness and is unmarked by gender, race, etc.

The turn to singularity comes in the wake of questioning the category of the subject and its pretended neutrality.[41] Singularity provides a way of talking about individuals other than as subjects. It recognizes the radical heterogeneity of individuals, the sheer fact that as an agglom-eration of matter, history, experience, whatever, you just are not some-one else; there is nothing you can be presumed in advance to share with someone else. So when a white-lesbian-woman from the American Midwest (the listing of markers of difference can of course be extended) interacts with, say, a straight-black-man from Liberia, they do not do so on the basis of a shared subjectivity (or even a shared subjective oppression) that would make them transparent to each other in dis-cussion. Rather, singularities *negotiate,* and the structure of singularity is very odd, since it is not repeatable. Hence a singularity cannot achieve total self-consciousness, since if it did know itself, the self that it knew would not be the same self as the self that did the knowing.

To put this another way, the singularity is a *minimal node of specificity,* which is not structurally homogenized as a subject. This does not make the singular individual a kind of "free radical," to use the language of physics. Singularities are homogenized in mass culture (which makes them into consumer subjects instead of traditional, productive subjects of the public sphere or civic society). In this regard, consumerism is a major index of the insufficiency of the notion of the subject, since traditional accountings for "the subject" cannot even explain why we like to shop, although we know it is a mode of self-victimization not a free and autonomous act: we buy what we are sold, not what we want, and then we end up wanting it. Hence it was necessary for subject-centered theories to develop the notion of ideology and to claim that all shopping for other than necessities of survival was the product of ideological trickery exerted on naive dupes—another narrative of the Fall.

While what I have just outlined may seem like an unnecessarily complicated argument to some, I would argue that the advantage of speaking in terms of singularities is that it offers us a way of discussing the contradictory and multiple ways in which relations of desire (for commodities and other things), power, and knowledge flow among individuals, without having to presume that there is a stable, natural, or logical order of such relations that we have lost and to which we should return. To speak of the "peripheral singularity" is to insist that there is no ideal individual that might achieve either total self-consciousness or a harmonious, balanced relation to others and the world. Peripheral singularities do not stand at the center of culture.

The notion of culture had proposed such a centered subject, who was indeed invoked ideologically to suggest that the logic of cultural participation provided a ground of equality that transcended economic expropriation. The contemporary capitalist economy has laid this ideological veil aside. Thus, although exclusions from cultural representation continue, they can now be thought of as vestigial. The laying aside of cultural taboos proceeds apace. Madonna, the icon of the Virgin, appears on screen in bed with gay black men, and the spectator situates her- or himself culturally in terms of how shocking this seems. This is what Debord meant by the society of spectacle: the recirculation of what lies outside the system as a value *within* the system, as "shock-value." As Madonna knows, culture is made up of roles and their combinations, not of identities. Everyone can, in principle, participate in culture, have their Warholian fifteen minutes. They can do so because such participation no longer has the meaning for society that it used to, because society is no longer organized in the interest of realizing cultural identity, which has now become an obstacle to the flow of capital rather than its vehicle.

Rather than denouncing this process in the name of hidden or yet-to-be-realized identities, we need to rethink the question of agency, to ask what can be the kinds of agency that can arise among *relays or roles* rather than self-identical subjects. And lest I seem to be merely denouncing Cultural Studies, let me make clear that work in Cultural Studies is structured by this tension: by a general tendency to engage in ideology-critique while realizing its limitations. Sometimes this appears as bad faith (the surreptitious hope that agencies will coagulate into a subject of history, that the theory of "cultural construction" will ground a new historical project). Sometimes it appears as the attempt to do something other than business as usual.

The notion that culture matters is ineluctably linked to the ascendancy of the nation-state as a political formation, and the decline of the nation-state means that the question of power is no longer structured in terms of the inclusion or exclusion of subjects from cultural participation. Instead of subject positions, we should speak of singularities that appear as peripheral in relation to a virtual cultural center that is indifferent to them as subjects (in a way the nation-state was not). In other words, we can write "excellence" at the center of the diagram where once there was "culture." Positions can be mapped in terms of degrees of excellence, and such mapping is the work of bureaucratic institutions such as the University. However, these institutions are no longer cultural in the strong sense, in that our position in relation to them is not a determinant of meaning, since "excellence," as we have seen in Chapter 2, is not referential but a unit of value internal to the system, the elemental unit of a virtual scale.

This, then, is what it means for me to say that Cultural Studies arises as a quasi-discipline once culture ceases to be the animating principle of the University and becomes instead one object of study among others. The problem of participation becomes most acutely the object of reflection when we no longer know what it would mean to participate, when there is no longer any obvious citadel to be captured. It does not mean that Cultural Studies is foolish, that those who practice it have missed the point. Rather, if culture is everything, then it has no center, no referent outside itself—and facing up to this dereferentialization seems to me to be the task incumbent upon Cultural Studies.

The chance to face up to this issue arises because the endeavor of Cultural Studies is the contemporary way to speculate on the question of what it means to be *in* the University, with the added complication that, unlike German Idealism, speculation itself is not already the answer to the question. Such is the situation of the posthistorical University, the University without an idea. The question remains, then, of how to understand the work that Cultural Studies does—how to conceptualize the mass of analyses as something other than fascinating symptoms of nostalgia for what the University once was. How, that is, can Cultural Studies do something other than critique culture excellently?

~ 8

The Posthistorical University

How are we to reimagine the University, once its guiding idea of culture has ceased to have an essential function? The last part of this book will seek to sketch the framework within which the transnational comparative analysis of the University might proceed. The general line of this argument will have to take account of the fact that although the University continues to exist, we can no longer continue to understand it solely in terms of its relation to culture. Once transnational capitalism has eroded the meaning of culture, and once the institutional system begins to show itself capable of functioning without reference to that term, then the role of education cannot primarily be conceived in terms of cultural acquisition or cultural resistance. This does not mean that those in the University should abandon critical judgment, become passive observers or even eager servants of capital. As I shall argue, the question of value becomes more significant than ever, and it is by raising value as a question of *judgment* that the discourse of excellence can be resisted. Evaluation can become a social question rather than a device of measurement. Yet to do this will no longer be to point to a notion of what constitutes true value, what really authorizes teaching, since what is at stake is no longer the nature of value but its *function*.

Where excellence brackets the question of value in favor of measurement, replaces questions of accountability or responsibility with accounting solutions, I shall argue that holding open the question of value is a way of holding open a capacity to imagine the social other-wise. Crucially, this is not the same thing as proposing a true model of the social that is based on, or developed in, the University. Rather than being a central locus of investigation into cultural value, the University thus becomes one site among many others where attempts are made to hold judgment open as a question. But I am getting ahead of myself. First I would like to return to the problem of critique, so as to link the problems that I have identified with the disciplinary project of Cultural Studies more generally to the question of how to think after culture.

The decline of the nation-state, and of culture as a national ideology, not only shifts the traditional role of the University but also makes it difficult to discern the terms in which we might analyze such a shift. I have already described one destiny of the contemporary or posthistor-ical University, the University of Excellence, where excellence names a non-referential principle that allows the maximum of uninterrupted internal administration. And I have sought to suggest that this devel-opment needs to be resisted. But to seek to resist it through critique, by remobilizing the critical function of the University, remains alas Kantian if not Luddite.

The problem of critique as reinforcement of the system has been sketched with admirable economy and polemical force by Theodor Adorno in "Cultural Criticism and Society."[1] His complex essay traces the breakdown of traditional forms of cultural critique in the face of contemporary culture's abandonment of ideological pretense. Neither the anti-exclusionary assault on high culture as the (bourgeois) part standing in for the whole, nor the assault on mass culture as "bread and circuses" that mask the true nature of expropriation will do. In this context, the critique of culture as an ideology becomes obsolete, since there is no outside to cultural ideology. Culture no longer hides anything; there is nothing behind culture for ideology critique to find, although "the materialistic transparency of culture has not made it more honest, only more vulgar" (34). This means that the analysis of culture can no longer assume a stable ground, can no longer assign its products to the machinations of particular vested interests. To use Adorno's words, "Today, ideology means society as appearance. Al-though mediated by the totality behind which stands the rule of partiality, ideology is not simply reducible to a partial interest. It is, as it were, equally near the center in all its pieces" (31).

As Adorno recognizes, the cultural critic either assumes a transcendent position that criticizes culture as false or unnatural (without realizing that the notion of the "natural" is itself generated by the culture under critique), or takes up an immanent position that offers culture a self-consciousness it already possesses, that increases its vulgarity rather than its honesty. "There are no more ideologies in the authentic sense of false consciousness, only advertisements for the world through its duplication and the provocative lie which does not seek belief but commands silence" (34). The critique of culture depends on the assumption that culture is organized in terms of truth and falsehood rather than in terms of successful or unsuccessful performance. What is more, critique depends on the idea that there is a quasi-religious belief in the icons of culture, and it loses its force once the system is prepared to make any cultural icon the site of economic profit. So the British royal family becomes a soap opera rather than an ideological excuse for popular submission, while on MTV Beavis and Butthead can perform semiotic analyses of gender roles in video clips for the amusement of those viewers whom cultural critique presumes are the blind dupes of these same video clips.

Hence the problem of Cultural Studies: its analyses of culture do have an effect, but as sites for further investment by a system that is no longer cultural in the traditional sense. Rather than posing a threat, the analyses performed by Cultural Studies risk providing new marketing opportunities for the system. Practices such as punk music and dress styles are offered their self-consciousness in academic essays, but the dignity they acquire is not that of authenticity but of *marketability,* be it in the cinema, on MTV, or as a site of tourist interest for visitors to London. The travel guide is a prime example of the way cultural particularity no longer offers an authentic alternative to the market system but is now a form of access to the status of the commodity. Cultural particularity has no referent outside the system in which it circulates. To put it bluntly, the shock value of punk is not lasting in a cultural sense, since it soon becomes possible to be "excellently punk." To say that it is not lasting does not mean, however, that there is no point in trying to do something new, only that it is naive to presume that in so doing one gains access to a real culture outside the system or that one disrupts absolutely the circuit of appropriations.

I do not think, then, that we can aim to replace the idea of culture with a return to the idea of reason, to give culture back its reason and make history the site of rational analysis. Thus when Anthony Easthope hails Cultural Studies as a new more scientific paradigm, an analysis of culture stripped of the superstitious veils of the aesthetic ideology and standing naked in the hard light of reason alone, I fear that the critical force of Cultural Studies may turn out to be animated by Kantian nostalgia. And I find confirmation of this worry in the hard disciplinary line taken by those such as Cary Nelson, for whom the disciplinary problematic of Cultural Studies turns out to be a question of border disputes, a question of making sure that one wins the conflict of the faculties.[2]

What I want to suggest, and this suggestion comes at the very beginning of what must be for me a long process of thinking, is that we should seek to turn the dereferentialization that is characteristic of the posthistorical University to good advantage. That is to say, we should try to think what it may mean to have a University that has no idea, that does not derive its name from an etymological confusion of unity and universality. For Humboldt, the University should name the idea of the totality that fuses the originary unity of science as principle with its ultimate universality as ideal, its spread through *Bildung*.[3] And I think that the beginning of a shift away from such a vision must come in a reflection upon the intersection of community and communication that culture names.

Let me sum up the argument on the University of Culture that I sketched in Chapter 5 by saying that the University of Culture is grounded in a notion of *communicative transparency.* For the German Idealists, this transparency allows the fusion of ethnic community and absolute idea. The fusion takes place at multiple levels. Pedagogically, Fichte refers to teaching as the self-unveiling of the students to the professors and of the professors to the students. Self-unveiling has nothing to do with classroom nudity but with a dialogue that is supposed to fuse the teachers and the students into a single corporate body with "a common spiritual existence . . . in which they have learned early on to know each other in depth and to respect each other, where all their reflections take off from a base which is identically known by all and which provides no matter for dispute among them."[4] This is the community of the University, the endless dialogue of which Humboldt and Schleiermacher speak. It is a community whose dialogue is about nothing, in the sense that no issues for dispute are engaged. There are no differends, no radical and incommensurable differences, only arguments as to the exact nature of what it is that we agree on.

Schleiermacher even makes the curious argument that the magisterial *ex cathedra* lecture course is a form of dialogue, a sanctuary that grounds the community of the University.[5] He claims that such a course displays the spirit of dialogue, even if it does not take on its external form. For Schleiermacher, the *ex cathedra* lecture awakens the idea of intellectual community in its hearers and enacts the process of knowledge rather than transmitting knowledge as a product. Communication is thus not the vehicle for transmitting positive knowledges; it is itself the enactment of the process of *Bildung*. The University community has its foundation in the capacity to share in a process of knowledge. Communication unites speaker and listener in the process of the revelation of the idea; it does not simply serve as a vehicle or bridge between them. In this sense, communication is *expressive* rather than transactional because the idea is revealed objectively as science by the speaker (in his or her enactment of the process of knowledge-acquisition) and subjectively as *Bildung* by the listener (in his or her awakening to the desire for consciousness).

The positions of Habermas, Lepenies, and Fish on the University actually represent the giving up of the expressive claim for revelation and a returning to a transactional model of communication. Unity is not expressed but implied negatively as the necessary positing of a horizon of consensus that, although it may not be empirically realized, is nonetheless the necessary precondition for all acts of communication. Consensus replaces ethnic identity as the grounds of a unified idea of culture. In the case of Cultural Studies, a horizon of *political* consensus does at times seem to play this role.

Thinking about what to do instead is more of a problem. I must

123

confess that I am attracted to Robert Young's suggestion that the University, both inside and outside the market economy, should "function as a surplus that the economy cannot comprehend."[6] The binary opposition is there, and the University will deconstruct it by being neither simply useful nor simply useless. All very good, and very much what Humboldt wanted: indirect utility, direct uselessness for the state. Of course, the question begging to be asked here is: Why does deconstruction end up restating Humboldt? If I find this an unsatisfactory conclusion to Young's fine study of Newman and Bentham on the University, it is because Young is perhaps still looking for a way to save the idea of the University, by proposing a deconstructive idea—the idea of the supplement—that will function analogously to the idea of culture. We could even sell the idea by suggesting to the state that culture has always been a dangerous supplement anyway. However, I do not think we can save the idea of the University by proposing new referents, even such troubling ones as the dangerous supplement. The technological University will reply by telling us to be excellently supplementary, by turning supplements into surplus value.

So what is the point of the University, if we realize that we are no longer to strive to realize a national identity, be it an ethnic essence or a republican will? In asking such a question I am not suggesting that I want to blow up the University, or even to resign from my job. I am neither pessimistic nor optimistic, since I do not think that the temporality implied by such terms is appropriate. Here I am entirely in agreement with Leo Bersani's critique, in *The Culture of Redemption,* of the idea that culture can redeem life.[7] Bersani's assault on the claims of literary modernism is a critique of the idea of culture that has provided the identity for the modern University. We need no new identity for the University, not even the supplement will save us. Rather we need to recognize that the dereferentialization of the University's function opens a space in which we can think the notions of community and communication differently.

A resistance to the technocratic University that does not ground itself in a pious claim to know the true referent of the University, the one that will redeem it, is difficult to characterize. The vast majority of those who speak about the University adopt one of two positions: either nostalgic calls for a return to the Humboldtian ideals of modular community and social functioning, or technocratic demands that the University embrace its corporate identity and become more productive, more efficient. Merely disdaining appeals to "excellence" will not do. The contemporary geopolitical situation seems to me to disbar any thought of return to the levels of state funding that characterized the Western University during the Cold War, when culture (in both the human and the natural sciences) was a field of superpower competition. The ensuing economic pressures mean that we cannot hope to expand toward a fuller realization of the Humboldtian ideal, even if the narrative of national culture still had a subject that could act as its referent.

The challenge of the present conjuncture is a difficult one, but I do not think that what is required of us is the building of a better institution, the production of another model of efficiency, another unified and unifying project. Being smart in the present situation requires another kind of thinking altogether, one that does not seek to lend work in the University a unified ideological function. In the final part of this book, I shall explore the ways in which we can understand the University today, as it abandons its role as the flagship of national culture but before it embarks irrevocably upon the path of becoming an excellent bureaucratic corporation. The University has to find a new language in which to make a claim for its role as a locus of higher education—a role which nothing in history says is an inevitably necessary one.

The three functions that are still invoked in the contemporary University are *research, teaching,* and *administration.* The last of these is, of course, the most rapidly expanding field in terms of the allocation of resources, and, as I have argued, its expansion is symptomatic of the breakdown of the German Idealist contract between research and teaching. Indeed, I would be inclined to argue that the University of Excellence is one in which a general principle of administration replaces the dialectic of teaching and research, so that teaching and research, as aspects of professional life, are subsumed under administration.

A great deal of the current attack on the University claims that a too-exclusive focus on research is harming teaching. For the humanities this complaint is as old as the modern University.[8] However, the terms of its contemporary resurgence are, I have suggested, different in that the complaint is symptomatic of a more fundamental breakdown: the breakdown of the metanarrative that centers the University around the production of a national subject. The University no longer has a hero for its grand narrative, and a retreat into "professionalization" has been the consequence. Professionalization deals with the loss of the subject-referent of the educational experience by integrating teaching and research as aspects of the general administration of a closed system: teaching is the administration of students by professors; research is the administration of professors by their peers; administration is the name given to the stratum of bureaucrats who administer the whole. In each case, administration involves the processing and evaluation of information according to criteria of excellence that are internal to the system: the value of research depends on what colleagues think of it; the value of teaching depends upon the grades professors give and the evaluations the students make; the value of administration depends upon the ranking of a University among its peers. Significantly, the synthesizing evaluation takes place at the level of administration.

In these terms, the oft-repeated claim that the University is too research oriented and has given up on teaching is actually the product of a nostalgia for a subject whose "experience" might serve to register and synthesize the University as a whole—a student whose *parcours* could embody and unify higher education. I shall argue that this student has never existed and that 1968 proclaimed "his" non-existence (among other things, by reminding us that the supposedly universal student was gendered). In discussing how to divert the dereferentializing process of capitalist bureaucracy into a way to make the University a more interesting place to be, I shall focus on how a general administrative logic of evaluation replaces the interplay of teaching and research as central to the functioning of the University. This will not be merely a denunciation of the evaluative logic of excellence, for it should be clearly stated that the discourse of excellence has its advantages. For instance, it is what has permitted the speed with which feminism and African-American studies have risen to powerful positions in the disciplinary order.

The breakdown of the old disciplinary structure seems to me no great

126

loss as such. It is a matter of in whose interests the changes occur. As a faculty member, I want us to be careful that the surplus value released by the erasure of old job demarcations gets shared among the faculty and students, and does not simply accrue to the administration. A great deal of money can be saved, for example, by fusing the humanities under the rubric of "Cultural Studies" (support staff, teaching credits, physical plant, etc.), and we have to demand that University administrators plough back these savings into funding pedagogical initiatives (such as short-term concentrations for teaching and research, mini humanities centers) that allow interesting work to be done.

Now that we can no longer make a redemptive claim for research, can no longer believe that the imagined community of scholars mirrors in microcosm the potential community of the nation-state, we have to think how to reimagine the notion of community itself. Hence I shall argue that, far from community being the locus of unity and identity, the question of the proximity of thinkers in the University should be understood in terms of a *dissensual community* that has relinquished the regulatory ideal of communicational transparency, which has abandoned the notion of identity or unity. I shall attempt to sketch an account of the production and circulation of knowledges that imagines *thinking without identity*, that refigures the University as a locus of dissensus. In these terms, the University becomes one place among others where the question of being-together is posed, rather than an ideal community. My call is for a more radical and uncomfortable dissensus even than that proposed by Gerald Graff's call to "teach the conflicts." For behind Graff's laudable desire to displace the monologic authority of disciplinary discourse lies a desire for final consensus, the consensus that would permit the determination and transmission of "the conflict" as a unified object of professorial discourse.

Second, I shall call for a revaluation of teaching, a rethinking of the question of value in relation to teaching, specifically in relation to the question of time. The time of education is still addressed in general under the terms of a modernist metanarrative that has lost its purchase: the passage from ignorance to enlightenment in a particular time span. And it is in terms of time, "credit hours," that teaching is reduced to the logic of accounting. In "Analysis Terminable and Interminable,"

Freud already pointed out that education, like psychoanalysis and government, is an impossible profession, systemically incapable of closure. And yet the treatment of pedagogic time as exhaustively accountable is a major feature of the push to excellence. "Time to completion" is now presented as the universal criterion of quality and efficiency in education. Even though the Mellon report that caused the push for on-time completion in the United States and Canada has been discredited (the massive shortfall in professors occasioned by retirement that it predicted has been more than made up for by "downsizing"), the drive to push out Ph.D.s within four years continues unabated, despite the fact that there are no jobs for them to occupy, either in the University or elsewhere.

As I asked rhetorically in discussing the *Maclean's* report: How long does education take? The question becomes the more pressing since the age of the student population is becoming less and less homogeneous, since returning students are becoming an important resource for the University, one whose admission requires that we rethink the temporal structure within which we imagine teaching as a process. We might ponder the fact that the drive to on-time completion of the Ph.D. is accompanied by instructions to faculty (at my University at least) to stop giving "incompletes" to graduate students, to hurry up and tell them that their studies are completed, to stop thinking. In criticizing this interest in speed and efficiency, I am not arguing for some romantic ideal of eternal learning (to do so would be to presume that one could ignore institutional factors). I am merely suggesting that the complex time of thought is not exhaustively accountable, is structurally "incomplete." Thus, in Chapters 9 and 10 I shall argue for a pedagogy that refuses to justify the University in terms of a metanarrative of emancipation, that recognizes that thought is necessarily an addiction from which we never get free.

It is with regard to the *institution* that I think we need most urgently to rethink the terms within which we address the function of the University. In particular, the recognition that the University as we know it is a historically specific institution, is one with which academics have a hard time coming to terms. History grants no essential or eternal role to the modern research University, and it is necessary to contemplate the horizon of the disappearance of that University. Not to embrace the prospect of its vanishing, but to take seriously the possibility that the University, as presently constituted, holds no lien on the future. As I have suggested, the present model is in its twilight, and I do not think we can continue to make redemptive claims for the role of the University of Culture, be that culture humanistic, scientific, or sociological. Rather than offering new pious dreams of salvation, a new unifying idea, or a new meaning for the University, I will call for an institutional pragmatism. This pragmatism recognizes that thought begins where we are and does away with alibis. By thinking without alibis, I mean ceasing to justify our practices in the name of an idea from "elsewhere," an idea that would release us from responsibility for our immediate actions. Neither reason, nor culture. Neither excellence, nor an appeal to a transcendence that our actions struggle to realize, trying as we may to justify our deeds and absolve ourselves.

Such a pragmatism, I shall argue, requires that we accept that the modern University is a *ruined* institution. Those ruins must not be the object of a romantic nostalgia for a lost wholeness but the site of an attempt to transvalue the fact that the University no longer inhabits a continuous history of progress, of the progressive revelation of a unifying idea. Dwelling in the ruins of the University thus means giving a serious attention to the present complexity of its space, undertaking an endless work of *détournement* of the spaces willed to us by a history whose temporality we no longer inhabit. Like the inhabitants of some Italian city, we can seek neither to rebuild the Renaissance city-state nor to destroy its remnants and install rationally planned tower-blocks; we can seek only to put its angularities and winding passages to new uses, learning from and enjoying the cognitive dissonances that enclosed piazzas and non-signifying *campanile* induce.

This pragmatism, then, involves two recognitions. First, an awareness of the complexity and historically marked status of the spaces in which we are situated, while recognizing that these are spaces that we cannot inhabit, from which we are alienated, so that neither nostalgia nor revived organicism is a viable option. Second, a refusal to believe that some new rationale will allow us to reduce that complexity, to forget present complexity in the name of future simplicity. The pragmatism that dwells among the ruins of an institution it can no longer inhabit will be the matter of Chapter 11.

Yet before moving to such considerations, I want to say something about the question of evaluation in general. The criterion of excellence has been the object of my scorn, but that does not mean that those in the University do not need to bother themselves with such matters, that evaluation is beneath our dignity. Rankings such as those proposed by *Maclean's* will continue to be published, and the question remains of how the calls for integration and productivity are to be answered. This is also the question of how funds are to be obtained in the face of two terrifying prospects: dwindling public funds and burgeoning interest among transnational corporations in Universities as sites for investment. The administrators already have what seems to them an excellent answer to the question of evaluation, so that ignoring it will not make the question go away. As a native of Great Britain, I have already watched the evisceration of the humanities because they were unable to say anything more compelling than bleating about "leisure" and "cultivated individuals." And things do not necessarily bode well for the once-secured funding of the sciences either. The cancellation of the Superconducting Super Collider project likewise indicates that the U.S. government is no longer concerned with superpower cultural rivalry for the biggest toys, something which means that the natural sciences are no longer able to write their own research ticket, to presume an infinite investment of the national will in the production of scientific knowledge.

Those in the University are called upon to judge, and the administration will do it for them if they do not respond to the call. Responding does not, however, mean proposing new criteria, but finding ways *to keep the question of evaluation open,* a matter for dispute—what Lyotard would call the locus of a differend.[9] Let us take the example of student evaluations, which are becoming more and more common in the universities of North America, and are clearly linked to the repositioning of the student as a consumer of services. In order to permit standardization and integration under a common index of value, administrations push for the introduction of standardized, multiple-response questions across the board that will allow the calculation of a quotient of consumer satisfaction, preferably modeled on the consumer survey.

Arguing against the use of such standardized forms does not mean resisting the question of evaluation, merely the refusal to believe that the question of quality in education is susceptible to statistical calculation. The point here is to refuse to equate accountability with accounting. To give an example from my own department: the proposed form asked a number of questions to be answered on a scale of 1–4, all the answers being combined to give an average score for satisfaction on the same scale. Anything below 3 would be cause for concern. This, of course, makes the task of evaluating teaching extremely easy and is attractive to anyone who has ever sat upon a salary committee in a North American University, where merit raises are partially determined in respect to "quality of teaching." Such a score would put an end to interminable discussions about teaching merit and would be easy to convert into a cash equivalent, at a ratio of x dollars for each point above 3.0. Not to mention the use of such data in matters of promotion and tenure, which extend to universities where the practice of merit raises has not been introduced.

It seems to me that an argument can be made for the illegitimacy of such modes of evaluation on two counts. First, concerning the nature of the questions, which make a mistake in logic by presuming that evaluations can be directly deduced from descriptive statements. Logically speaking, this is a confusion between a statement of fact and a statement of value. Hence, for example, one of the questions proposed was "Did the professor respect the syllabus?" The statement presumes that such a state of affairs is automatically a good thing (respecting a contract), whereas we are, I think, entitled to suggest that it may be appropriate for a professor to tear up the syllabus and start again if it seems pitched at the wrong level for the class. These kinds of problems haunt many of the questions on student evaluation forms, and it is impossible to imagine how simply to ignore them. Is the answer, then, for there to be only one question: "Did you think this was a good course?" But that will obviously not solve the problem either, since it immediately asks us to consider whether student pleasure is the absolute criterion of value; after all, learning may be a painful experience.

The second order of problem is linked both to positioning the student as sole judge of the quality of education and to the assumption that such a judgment can be quantified. This is precisely the logic of consumerism. The answer to the question of student evaluation seems to me a model for an approach to the question of evaluation as a whole. First, it is necessary to recognize that what is called for is an *act* of judgment, hence one that is embedded within a discursive or pragmatic context—a context that must be acknowledged when the judgment delivered is, in its turn, judged. Second, we must recognize that the question of what is to be done with such evaluations, how they are to be understood, is itself a matter for further judgment. No judgment is final; there is always another link in the chain. Questions of value are systemically incapable of closure. Third, the judge at each stage in the process must be called upon to take responsibility for the judgment delivered, rather than hiding behind a statistical pretension to objectivity.

What, then, are the practical implications of this questioning of the process of evaluation? To begin with, those in the University have to speak among themselves and to others in terms that acknowledge the complexity of the problem of quality. An example of the damaging effects of oversimplification is the current perception that many professors work only six hours a week. People have no difficulty in recognizing that a baseball player is not paid in relation to the minutes he spends at bat, and that the judgment of value has many complex variables. No one argues that a catcher should be paid less because he gets to squat while others run. This is not to suggest that we need an intra-university World Series, merely that the question of value can be made more complex without an automatic loss of comprehensibility. To take another example from the sports world, the relative popularity of figure skating at the winter Olympics, compared with sports in which the winner is established beyond question by a temporal calculation, suggests that the simplicity of the calculation of merit is not such an obstacle.

Thus, what is required is a simultaneous recognition that the question of evaluation is finally both unanswerable *and* essential. That is to say, unanswerability is no excuse for ignoring the question. The late Paul de Man gave us the terms of a literary analysis that recognized the reading of literature as a necessary and impossible task; the same is true of the evaluation of universities. Students would be required to write evaluative essays that can themselves be read and that require further interpretation, instead of ticking boxes and adding up point-scores. The further interpretation and judgment of such evaluations will take time, but it will not take time away from the "real business of the University" (transmitting and producing knowledge). For such evaluation, judgment and self-questioning *are* the real business of the University. Thus universities should, as it were, be required to write essays in evaluation, not to elaborate banal and cliché-ridden mission statements (which are all the same from university to university) and then quantify how far they have lived up to them. This will mean a lot of work for University presidents, but I for one would rather have them thinking about questions of value than juggling indices of excellence and filling in charts of "goal achievement." I do not think it is too much to expect that those concerned with evaluation, at every stage of the process, from student to president, be capable of facing up to fundamental questions concerning the nature of value and quality, nor do I think that the time spent in such reflection will be wasted.

"Writing an essay" is, of course, a metaphor here, a metaphor for producing a judgment of value that seeks to grapple with and take responsibility for itself as a discursive act. This taking of responsibility thus invokes an accountability that is radically at odds with the determinate logic of accounting, since it argues that taking responsibility for one's actions involves an obligation that exceeds the subject's capacity to calculate. Responsibility, then, is not a matter solely for the subject, a matter that can be calculated by a more self-conscious subject (I will discuss this logic of unaccountable obligation more fully in Chapter 10). Such writing means an engagement with the variables surrounding the judgment: the position of the judge, the recipient of the judgment, the criteria on which the judgment is based, and that upon which the judgment is passed. This engagement should lead to a number of important questions: Who am I to judge? To whom is the judgment addressed? What difference does that judgment make? What is the judge claiming to judge? What is the significance of the criteria implied by this judgment?

As the nature of these questions indicates, I am arguing that the entire judgment is itself delivered not as a statement of fact but precisely as a *judgment,* to be judged by others in its turn. This will not mean that judgments are any less effective. Rather, the effects of those judgments are themselves up for discussion. Judgment is better understood in relation to a continuing *discussion* rather than as a finality. To whom and to what the University remains accountable are questions we must continue to pose and worry over. Appeals to accounting—whether in the form of numerically scored teaching evaluations, efficiency ratings, or other bureaucratic statistics—will only serve to prop up the logic of consumerism that rules the University of Excellence. Value is a question of judgment, a question whose answers must continually be discussed.

9

The Time of Study: 1968

That the University needs to consider evaluation seriously became most apparent during the student revolts in the 1960s. At that moment, questions of value arose alongside the recognition that the University was indeed a bureaucratic system. The student revolts changed what the University meant in a sense that parallels, although also differs from, the shift introduced by the discourse of excellence. This is particularly true in France, the example on which I will focus, where a major part of the struggle in the universities in 1968 concerned the question of "modernization": issues such as changes in the administrative contract (control of student life, or of examinations), and the introduction of new disciplines (psychology and social sciences).[1]

That the events should have begun in France is itself structurally linked to the French University, which has never been modern in the strong sense of the German usage.[2] The French University draws its traditions from the Middle Ages rather than the Enlightenment.[3] Hence, where the students of the SDS in the United States were essentially demanding a nation fit for them to be in its University, demanding that the state live up to the terms of the Humboldtian contract, the French students did not accept the nation-state as a condition and thus put both the University (as an institution or an administrative system) and the possibility of its social articulation into question.

What actually happened in 1968 is, of course, a matter for interpretation. A great deal of energy has been applied to minimizing or mythologizing the student riots either as incoherent, juvenile, and hope-lessly idealistic or as the lost hope of revolution that brought the French state to its knees and was betrayed by the left-wing political establish-ment. Protests at the Nanterre campus of the University of Paris began in November 1967 in opposition to the Fouchet plan of 1966, which had proposed the reorganization of University studies into separate two- and four-year degrees, alongside the introduction of selective ad-mission criteria. Criticism, led by Daniel Cohn-Bendit, initially cen-tered around three major aspects of the plan: first, restricted entry to tertiary education; second, the implications of social engineering in the introduction of both the development of social science disciplines and job-oriented degrees; third, the question of social discipline in the Uni-versity system. The third issue arose because restricted admission was being proposed by Fouchet as the solution to overcrowding in the lec-ture rooms and student facilities. The link to the Vietnam war, as at Columbia University, was crucial here. The initial spark for the first occupation was the March 22, 1968, arrest of six members of the Na-tional Vietnam committee, in protest of which student activists occu-pied the administrative building of the Nanterre campus. The Nanterre campus was closed by authorities on March 28, around the same time as Rome University and the University of Madrid were closed in re-sponse to student protests. In late April and early May the student struggle spread around Paris, and the police stormed the Sorbonne on May 10. Likewise, the student occupation of Columbia was broken by extreme police violence.

What was special about France, though, was the spread of the student movement into a spontaneous strike (around nine million workers were on strike by May 22), a strike that occurred without, if not despite, the central committees of the Communist Party and the major, com-munist-controlled, French union federation (the CGT or Confédéra-tion Générale des Travailleurs). De Gaulle responded on May 24 by calling for a referendum, and on what is generally called "the night of the barricades," the revolutionaries, led by informal action committees, attacked and burned the Paris Stock Exchange in response. The Gaullist government then held talks with union leaders, who agreed to a package of wage-rises and increases in union rights. The strikers, however, sim-

136

ply refused the plan. With the French state tottering, de Gaulle fled France on May 29 for a French military base in Germany. He later returned and, with the assurance of military support, announced elections in forty days. This act effectively split the strikers off from the political machine once more, as the left establishment scented the possibility of riding the revolutionary wave into elected government. They were mistaken, however. Over the next two months, the strikes were broken (or broke up) while the election was won by the Gaullists with an increased majority.

This brief summary of events, which obviously ignores Czechoslovakia and many other places, foregrounds the students in order to insist that the link between students and workers was crucially a problematic one. The students were not cannon-fodder for a "real" struggle by workers, nor were the workers the ignorant army organized and directed by University-based theorists. There was not even one generally accepted version of what held the two together. The revolts were serially articulated rather than hierarchically structured, and the nature of the analogy between them was never singularly determined.

Many diagnoses of the causes of the revolt have been attempted, and my concern is not that of a historian. I want to stress the way in which the University emerged as an institutional question and suggest that this happened so cathartically in France because the University there was paradoxically positioned as a structure that had remained largely feudal. The students thus resisted both the existing feudal structure and the state's attempt to modernize it. This fed into a general critique of the nation-state. The critique, however, did not have to be grounded in the systematic suggestion of a "third way," because the particular historical circumstances allowed the left-wing parties of "progress" to be exposed as counter-signatories to the state's contract, as part of the problem of the nation-state rather than as its solution. So the question was not how to make the University into a proper state institution but how to think about the University outside the terms laid down by the nation-state, while also recognizing that the old feudal structure was dysfunctional.

In a sense, part of what happened in 1968 as revolution happens now as student apathy, which is another name for consumerism: a massive disaffection from the institution and from the modern contract between the University and the nation-state. As W. B. Carnochan notes, in the long term, student passivity is the exception rather than the rule, so that we should ask what it means that today students seem so passive.[4] Students in 1968 decathected by revolting; nowadays they do not cathect in the first place. I am not talking here about dropout rates so much as about the widespread sense among undergraduate students in North America that they are "parked" at the University—taking courses, acquiring credits, waiting to graduate. In a sense, this is their reaction to the fact that nothing in their education encourages them to think of themselves as the heroes of the story of liberal education, embarking on the long voyage of self-discovery. What they are engaged in is *self-accreditation,* preparing for the job market—which is why interdisciplinary "pre-professional" majors are becoming increasingly popular. In response to this condition of the University, it is no use being nostalgic for the days when bourgeois society was sufficiently closed and prosperous, when the University was sufficiently elitist. Rather, the question is how to think about teaching in the space of the University within such a context—a context which is, in its way, revolutionary. After all, one of the things that the student revolts of 1968 attacked was the complicity between sociology and marketing. Now universities offer majors in marketing.

Pierre Bourdieu, of course, denies that 1968 was anything more than a cosmetic change within the system, since, as we have seen in Chapter 7, for Bourdieu the analysis of the system must return every action to its motivation within the terms of the system. Everything for Bourdieu proceeds from a desire for cultural capital. Hence he presents every critique *of* the system as being a move *within* the system, and the same goes for his critique of 1968 in *Homo Academicus.* He dismisses the events of 1968 on the grounds that they were generated by an "emotional excitement" that led professors to listen to "unrepresentative" individual students and student leaders.[5] Bourdieu's tone leaves little doubt as to his contempt for such unruly behavior. More fundamentally, however, he also argues that the apparent "crisis" was not really a challenge to the "social totality" of the academic system but merely a "symbolic production" designed to allow a shift of power *within the system.* The crisis arose, according to Bourdieu, owing to the fact that an entire class of students and junior teachers had been led to "maladjusted expectations" by a system that could not deliver sufficient cultural capital to those it processed, by reason of their increasing number in a system that was fundamentally elitist.[6] Bourdieu concludes that any upheaval in the social order or the practice of pedagogy is merely a secondary symptom of this minor readjustment of the network of positions of power within the social totality.

John Guillory's *Cultural Capital* makes a similar argument concerning deconstruction and the introduction of literary theory as a supplemental canon for graduate study in English. Refusing all radical claims made in the name of theory, Guillory argues that literary theory must be understood as the introduction of a technically complex but reproducible practice of reading that answered to a specific institutional need in the North American University. Namely, literary theory is supposedly the development of a more and more specialized technical discourse that would lead graduate students to understand their training as preparation for a specialized technical-managerial role rather than for the role of the public intellectual.[7] For Guillory as for Bourdieu, an other to the system is thus unthinkable; a given action is only a move within the system, whose meaning resides in its effect within the rules of that system.

The problem with this account is not its cynicism so much as its a priori assumption that culture is a single system with closed boundaries. I think Guillory is right to diagnose a decline in the role of the public intellectual: there will be no more Lionel Trillings. This is not, however, the result of a Benda-like *trahison des clercs* so much as of a social shift that throws in doubt the possibility of such a role.[8] Guillory's tendency to the ad hominem attack in relation to de Man and his disciples seems to me highly problematic, in that he seeks to hold individuals *individually* responsible for their blindness to the fact that they are *not individuals* but tools of the system. For Guillory, it is the system alone that gives meaning to intellectual production. Given the attention that those working in the field of literary theory have traditionally paid to institutional questions (Derrida and Samuel Weber are exemplary figures here), this seems not only harsh but inaccurate. It would be more accurate to contend that a common feature of many of the texts produced under the rubric of literary theory is precisely a tendency to worry about the problematic role of the intellectual within a bureaucratic system of power. Derrida, de Man, Weber, Barbara Johnson, and others share a common concern to consider the ways in which the performative aspects of critical statements are inflected by the evacuation of the public sphere in contemporary capitalist society.[9]

The problematization of the public sphere, the sense that the general public may not exist, is addressed by the authors of an important recent collection, *The Phantom Public Sphere.*[10] In recognizing that the public is no longer available as such, Bruce Robbins's introduction calls for a "less backward-looking conversation" that will be capable of redefining a public sphere that is more complex and incommensurate in its multiplicities. I am less than convinced of this possibility, though. The issues of globalization and mass publicity, raised respectively by Arjun Appadurai and Michael Warner in the volume, seem to me to pose fundamental problems for the idea of a general public, however fractally fragmented.[11]

More precisely, the concept of a public sphere is anchored upon the notion of a liberal individual who participates in it, who can say with Terence that as a human, nothing human is alien to him (or her).[12] Such a subject is capable of the public exercise of reason. In Kant's terms in "What Is Enlightenment?" the public exercise of reason is the conversation of the individual with the universal—the public is an abstraction. As Kant remarks: "By the public use of one's reason I understand the use which a person makes of it as a scholar before the reading public. Private use I call that which one may make of it in a particular civil post or office which is entrusted to him."[13] Kant's description of the public is more or less what we would now call the private exercise of reason (the sort of thing that a dwindling class do at their word processors), while his version of the private includes such things as one's job—what we would think of as public life. This is rather confusing, until we realize that the public, for Kant, is not an empirical reality (society at large) but the rational possibility of a universal discourse governed by the rules of reason alone. The post-Kantian notion of the public sphere that Habermas sketches—

and his is the prevalent description today—introduces an anthropological and comparative generality, where Kant had insisted on the logic of absolute reason.[14] For Habermas, one converses with the world-at-large, not with the universal; public life becomes the possibility of open democratic discussion and the establishment of consensus among subjects.

Current developments in the global forms of capitalism and mass publicity seem to me to run directly against this notion of public life in that they combine a generalized consumerism with a logic of "narrowcasting." The question of systemic coherence can no longer be posed at the level of the culture of an individual subject, of a "general reader," as it were. As with the University, no subject is capable of embodying the "public" metonymically. And the questions of difference raised by considerations of gender and ethnicity are laudable reminders of this fact. The male WASP constructs himself as unmarked by signs of difference, as the white mythological center of culture from whom all others are different, and makes such blankness the condition of entry to the public sphere. As I have argued, there is no longer a general subject of culture; there are merely peripheral singularities within a unipolar system. So the question of intervention shifts, since the cultural metaphor for individual participation offered by the nation-state cannot simply be expanded to fit a global society, which does not amount to a worldwide nation-state. Or, in the words of Michael Warner, who, after having made the point that the bourgeois public sphere is grounded upon a disincorporation of voice that no longer holds in the print medium, argues:

> In each of these mediating contexts of publicity, we become the mass public subject, but in a new way, unanticipated within the classical bourgeois public sphere. If mass-public subjectivity has a kind of singularity, moreover, an undifferentiated extension to indefinite numbers of individuals, those individuals who make up the 'we' of the mass public subject might have very different relations to it. It is at the very moment of recognizing ourselves as the mass subject, for example, that we also recognize ourselves as minority subjects . . . The political meaning of the public subject's self-alienation is one of the most important sites of struggle in contemporary culture.[15]

Warner's discussion of the singularity of mass-public subjectivity, its address to individuals as singularities, seems to me correct, as is his awareness that the individual singularity is simultaneously addressed as a member of the mass *and* as a minority. This double address happens in a manner that cuts out or brackets the majoritarian generality of the public sphere in favor of the marketing techniques of demographic narrowcasting. Alongside national broadcasting (PBS, RAI, CBC, BBC), we have a series of narrowcast channels (like MTV or BET) that aggregate individuals temporarily as a demographic statistic rather than as a community or a society. And the tendency is furthermore for the national station to become one narrowcast channel among others, rather than the channel that claims to synthesize all the others in a general, national, TV station.

This process is obviously more advanced in the United States than elsewhere, but it does seem to be the path that is sketched out in Europe, with the emergence of cable and satellite as a carrier for private TV stations. The nation-state no longer serves as the structural analogy for all TV production, since narrowcast channels do not (like the British Independent Television channel ITV) any longer compete with the state-controlled broadcast channel for a national audience. Rather, the notion of a national audience to which TV would feed a general ideology (the universal lessons in citizenship of the Donna Reed Show) seems to be disappearing. Advertisers—and TV exists as a machine to create and package advertising time—are more and more interested in targeting specific demographic bands who might actually buy their products. General broadcast stations continue to exist and sell certain kinds of product. However, they are now one channel among others. In Europe, the nation-state has traditionally exercised more control (aided by language barriers), but the horizon of integration promises an open market for independent channels through satellite and cable.

Perhaps the most startling example of the effects of the withdrawal of the nation-state from the center of information-circulation comes in the case of radio with regard to the World Service of the BBC. A massive ideological weapon of the British State, with an unparalleled reputation worldwide, the World Service has traditionally broadcast centrally in English, with parallel programming in other languages, and a small amount of local programming for certain areas. Those of us in North America who depend upon it as one of the few sources of informed programming of events in Africa, for instance, will soon no longer benefit from this service that brought such ideological benefits (cultural capital?) to the British nation-state at a relatively low cost. The central broadcasting program is to be broken up, and the World Service will simply make programs to be sold to local stations around the world for rebroadcast. Thus, the cash nexus will be introduced, and the World Service will have to sell its programs locally on the market. Such a shift should give us pause. A nation-state, Britain, not noted for a lack of nationalism, is voluntarily abandoning a massive ideological weapon in the interests of short-term profit. And the reason for this? Because the long-term profits of national ideology are no longer calculable, because there is no longer a sustainable fiction of the political subject of the nation-state (and by analogy, of the world) to whom such ideology might be directed. The cash-nexus replaces the ideological conflict of the cold war; the demographic aggregate replaces the public sphere. Those of us who want news of Africa will go elsewhere, to the marketing and sales lists of specialized magazines, digitalized news networks, and internet surfing.

Such aggregations are temporary in that the individual is positioned as a consumer without memory, a gaping mouth, as it were, rather than as the subject of a narrative of self-realization. Now the "same" individual can be aggregated successively in multiple demographic bands, rather than occupying a supposedly self-consistent position in a generalized public sphere. Mass products simultaneously offer consumers both homogenization and specialness, and there is no longer a need for mass publicity to invoke a civil subject who would be capable of synthesizing these two contradictory pulls. Hence, for instance, the paradoxical double move of indifferentiation and individuation, the combination of shock value and mass marketing, in advertisements for the "United Colors of Benetton." Negotiating political actions in such a context will require a more supple thinking than the proleptic nostalgia of traditional appeals to the political as the sphere in which the human subject of history realizes its true identity and liberates itself as educated, as proletarian, or as capable of enrichment.[16]

The insistence that the subject whose body is marked by difference cannot finally be assimilated into the virtual politics of the public sphere is particularly relevant to the University. For if the decline of the idea of culture is the decline of the University as prime model for the community of the public sphere in the nation-state, the invocation of excellence is, as we have seen, the attempt to rephrase the virtual public sphere in economic rather than political terms. To put this another way, excellence pretends indifference to the gendering or other forms of marking of the bodies that it evaluates. And it does this by appealing to an internal logic of accounting rather than to the microcosmic model of social accountability (of a communitarian bond).

1968 marks the entry of the student body into the sphere of the University, an entry that meant the University could no longer be understood in terms of the story of an individual subject's passage through it. My pun on "body" is not incidental either. The questions of gender, class, and ethnic difference among the students were all repeatedly and urgently part of the student program. The students began by refusing the myth of "the student" as a disembodied or virtual entity, which took the practical shape of refusing the antiquated disciplinary rules concerning sexual practices, the right to decorate rooms, and the right to offer education to immigrant Magrebhins. The student discontent in the France of 1968, which David Caute dismisses as "petty frustrations," is less marginal than he thinks to the "wider grievance against technological authoritarianism."[17] However, as Christopher Fynsk has pointed out, the events of May 1968 can also easily serve as a generative myth for a politics of rejection that masks the ease with which leftist intellectuals inhabit the educational system.[18] Understanding 1968 requires recognizing how the "events" broke with a certain narrative of the University education as the individual experience of emancipation in the passage of a virtual student from ignorance to knowledge, from dependence to autonomy and competence. 1968 broke with that narrative precisely insofar as the students were revolting as students, not as would-be professors.

I think that the eruption of the students put an end to a certain idea of the University, insofar as the students were not seeking autonomy. Or to put it more bluntly, they did not identify autonomy with freedom. They knew, as some professors do, that the pedagogic relation is not something we can have done with. I do not mean anything as banal as "you never stop learning," although that is probably true. Rather, the pedagogic relation is dissymmetrical and endless. The parties are caught in a dialogic web of obligations to thought. Thought appears as the voice of an Other that no third term, such as "culture," can resolve dialectically.

The transparent University of Culture had allowed the German Idealists to propose that the time of study was both a single moment and an eternity: the single moment of the awakening of consciousness and the eternity of absolute knowledge (the awakening of consciousness at the time of redemption). What I am arguing for is the possibility that the students of 1968 imagined a University without redemption. Such a vision of the University implies that students are not simply intellectuals or managerial professionals in waiting. Rather, the University implies the time of pedagogy: a thought or study in excess of the subject, which rejects the metanarrative of redemption.

The problematic I have sketched is one that requires the greatest vigilance. It is no longer possible to think of the politics of the University as if the institution were a simple tool or instrument that should be turned to other ends. To think that the politics of the University can be sorted out by campus radicalism is to compound misjudgment with the worst sort of willful memory lapse.[19] The realization of 1968 is that the functioning of the University, the question of its role, is not a self-evident one. The University cannot be assumed in advance as either the positive or negative framework for critical activity, nor should it be assumed that such activities are ever free of the implication that the University is an institution. As an institution it has a history—and a history that is structured by the contradictions attendant upon the performative act of the foundation of any institution. The history of an institution is persistently marked by the structural contradiction of its founding. The institution is founded, is grounded, in being called forth into existence as a radically new institution. It will exist in a place where it did not exist before, and hence its foundation is never natural or assured. It did not spring up. In this sense, all institutions, as founded, are unfounded.[20] What the campus radicals of 1968 had already realized was that the University should be analyzed as a *bureaucratic system.* The students made a series of claims about this. Their common thread was a resistance to the imposition of an analogy between the production, distribution, and consumption of *commodities,* and the production, distribution, and consumption of *knowledge.*

In speaking of a common thread here, I must be very careful. The student revolt was extremely incoherent, composed of many different tendencies with heterogeneous and incompatible aims. This is true not just of the student revolt in France or the United States, but also of the various events around the world. In discussing the position of "the students," I am not claiming somehow to have access to what is most essential about the position of the student. I am speaking as someone who has been a student in a particular historical period and who is a professor in another; someone who talks to students regularly and who does not claim to understand them any better (or any worse) than they understand themselves. So when I write "the students," it is merely to suggest a certain kind of trouble attendant on the structural position of the students in the institution of the University. Likewise, I draw on the writings of Daniel and Gabriel Cohn-Bendit and others in the movement of March 22, not because they express some eternal verity concerning the nature of the students, but because they mark off one point of resistance among others, one point at which "the students" came to name an instance that was out of step with the march of the University system.

As students and teachers, we should protect the discomfort we feel at our situation. We should be very distrustful of any claims to have solved the problem of the University, of any panaceas that offer to resolve institutional problems, to let us forget the problem of the politico-institutional structures within, upon, and against which we work. In May 1968 the students sought in the pedagogic relation the grounds for a new social orientation. Socrates knew that pedagogy took place under the sign of *eros* rather than of *logos* (sexual harassment is, of course, an example of the illegitimate attempt to unify *eros* and *logos*). The students refused a logocentric pedagogy, refused to reduce their activity of learning to either a matter of the transmission of information (a process of training for bureaucratic roles within the state) or a timeless and apolitical activity. And at the same time, they refused to become intellectuals who claim to incarnate the *logos,* to speak for others because they have understood them fully in a way that those others have not understood themselves. What some of the students seem to have known in 1968 is that they do not even speak for themselves.

The Cohn-Bendits' account of the student uprising in *Obsolete Communism: The Left-Wing Alternative* is so important because it draws attention to the French student movements as the persistent and conscious refusal of vanguardism in favor of institutional pragmatism: "The type of organization we must build can neither be a vanguard nor a rearguard, but must be right in the thick of the fight."[21] The Cohn-Bendits recognize that further study is required. The students are not simply heroic militants. Their militancy challenges the representational claim of democracy, the claim that liberal democracy achieves exhaustive representation, reflects itself to itself. The students in 1968 motivate a society to rebel *against its own elected representatives,* against the democratically elected government. What is more, they do so in the name of an uncertainty about who they are and not in the name of militant certainty. As the Cohn-Bendits remark, "they are not a class, and they have no objective interests to defend" (54). They sum up this uncertainty with an honesty that is striking in a polemical work: "There are 600,000 of us; sometimes treated as mere children, sometimes as adults. We work, but we produce nothing. Often we have no money, but few of us are really poor. Although most of us come from the bourgeoisie, we do not always behave like them. The girls among us look like boys but are not sure whether they really want to be boys. We look upon our professors as part father, part boss and part teacher, and can't quite make up our minds about them" (41).

The students are neither adult nor child, and what matters about 1968 is that the narrative of *Bildung*—of simple passage from infancy to adulthood, from dependency to emancipation (the Kantian narrative of enlightenment that characterizes the knowledge process itself in modernity)—has been rejected by the students in the name of an uncertainty. An uncertainty about maturity, about labor, about wealth, about class, about gender. This ambivalence goes along with a radical pragmatism: the refusal of vanguardism that wants to fight "on the spot," in the thick of things. That is to say, the students refuse to be intellectuals, to proleptically embody the subject of history.

1968 thus names a recognition that "the student" is not, has never quite been, a modern subject.[22] In this sense, the position of the students has always been that of a troubled relation to the public sphere. The public sphere is proposed as the birthright of citizens, but the students have to go through a period of training in order to accede to their birthright. Even the necessity of training marks that accession as troubled. Henceforth, the students will only participate at the price of forgetting their education, taking it to be over.

Socially displaced by the strange temporality of education, students are positioned so as to provide a critique of the possibility that society might represent itself to itself, might define itself through the autonomous exercise of its own will. (This is the presumption on which the claim to authority made by modern representative democracy is based.) I would argue that the revolt of 1968 was structured by the way in which students are positioned as capable of enacting the sense in which we are and are not part of society, that we always function in society before we understand what it means to do so, and that we do so until death. The social predicament of modernity that students expose is one of difference (the fact that there are others) and of temporal non-equivalence (deferral). Born too soon without knowledge, and yet born too late to live that knowledge except as tradition received from elsewhere, students name the temporal predicament of modernity. On the one hand, too soon: they are born into culture, but they still have to learn to speak its language. On the other hand, too late: the culture they are born into precedes them, and they cannot make its anteriority their own; they can only handle the fragments of its language.

Thus, thinking about the position of students can remind us that neither nostalgia nor education can settle accounts with culture in a non-Idealist sense. Culture here is both tradition and betrayal; we are handed over to culture even as it is handed to us. Modernism tries to forget this predicament in two ways: by the *conservatism* that says we can live the tradition (it is not too late) and by the *progressive modernism* that says we can make an entirely fresh start, forget the tradition and move on to build a bright new world (it is not too early, we can teach ourselves). In each case, conservatives and progressives talk about culture as if it ought to be, or is, synonymous with society. Conservatives say that culture ought to provide the model for society, that we should live in a world of high culture or of organic villages. In short, they believe that culture should determine society. Progressives tend to say that culture *is* society, or else it is merely ideological illusion, that the self-definition of the human community should define the model of our being-together.

Students know both that they are not yet part of culture and that culture is already over, that it has preceded them. Neither nostalgia nor education can solve the students' malaise. They cannot simply mourn a lost culture (conservatism) nor can they forget the tradition and move on to build a bright new world (progressive modernism). The tradition can neither be lived as culture nor forgotten as superstition: neither Schleiermacher nor Kant. "We" cannot make our own salvation. The pedagogic relation is not one of transparency, be it as expressive revelation (the German Idealists), as the transmission of information (the technocrats), or as the establishment of professional consensus (Fish and Habermas). The events of 1968 offer the terms of a pedagogy that is neither conservatively nostalgic nor progressively modernist. The events break with the ideology of communication and insist upon the specific chronotope of the educational relation. This is a temporality that is radically unaccountable. The task we have before us, then, is understanding the situation of the contemporary University without falling into either nostalgia for national culture or the discourse of consumerism. That will also be the task of the final three chapters, in which I take up in turn questions of pedagogy, institutions, and community.

⁓ 10

The Scene of Teaching

The replacement of culture by the discourse of excellence is the University's response to 1968. In the face of student critiques of the contradiction between the University's claim to be a guardian of culture and its growing commitment to bureaucracy, the University has progressively abandoned its cultural claim. Forced to describe itself as either a bureaucratic-administrative or an idealist institution, it chose the former. And consequently there is no way back to 1968; a repetition of the radical postures of the late 1960s is not adequate to resist the discourse of excellence. This is because the discourse of excellence can incorporate campus radicalism as proof of the excellence of campus life or of student commitment—something that even *Maclean's* does in its evaluations.

This is not to say, however, that no resistance to the discourse of excellence is possible. Rather, we need to think differently about the shape such resistance must take. What we stand to learn from the events of 1968 is that the emergence of the student who has a problematic relation to modernity offers a resource for resistance. This resource will emerge in the scene of teaching, which will be the focus of this chapter. What is at stake here is what I hinted at earlier: the *value* in teaching. To whom or to what are teachers, students, and institutions accountable? And in what terms? In the University of Excellence, the problem of value is bracketed, and statistical evaluation (of the measure of excellence) is presumed to provide definitive answers that then feed into funding, resources, and salary decisions. This chapter will explore how we can keep the question of value open in relation to pedagogy, which means neither accepting the accounting logic of the bureaucrats nor simply ignoring it in the name of a transcendental value to education. Pedagogy, I will suggest, has a specific chronotope that is radically alien to the notion of accountable time upon which the excellence of capitalist-bureaucratic management and bookkeeping depend. Such a pedagogy can provide a notion of educational responsibility, of accountability, that is markedly at odds with the logic of accounting that runs the University of Excellence.

To understand how this can indeed be the case, it is important to situate the scene of teaching as part of the larger tableau of how education itself is understood. When people address the question of education, they tend to do so from one of three points of view. First, the administrator is concerned to understand education as a process in which the production and distribution of knowledge will repay the costs in time and capital expended. Second, the professor wants to justify a life spent in the pursuit of objectives that, analyzed in terms of cost and benefit, seem to produce little personal payoff. So she or he will tend to make large claims for her or his power to train a certain kind of student subject: critical, well-rounded, or empowered. Third, the student usually complains about an institution or a practice to which she or he feels forced to submit without first understanding why. From the student's perspective, the hierarchy seems not to acknowledge the student to whom it appeals (as product) in order to justify itself, although in a consumer society these complaints become harder to ignore.

Each of these descriptions of education performs an initial gesture of centering in that each assumes that its perspective stands at the *center* of the educational process. The question of value is thus always posed from a subjective standpoint that is taken to be central: how to evaluate teaching *for* the University administration, *for* the teacher, or *for* the student. It would even be possible to take this argument a step further and say that the administration usually intervenes a second time as a meta-evaluator that produces a synthesized metasubjective standpoint. By weighing the various costs and benefits, the meta-evaluator tries to

151

offset advantages of one position against disadvantages of the others. The final goal here is to perform a synthesis of the three different interests, even where they seem to be conflicting or competing.

However common it is to approach the evaluation of teaching in these ways, the structure of responsibility, of accountability, is much more complex and intertwined, and I shall argue that no such synthesis is possible. My aim in focusing on teaching—and in relating that focus to the kind of attention this book pays to institutions—is not to put teaching "back at the center of things." As my analysis has shown, the constitutive moment of the modern University is the placing of an idea at the center of things, making both teaching and research depend upon this idea. However, in the posthistorical University, bureaucratic administration becomes central, because the very emptiness of the idea of excellence makes the integration of activities into a purely administrative function. Teaching actually thus becomes a triple administrative function. First, the simple administration of students by teachers (keeping them off the streets). Second, the training of the administrative or managerial class (the self-reproduction of the administrative system). Third, the administration of knowledge (the functional programming of students). There is even a fourth function, if you like, in that subsequently teaching is administered through the process of evaluation.

The administration of knowledge is, of course, the only point at which anything like a question of content enters: the question of what knowledge is to be managed by teachers and *administered* to students. But the question of content is short-lived, since in order to be administered to students, knowledge has to be made into *manageable* doses. Thus the textbook takes on a new form in the University of Excellence. It tends to become shorter and to require less of the student. In fact, it tends toward virtuality, as we have seen in Chapter 6 in reference to the question of the literary canon. Teaching administers students. It accredits students as administrators, and it trains them in the handling of information. It probably does all these things rather successfully.

It would be wrong, then, to suggest that teaching does not matter in the University of Excellence, for it is as closely tied to the logic of administration as it had previously been to the logic of cultural reproduction (the reproduction of subjects of culture). In order to open up the question of pedagogy we do not need, therefore, to *recenter* teaching but to *decenter* it. By the decentering of the pedagogic situation I mean to insist that teaching is not best understood from the point of view of a sovereign subject that takes itself to be the sole guarantor of the meaning of that process, whether that subject is the student, the teacher, or the administrator. Decentering teaching begins with an attention to the *pragmatic scene of teaching*. This is to refuse the possibility of any privileged point of view so as to make teaching something other than the self-reproduction of an autonomous subject. Neither the administrator taking the system in hand, nor the professor taking the student in hand, nor the student taking him- or herself in hand will do the trick.

In order to pose the question of the grounds of value in teaching in terms that respect the complexity of the obligation involved, it will also be necessary for me to resist the temptation of believing in my own autonomy. That will involve resisting the lure of speaking from a position in which the intellectual subject takes itself to incarnate the singular voice of the universal. Instead, I would emphasize that pedagogy cannot be understood apart from a reflection on *the institutional context of education*. This reflection refuses both the isolation of education in relation to wider social practices and the subjugation of education to predetermined or externally derived social imperatives.[1] Institutional forms are always at work in teaching: forms of address, rooms, conditions of possibility. But the reminder of the institutional question is a warning against imagining that attention to pedagogic pragmatics can be essentially divorced from an attention to institutional forms.[2] Paying attention to the pragmatics of the pedagogic scene, without losing sight of institutional forms, is important, because it refuses to make the pedagogical relation into an object of administrative knowledge. Understanding teaching is not a matter of drawing flow charts that track and police the movements of knowledge, power, or desire. Such charts, even when drawn up with the best of intentions, tend always to install a single and authoritative point of view, reducing teaching to an object of knowledge for a sovereign subject who will play the role of policeman.

This reduction of the goals of teaching to the concerns of a sovereign subject is also nothing new; it has simply taken different forms over the years. The Enlightenment proposes education as the site of emancipation, the freeing of the student from all obligations, including that to the teacher. The modern bureaucratic state proposes to reduce the relation to that of the development and training of technocrats through the transmission of education. These attempts can be summarized under the rubric of the ideology of autonomy. I want to suggest, however, that pedagogy also can be understood otherwise: other than as the inculcation or revelation of an inherent human autonomy, other than as the production of sovereign subjects.

Such a consideration of pedagogy must begin by recognizing that the modernist project of autonomy and universal communicability is not provisionally but fundamentally incomplete. No authority can terminate the pedagogic relation, no knowledge can save us the task of thinking. It is in this sense that the posthistorical University can perhaps relinquish the presumption to unite authority and autonomy in a community unified by an idea: be it the idea of reason, culture, communication, or professional excellence. My aim, then, is an anti-modernist rephrasing of teaching and learning as sites of *obligation*, as loci of *ethical practices*, rather than as means for the transmission of scientific knowledge. Teaching thus becomes answerable to *the question of justice*, rather than to the criteria of truth. We must seek to do justice to teaching rather than to know what it is. A belief that we know what teaching is or should be is actually a major impediment to just teaching. Teaching should cease to be about merely the transmission of information and the emancipation of the autonomous subject, and instead should become a site of obligation that exceeds an individual's consciousness of justice. My turn to the pedagogical scene of address, with all its ethical weight, is thus a way of developing an accountability that is at odds with accounting.

This is a complex move, and I want to slow down and explain it more precisely. First of all, the scene of teaching should be understood as a radical form of dialogue. This is not a Habermasian claim for communicative rationality in which the dialogues of teachers and students are really divided monologues. I would argue that the dialogues between teachers and students are not synthesized in a final agreement (even an agreement to disagree) that evidences the capacity of the informed and rational subject to occupy both sides of a question. That is to say, the dialogue of teaching is not organized dialectically so as to arrive at a single conclusion that will be either the vindication and reinforcement of one position (Socrates' opponent is forced to agree with Socrates) or a synthesis of the two (Joyce's "jewgreek is greek-jew").[3] The dialogue does not thaw and resolve into a monologue, nor is it controlled solely by the sender as a formal instrument in the grasp of the writing subject, like Mallarmé's use of the *mise en page*. In this respect, I am evoking the dialogue form in order to refuse the modernist privileging of the sender over the addressee, to refuse the figure of the lone artist who synthesizes reality through either a rational understanding or a romantic effort of will.

To pay attention in this way to the addressee is not simply to attempt to determine the conditions of reception of a discourse, which would be another way of creating a monologue. The listener is not an empty head, as in the line drawings that illustrate Saussure's account of communication. Saussure would have communication be the passage of a message from a sender to a receiver who is silent, who exists only as receptacle. A message is passed from a sender (full vessel emptied) to a receiver (empty vessel filled). Dialogue would then be merely the exchange of roles between two persons, so that the first sender becomes in turn the empty receiver, and so on. By contrast, Bakhtin seems to me correct when he observes that "it is not a mute, wordless creature that receives such an utterance but a human being full of inner words. All his experiences—his so-called apperceptive background—exist encoded in his inner speech, and only to that extent do they come into contact with speech received from outside. Word comes into contact with word."[4]

I am thus inclined to leave Saussure's model of communication behind in favor of what Bakhtin has called dialogism. This is an often misunderstood and misused term. Bakhtin's dialogism is not simply the capacity for reversed or serial monologue, the exchange of roles that allows interlocutors to take turns at being monologic senders (as it is for Socrates). The addressee's head is full of language so that the story of communicative transmission cannot adequately describe what happens in linguistic interaction. Inter*discursive* rather than inter*subjective*, the addressee is not a virtual point of consciousness (the *tabula rasa* of a listening pineal gland, as Descartes might have it). All consciousness is consciousness of language in its heterogeneous multiplicity. Understanding and misunderstanding, as it were, are entwined as the conditions of linguistic interaction. Communication cannot be the transfer of a prefabricated meaning, since the meaning of words does not remain the same from one utterance—or more precisely, one idiolect—to the next. What a sender says takes its place amid a crowd of idiolects in the listener, and their conversation acquires its sense in a discursive act of which neither is the master. Thus, to recognize the addressee is to inscribe within discourse a radical aporia. It is to speak in a way that respects what might be called the abyssal space of reading by the other: the fact that we never know to whom our words may speak. Teaching, then, is not primarily a matter of communication between autonomous subjects functioning alternately as senders and receivers.

The difference between Saussure's monologic model of communication and Bakhtin's dialogism may not seem all that significant in a discussion of pedagogy. But it actually tells us a great deal about misplaced pedagogical commitments to autonomy, helping us to understand—and avoid—three pitfalls that attend the pedagogic relation: First, the hierarchy that makes the professor an absolute authority and the students so many receptacles for the transmission of a preconstituted and unquestionable knowledge. Second, the claim that teaching raises no difference between teachers and students, the demagoguery that suggests there is nothing to learn. Third, the reduction of education to the development and training of technocrats without questioning the purposes and functions to which that training is dedicated. All three of these seek to put an end to questioning, most obviously in the first and third cases, but more insidiously in the second, where thought is sacrificed rather than questioned—sacrificed precisely because it might question the presumption of an indifferent egalitarianism.

What these misplaced pedagogic commitments have in common is an orientation toward *autonomy*, an assertion that knowledge involves the abandonment of a network of ethical obligations: to have knowledge is to gain a self-sufficient, monologic voice. The first replicates on a large scale all of the problems with Saussure's model of communication. The authoritative voice of the *magister* rests upon his or her (usually his) privileged relation to the meaning of knowledge. This relation is secured against any irruption of the pole of the addressee—authoritative discourse means that it makes no difference to whom he or she is talking. The pole of the addressee is empty, an empty vessel. And the end of the process will be a replication of that autonomy, as the student becomes another professor, in turn. Thus, student autonomy is the end product of the pedagogical process, which is nothing more than the replication of the autonomy of the master.

Second, in the demagogic mode, the students' autonomy is assumed as an a priori given, is asserted from the beginning as the unrecognized condition of possibility of education. Students have the autonomy to decide what it is they know, what it is they should or should not learn; they have no particular relation to the professor. This might look like a claim for the recognition of the student addressee, but it actually returns to Saussure. The addressee is merely redescribed as always already the sender of any message, able to listen to a message only insofar as he or she has, in fact (or *in potentia*), already sent it to him- or herself.

Third, in the technocratic mode of training, autonomy is accorded to the referent, to a technical knowledge that is indifferent to the specificity of its inculcation. In this instance, the pedagogic relation is once again reduced to a mere replication that accords with Saussure. This time the replication is of the bureaucratic state as it fits subjects to tasks. The educational subject is the system, and the autonomy that the student gains through education is the freedom to occupy a preconstituted place in the system, which we usually describe in terms of the illusion of "working for oneself."

The common narrative that underlies these three accounts of the function of education argues that the goal of education is the achievement of a certain mimetic identity by the student: either as replication of the professor or as replication of a place in the system. And with this identity comes autonomy, or to put it more clearly, *independence*—the end of dependence, the end of obligated relations to others. The student has acquired a certain freedom, a position of self-sufficient identity. She or he has been granted it by the professor, by the consensus of her or his peers, and by the employer. She or he will not have to listen any more—indeed, should not listen any more, since listening would be tantamount to questioning, which indicates, by a twist in logic, dependence.

This is part of the long narrative of education that the Enlightenment, above all in French secondary schools, inculcated: that knowledge would make mankind free, that education is a process of transforming children into adults. Education, that is, transforms children, who are by definition dependent upon adults, into independent beings, the free citizens that the modern state requires. They will judge for themselves. They will vote individually, in private, in little boxes that cut them off from all relation to others. Hence, the French educational system has always privileged primary education rather than the University, since the state's interest in education is above all in the production of citizen-subjects. The subject's "freedom" is the freedom to be subjected to a state. Subjection is held to be no constraint by virtue of the fiction that the existence and nature of that state holds only insofar as it is the object of the free choice of subjects—a fiction of representation whose limits appear the moment one remarks, "but I didn't vote for that."[5] If we are perhaps ready to recognize that this freedom is bought at the price of subjection to the abstract entity that is the modern state, we have yet to think through its implications for our understanding of pedagogy.

In place of the lure of autonomy, of independence from all obligation, I want to insist that pedagogy is a *relation, a network of obligation.* In this sense, we might want to talk of the teacher as *rhetor* rather than *magister,* one who speaks in a rhetorical context rather than one whose discourse is self-authorizing. The advantage here would be to recognize that the legitimation of the teacher's discourse is not immanent to that discourse but is always dependent, at least in part, on the rhetorical context of its reception. The *rhetor* is a speaker who takes account of the audience, while the *magister* is indifferent to the specificity of his or her addressees.

Yet the invocation of "rhetoric" leaves room for a certain reservation with regard to the embrace of sophistic rhetoric as a *model* for the pedagogic scene. The appeal to persuasion risks turning the pedagogic relation back into a site of subjective calculation. This is the epistemology of Stanley Fish, in which the act of rhetorical persuasion is an agonistic contest of subjective wills who continue to use language instrumentally, as the instrument of persuasion that will create an effect of conviction and cause the addressee to become, for him- or herself, what he or she is for the speaker. Fish's rhetoric does not display a prudent respect for the pole of the addressee; instead, it seeks to erase the pole of the addressee, to render it identical to the pole of the speaker. That is to say, the listener is made to adopt the same "position" as the speaker. The pole of the addressee is recognized only as the object of a calculation by the speaker.

If the rhetorical pragmatics of the pedagogue are not directed at conviction, how then are we to characterize the ethical obligation that teaching aims to evoke? What is more, how are we to avoid focusing solely on teaching as an intersubjective relation? It is important to underline here that teaching is not exhausted in the achievement of intersubjective communication. The student-teacher relation is not one of magisterial domination, nor is it one of dyadic fusion in which mutual understanding would serve as an end in itself (the mutual unveiling of teachers and students of which Fichte speaks in his writings on the University).[6] Neither convincing students nor fusing with them, teaching, like psychoanalysis, is an interminable process.

What prevents a fusion between teachers and students and makes teaching interminable (structurally incomplete) is that the network of obligation extends to all four poles of the pragmatic linguistic situation: the sender, the addressee, the referent, and the signification.[7] The referent of teaching, that to which it points, is the name of Thought. Let me stress that this is not a quasi-religious dedication. I say "name" and I capitalize "Thought" not in order to indicate a mystical transcendence but in order to avoid the confusion of the referent with any one signification. The name of Thought precisely is a name in that it *has no intrinsic meaning.*[8] In this sense, it is like excellence. However, Thought differs from excellence in that it does not bracket the question of value.

What I would like to suggest is that we recognize that, with the decline of the nation-state, the University has become an open and flexible system and that we should try to replace the empty idea of excellence with the empty name of Thought. The first difference between the two emptinesses is that Thought, unlike excellence, does not masquerade as an idea. In place of the simulacrum of an idea is the acknowledged emptiness of the name—a self-conscious exposure of the emptiness of Thought that replaces vulgarity with honesty, to rephrase Adorno. And a second difference, proceeding from this, is that Thought does not function as an answer but as a *question.* Excellence works because no one has to ask what it means. Thought demands that we ask what it means, because its status as mere name—radically detached from truth—enforces that question. Keeping the question of what Thought names open requires a constant vigilance to prevent the name of Thought from slipping back into an idea, from founding a mystical ideology of truth. We can only seek to do justice to a name, not to find its truth. Since a name has no signification, only a designatory function, it cannot have a truth-content. The meaning-effects of a name are structurally incapable of final determination, are always open to discussion.

As a horizon, the name of Thought cannot be given a content with which consciousness might fuse, or a signification that would allow the closure of debate. Debate may occur as to its signification, but this will always be an agonistic contest of prescriptives about what Thought should be. Nothing in the nature of Thought, as a bare name, will legitimate any one or other of these accounts. To put this another way, any attempt to say what Thought should be must take responsibility for itself as such an attempt. The name of Thought, since it has no content, cannot be invoked as an *alibi* that might excuse us from the necessity of thinking about what we are saying, when and from where we are saying it.[9] Hence, for instance, I admit that these reflections are written from the point of view of someone who is, professionally, a teacher, though he does not know in any absolute sense what is the signification of the name of teacher. Thought is one of many names that operate in the pedagogic scene, and the attribution of any signification to it is an act that must understand itself as such, as having a certain rhetorical and ethical weight.

In the classroom, Thought intervenes as a third term alongside speaker and addressee that undoes the presumption to autonomy, be it the autonomy of professors, of students, or of a body of knowledge (a tradition or a science). Thought names a differend; it is a name over which arguments take place, arguments that occur in heterogeneous idioms. Most important, this third term does not resolve arguments; it does not provide a metalanguage that can translate all other idioms into its own so that their dispute can be settled, their claims arranged and evaluated on a homogeneous scale. As a name, Thought does not *circulate;* it waits upon our response. What is drawn out in education is not the hidden meaning of Thought, not the true identity of students, not the true identity of the professor (replicated in the students). Rather, what is drawn out is the aporetic nature of this differend as to what the name of Thought might mean: the necessity and impossibility that it should be discussed, despite the absence of a univocal or common language in which that discussion could occur. Thought is, in this sense, an empty transcendence, not one that can be worshiped and believed in, but one that throws those who participate in pedagogy back into a reflection upon the ungroundedness of their situation: their obligation to each other and to a name that hails them as addressees, before they can think about it.

Thus, to attribute a signification to Thought, the act of saying what it means to think, is inevitably a political question in the minimal sense of an agonistic moment of conflict, where a difference is opened concerning the nature of discourse. To put this another way, "What is called thinking?" is never simply a theoretical question, one that a fully grounded epistemology might answer.[10] Our reflections on teaching as a practice must insist on a pedagogic scene structured by a dissymmetrical pragmatics, and this unequal relation must be addressed in terms of ethical awareness. The scene of teaching belongs to the sphere of justice rather than of truth: the relation of student to teacher and teacher to student is one of asymmetrical obligation, which appears to both sides as problematic and requiring further study.

The condition of pedagogical practice is, in Blanchot's words, "an infinite attention to the other."[11] Not the attention of individual subjects to individual objects, for we are not returning to the Enlightenment privileging of autonomy. No individual can *be* just, since to do justice is to recognize that the question of justice exceeds individual consciousness, cannot be answered by an individual moral stance. This is because justice involves respect for an absolute Other, a respect that must precede any knowledge about the other.[12] The other speaks, and we owe the other respect. To be hailed as an addressee is to be commanded to listen, and the ethical nature of this relation cannot be justified. We have to listen, without knowing why, before we know what it is that we are to listen to.[13] To be spoken to is to be placed under an obligation, to be situated within a narrative pragmatics. Even a preliminary discussion of the framework within which discussions are to be undertaken requires this initial respect, a respect that is senseless in that it has no constative content. Nor is this "respect" a matter of deference; it is the simple fact of alertness to otherness, something that the German word *Achtung* conveys, linking as it does respect and warning. *"Achtung! Ein andere"* is perhaps the (post-Kantian) rule of this ethics, a respect for the Other rather than for the Law—which is to say that this is not a subjective attitude of respect for the institutions of state, since the subject does not find itself reflected in the other it respects.

In the classroom, the other should not serve to erase the addressee; the pragmatic instance that the other occupies is not simply the pretext for a communication between the philosopher-master and the tradition of Western Thought (or the unconscious). There is some other in the classroom, and it has many names: culture, thought, desire, energy, tradition, the event, the immemorial, the sublime. The educational institution seeks to process it, to dampen the shock it gives the system. *Qua* institution, education seeks to channel and circulate this otherness so that some form of profit can be made from it. Yet shock arises, since it is *the minimal condition of pedagogy,* and it opens a series of incalculable differences, the exploration of which is the business of pedagogy. Education, as *e ducere,* a drawing out, is not a maieutic revelation of the student to him- or herself, a process of clearly remembering what the student in fact already knew. Rather, education is this drawing out of the otherness of thought that undoes the pretension to self-presence that always demands further study.[14] And it works over both the students and the teachers, although in a dissymmetrical fashion.

The demand that the pole of the addressee should be respected is not a demagoguery. A refusal to make the students into the locus of a simple reproduction, either of the professor or of the faithful servants the system requires, does not mean that the students occupy a position of autonomy or authenticity, or that in order to be educated they need only to affirm who they already are. *Pace* Paulo Freire, radical pedagogy must avoid subjugating education to a Marxist grand narrative. The students are not a proletariat by analogy; they do not incarnate the repressed meaning of the educational process.[15] To mount an attack on the professors' authority, on the professor as the transcendent subject of the educational process, must not simply be to seek to replace the professor by the student. This would be the demagogic version of 1968: the inversion of hierarchy so that the students embody the real University.

The question of the University cannot be answered by a program of reform that either produces knowledge more efficiently or produces more efficient knowledge. Rather, the analogy of production itself must be brought into question: the analogy that makes the University into a bureaucratic apparatus for the production, distribution, and consumption of knowledge. For what is at stake here is the extent to which the University *as an institution* participates in the capitalist-bureaucratic system.[16] It seems to me dishonest to pretend that it does not. The University as an institution can deal with all kinds of knowledges, even oppositional ones, so as to make them circulate to the benefit of the system as a whole. This is something we know very well: radicalism sells well in the University marketplace. Hence the futility of the radicalism that calls for a University that will produce more radical kinds of knowledge, more radical students, more of anything. Such appeals, because they do not take into account the institutional status of the University as a capitalist bureaucracy, are doomed to confirm the very system they oppose. The ideological content of the knowledges produced in the University is increasingly indifferent to its functioning as a bureaucratic enterprise; the only proviso is that such radical knowledges fit into the cycle of production, exchange, and consumption.

Produce what knowledge you like, only produce more of it, so that the system can speculate on knowledge differentials, can profit from the accumulation of intellectual capital.

It is perhaps worthwhile to distinguish once again my analysis from Bourdieu's concept of "cultural capital," which animates John Guillory's analysis of the University in *Cultural Capital.*[17] For Guillory, as for Bourdieu, cultural capital retains a primarily ideological function despite the fact that the concept of cultural capital seems relatively indifferent to the ideological content of cultural production. As we have seen, this is because cultural capital is conceived as circulating within a cultural system that is closed off by national boundaries. In order for symbolic status to be quantifiable, to be analyzed as an analogue of financial value, the system within which it is distributed must be closed. Hence Bourdieu and his epigones tend to limit the field of their studies, often appealing to a need for contextual specificity. From such a narrow perspective, the University necessarily appears as an ideological apparatus of the nation-state rather than a potentially transnational bureaucratic-capitalist enterprise.

My argument is that the University is developing toward the status of a transnational corporation. To recognize the transnational framework within which the question of the University is posed is to have to acknowledge that teaching cannot be understood either as structurally independent of a generalized system of exchange or as exhaustively contained within any one closed system of exchange. This, it seems to me, is the situation in which we find ourselves now, one of both limitation and openness. We are more free than we used to be in our teaching, but we can no longer see what it is that our freedom is freedom from. How can we raise the question of accountability without always already giving in to the logic of accounting? In some sense, we cannot. People have to be paid, get scholarships, etc. The question, then, is how we can raise the question of accountability as something that *exceeds* the logic of accounting. The exponential growth in the commodification of information itself, thanks to new technologies, renders the current situation even more acute.

If pedagogy is to pose a challenge to the ever-increasing bureaucratization of the University as a whole, it will need to decenter our vision of the educational process, not merely adopt an oppositional stance in teaching. Only in this way can we hope to open up pedagogy, to lend it a temporality that resists commodification, by arguing that *listening to Thought* is not the spending of time in the production of an autonomous subject (even an oppositional one) or of an autonomous body of knowledge. Rather, to listen to Thought, to think beside each other and beside ourselves, is to explore an open network of obligations that keeps the question of meaning open as a locus of debate. Doing justice to Thought, listening to our interlocutors, means trying to hear that which cannot be said but that which tries to make itself heard. And this is a process incompatible with the production of (even relatively) stable and exchangeable knowledge. Exploring the question of value means recognizing that there exists no homogeneous standard of value that might unite all poles of the pedagogical scene so as to produce a single scale of evaluation.

Such an exploration may prove surprising. Contrary to conventional wisdom, an audience does not preexist an event. The event makes the audience happen, rather than the event happening in front of an audience. Making an audience for this kind of pedagogy "happen" is the task that faces those of us who find ourselves in the contemporary University—teachers and students alike. That audience is not a general public; it is an agglomeration of people of widely differing ages, classes, genders, sexualities, ethnicities, and so on. It is not simply composed of students; it will have to include funding agencies, both state-controlled and private. Creating and addressing such an audience will not revitalize the University or solve all our problems. It will, however, allow the exploration of differences in ways that are liberating to the extent that they assume nothing in advance.

~ 11

Dwelling in the Ruins

Up to this point, my description of the current situation may seem to have rather dire consequences for the University in general and for the humanities in particular. However, such is by no means the case. A certain amount of crystal-ball gazing might lead us to want to say things such as: the humanities will in twenty years' time no longer be centered in the study of national literatures. And these predictions might prove more or less correct. However, my argument is less concerned with the precise disciplinary shape that the University of the twenty-first century will assume than with what that shape will *mean,* which is to say, how it will be given meaning as an institutional system. This is why my analysis thus far has tended to ignore the uneven and combined development that is the actual form of the appearance of the tendencies that I have sought to isolate. And it is also the reason for my own habit of privileging self-description (such as prospectuses) over empirical study in the analysis of how universities work. I will cheerfully admit that in all probability far less will have changed in the daily life of professors and students than one might expect. Significant shifts, though, are taking place in the way in which everyday practices are organized and ascribed meaning. These shifts are even taking place at a remarkably intense rhythm (rhythm rather than speed, since these shifts are not linear but interruptive). For purely heuristic purposes, I subsume these shifts under the name "dereferentialization," which marks a decline in the ideological function *of* the University that is intimately linked to the symptomatic rise of ideology-critique as a methodology inside the University.

This process of dereferentialization, though, is not a historical necessity for Thought. That is to say, I do not invoke dereferentialization as an alibi for retirement from the University. Instead, it seems to me that an engagement with and transvaluation of this shift can allow innovative and creative thinking to occur. But for any such innovation to occur, we must address two issues: the place of the University in society at large, and the internal shape of the University as an institution. Within modernity, the University held a central place in the formation of subjects for the nation-state, along with the production of the ideology that handled the issue of their belonging to that nation-state (culture). Its internal organization as a community was meant to reflect that structure of belonging or community in which a general culture of conversation held together diverse specialties in a unity that was either organic (Fichte), societal (Newman), or transactional (Habermas).

In all of these accounts, the University held the promise of being a microcosm of the nation-state. In my final two chapters, I want to ask what can be done with and in a University that, along with the nation-state, is no longer central to the question of common life. This involves two questions: that of the institution's function as an institution, and that of the community that the institution may harbor. I shall not argue, though, for either a new institution or a new community, but rather for a rethinking of both terms. If my preference is for a thought of *dissensus* over that of consensus—as I shall argue in the next chapter—it is because dissensus cannot be institutionalized. The precondition for such institutionalization would be a second-order consensus that dissensus is a good thing, something, indeed, with which Habermas would be in accord. A version of this tendency is persuasively argued for in Gerald Graff's *Beyond the Culture Wars: How Teaching the Conflicts Can Revitalize American Education.*[1]

For my part, I will propose a certain pragmatism, a pragmatism that does not simply accept the institution's lack of external reference and glory in it (as does Stanley Fish in *There's No Such Thing as Free Speech*), but that tries to make dereferentialization the occasion for *détourne-*

ments and radical lateral shifts.[2] Such moves may be critical, but they will not appeal to a transcendent self-knowing subject capable of standing outside his or her own behavior and critiquing it. To refer back to another term I have already introduced, such an institutional pragmatics will be without *alibis*, without "elsewheres," a truth whose name might be invoked to save us from responsibility for our actions. Here lies another of my differences with Fish and Rorty: this is a pragmatism that does not believe that it adds up to its own alibi, or that its denial of the grand narratives is not itself a project. To put this another way, being a good pragmatist is not in itself a guarantee that one will always be right. It may be pragmatic to abandon pragmatism, so pragmatism cannot function as a project in the modernist sense. Hence institutional practices—even in an institution stripped of Platonic illusions—cannot be their own reward. If I have certain principles (more accurately, certain habits or tics of thought), they are not grounded in anything more foundational than my capacity to make them seem interesting to others, which is not the same thing as convincing other people of their "rightness."

Institutional pragmatism thus means, for me, recognizing the University today for what it is: an institution that is losing its need to make transcendental claims for its function. The University is no longer simply modern, insofar as it no longer needs a grand narrative of culture in order to work. As a bureaucratic institution of excellence, it can incorporate a very high degree of internal variety without requiring its multiplicity of diverse idioms to be unified into an ideological whole. Their unification is no longer a matter of ideology but of their exchange-value within an expanded market. Administering conflict thus does not mean resolving it, as one might take the example of the Cold War to have demonstrated. The non-ideological role of the University deprives disruption of any claim to automatic radicalism, just as it renders radical claims for a new unity susceptible to being swallowed up by the empty unity of excellence.

Those of us who, like me, have found the University a place where the critical function has in the past been possible, have to face up to the fact that our current gains in critical freedom (unimaginable shifts in the institutional face of new programs, etc.) are being achieved in direct proportion to the reduction in their general social significance. This is not in itself any reason to abandon projects for change or innovation. Far from it. But what is required is that we do not delude ourselves as to their significance, that we do not satisfy ourselves with rebuilding a ghost town. Energies directed exclusively toward University reform risk blinding us to the dimensions of the task that faces us—in the humanities, the social sciences, and the natural sciences—the task of rethinking the categories that have governed intellectual life for over two hundred years.[3]

We have to recognize that the University is a *ruined institution,* while thinking what it means to dwell in those ruins without recourse to romantic nostalgia. The trope of ruins has a long history in intellectual life. The campus of the State University of New York at Buffalo is decorated by some artificial concrete ruins that allude to Greco-Roman temple architecture, something that might seem incongruous in North America were it not that it coincides with a history that I have already sketched. This history is that of modernity's encounter with culture, where culture is positioned as the mediating resynthesis of knowledges, returning us to the primordial unity and immediacy of a lost origin—be it the total sunlight and dazzling whiteness of an artificial Antiquity or the earthy social unity of the Shakespearean Globe.[4] This story has been with us since at least the Renaissance, which actually took place in the nineteenth century as the nostalgia of Burckhardt, Pater, and Michelet for an originary moment of cultural reunification; and I have discussed its incarnations elsewhere.[5]

Du Bellay's sonnet cycle "The Ruins of Rome" claims to be the first illustration of the Renaissance of France as a linguistically unified nation-state, the Renaissance for which he calls in his *Défense et illustration de la langue française.* The claim to new origin and national specificity is somewhat vitiated in that his arguments are largely a pirate translation from an Italian dialogue by Speroni. France, says du Bellay, can arise as a modern nation-state by giving a new life and critical dignity to the national language, a task he undertakes on the ground plan offered by the ruins of Rome. A lost splendor will endow the building of a renewed vernacular, much as the stones of Roman monuments were taken and used for building Renaissance palaces.

Where du Bellay saw in the ruins of Rome the foundations of modernity, the Romantics appreciated ruins as ruins, even constructing artificial ones in the grounds of stately homes, just as the monster in Mary Shelley's *Frankenstein* constructs his subjectivity in part from overhearing the reading of Volney's *Ruins of Empires*. According to this romantic story, the fragmented subject (the monster, himself pieced together by technology from bits of past bodies that have lost their organic life) aesthetically appropriates the scattered shards of a now broken and lifeless tradition. That which he cannot live he apprehends aesthetically, thus performing a secondary synthesis both of the tradition (as object of aesthetic appreciation) and of his own subjectivity (as subject of that act of appreciation). Art redeems a fractured and merely technical life; a unified life that can no longer be lived is resynthesized as art.

The Romantics, appreciating ruins *as ruins* rather than as traces of a renascent past, recuperate tradition as aesthetic sensation through a subjective attitude of nostalgia. The Buffalo simulacrum of Greco-Roman culture as the foundation of the North American State University seems to propose an uneasy mixture of the two: a grounding of both the arts and the sciences in a particular tradition (and certainly not a Native American one). The simulation of ruins has to do with the Romantic aesthetic appreciation of the past, and their positioning beside the concrete buildings of the new University is indebted to a hermeneutic claim for knowledge as an interactive encounter with tradition. In either case, ruins are the objects of subjective appropriation and mastery, whether epistemological or aesthetic.

Freud's point in comparing the unconscious to the ruins of Rome was that the present did not ever achieve the modernist task of being simply present, of condemning the past either to become present (be reborn) or to enter utter oblivion.[6] Hence, in *Civilization and its Discontents*, he revises the allusion to insist upon its limitations: the figure of the building constructed from ruins is inadequate, he says, because it fails to convey the sense that, in the unconscious, two buildings from heterogeneous historical periods are impossibly co-present.[7] The past is not erased but haunts the present. Thus, the traumatic return of repressed memory is a constant threat. To inhabit the ruins of the

University must be to practice an institutional pragmatism that recognizes this threat, rather than to seek to redeem epistemological uncertainty by recourse to the plenitude of aesthetic sensation (nostalgia) or epistemological mastery (knowledge as progress). The ruins of culture's institution are simply there, where we are, and we have to negotiate among them.

This is a different way to think about our relation to tradition than that proposed by the German Idealists (in which hermeneutic reworking returned the tradition to a new unity and vitality, a renaissance).[8] We should not attempt to bring about a rebirth or renaissance of the University, but think its ruins as the sedimentation of historical differences that remind us that Thought cannot be present to itself. We live in an institution, and we live outside it. We work there, and we work with what we have at hand. The University is not going to save the world by making the world more true, nor is the world going to save the University by making the University more real. The question of the University is not that of how to achieve a stable or perfect relation between inside and outside, between the ivory tower and the streets. So, let us treat the University as we treat institutions. After all, I do not need to believe a story about Man (universal subject of history) creating power by taming nature and bending it to his will in order to switch on the light, nor does my incredulity mean that the light will go off. Nor does continuing to believe this story keep the light on if I cannot afford to pay my electricity bill. Enlightenment has its costs.

Although this may seem to make light of institutions, it actually involves a political recognition that institutions have a weight that exceeds the beliefs of their clientele. What I mean by dwelling in ruins is not despair or cynicism; it is simply the abandonment of the religious attitude toward political action, including the pious postponement or renunciation of action. Remember Leonard Cohen's dictum: "they sentenced me to twenty years of boredom, for trying to change the system from within."[9] Change comes neither from within nor from without, but from the difficult space—neither inside nor outside—where one is. To say that we cannot redeem or rebuild the University is not to argue for powerlessness; it is to insist that academics must work without alibis, which is what the best of them have tended to do.

To return to my analogy of the Italian city, this means neither razing the old to build a rational city on a grid, nor believing that we can make the old city live again by returning to the lost origin. Structurally, each of these options presupposes that the city is not where we live, that we are somehow out in the suburbs, wondering what to do with uninhabited ruins. The city is where we dwell. The ruins are continuously inhabited, although they are also from another time whose functionality has been lost. Even if the University is legible to us only as the remains of the idea of culture, that does not mean that we have left its precincts, that we view it from the outside. The question that is raised by the analogy is how we can do something other than offer ourselves up for tourism: the humanities as cultural manicure, the social sciences as travelogue, the natural sciences as the frisson of real knowledge and large toys. If the process of consumerization seems more advanced in the humanities, this may only be a matter of a funding-induced perspective. How much does our vision of what science education achieves owe to Disney? Our idea of the natural sciences is already deeply structured by the mass media, through organizations such as NASA and the Epcot Center, in a way that makes the production of scientific knowledge deeply entrenched in the reproductive systems of mass culture.[10]

The cancellation of the Superconducting Super Collider suggests that the end of the Cold War does not simply have effects on the readiness of states to fund national competition in the realm of humanistic culture. Indeed, there is an increasing problem with what education in the natural sciences might consist of, what kind of subject it might be directed to. Information technology combines with the drying up of funds to suggest that there may no longer be an open market for graduate students educated in the pure sciences, while vocational engineering schools seem more adapted to the market. Hence, the question of to whom an education in physics or chemistry may be directed has no obvious answer. American physics departments in particular may have as much reason as the humanities to fear trial by "marginal utility" or "market forces" in funding battles, once there is no longer a quasi-inexhaustible defense budget. Incidentally, the highest percentage of post-graduate unemployment in Canada is not in the humanities but among physics majors. All of which suggests that the dualist split be-

172

tween humanities and natural sciences that has been the most apparent structural reality of the University in the twentieth century is no longer the practical certainty it once was. Not that it has ever really been so. English was initially perceived in the United States as a practical and businesslike alternative to the classics.[11] Of course, as Graff points out, the study of English literature was soon professionalized under the German model of *Geisteswissenschaft* as an autonomous field of research in order that its teaching might accede to the dignity of a "science," a field of knowledge.[12]

Earlier in this book, I dropped dark hints about the fate of departments of philosophy, which seem to be heading down the path already followed by classics, once the sumptuary laws that made a University without a strong philosophy department unthinkable have been dropped in favor of market imperatives. This may not be a bad thing, since it does not necessarily mean that a set of questions about the nature and limits of thinking, about the good life, etc., which were once asked under the heading of "philosophy," have ceased or will cease to be asked. It simply means that nothing in contemporary society makes it evident that individuals should be trained to ask such questions. Instead, philosophy departments are spinning off into applied fields in which experts provide *answers* rather than refining questions—medical ethics being the most obvious example, not least because the boom in medical ethics is the product of the interaction between biomedical technology and the economics of the U.S. medical insurance "system."

Instead, responsibility for questioning seems to have devolved onto literature departments insofar as those departments are themselves increasingly abandoning the research project of national literature. "English and Comparative Literature" tends to function in the United States as a catch-all term for a general humanities department and is likely for that reason to be gradually replaced by the less weighted title "Cultural Studies." It is worth thinking about why Cultural Studies should win out over the traditional designations of "History of Ideas" or "Intellectual History." This has to do both with their relationship with the existing research project of the history department and also with the extent to which the term "studies" acknowledges that the professionalization of the academy today is no longer structured by research into a central idea. To put this another way, as my argument in Chapter 7 has demonstrated, the idea of culture in Cultural Studies is not really an idea in the strong sense proposed by the modern University. Cultural Studies, that is, does not propose culture as a regulatory ideal for research and teaching so much as recognize the inability of culture to function as such an idea any longer.

I am frankly not equipped to trace the parallel processes that may emerge in the natural sciences and social sciences, but the apparent horizon in arts and letters for the North American University can be roughly sketched as the development of an increasingly interdisciplinary general humanities department amid a cluster of vocational schools, which will themselves include devolved areas of expertise traditionally centered in the humanities, such as media and communications. Such vocational schools will tend to increase the social science component in traditionally humanistic fields of inquiry, a process in which the designation of Cultural Studies as a disciplinary endeavor that straddles the humanities (critique of aesthetic objects) and the social sciences (sociology, communications) will doubtless play a part. This is a historical irony, since such a prospect has striking similarities to the original plan of many land-grant universities, before most of them bought into the research University model as the way to acquire increased prestige and concomitant funding. Such a horizon of expectation is already being marketed to us under the slogan of the "Liberal Arts College within the University of Excellence." Needless to say, the liberal arts college is invoked here less in terms of its pedagogical tradition than in terms of its potential attraction to consumers.

Such is the role that the humanities are called upon to play in the University of Excellence, one that wavers between consumer service (the sense of individual attention for paying students) and cultural manicure. And the claims for scientific research in the humanities, for a *Geisteswissenschaft*, that have through the history of the modern University assured a dignity to the humanities, no longer find themselves reflected in and guaranteed by a guiding idea of culture for the University as a whole. Hence it is not the research model, I fear, that will save the humanities (or indeed the natural sciences), since the organization of the humanities as a field structured by a project of research no longer appears self-evident (with the decline of the nation-state as the instance that served as origin and telos for such organization). In a general economy of excellence, the practice of research is of value only as an exchange-value within the market; it no longer has intrinsic use-value for the nation-state.

The question remains of how Thought, in the sense in which I have described it in Chapter 10, may be addressed within the University. We should be clear about one thing: nothing in the nature of the institution will enshrine Thought or protect it from economic imperatives. Such a protection would actually be highly undesirable and damaging to Thought. But at the same time, thinking, if it is to remain open to the possibility of Thought, to take itself as a question, must not seek to be economic. It belongs rather to an economy of waste than to a restricted economy of calculation.[13] Thought is non-productive labor, and hence does not show up as such on balance sheets except as waste. The question posed to the University is thus not how to turn the institution into a haven for Thought but how to think in an institution whose development tends to make Thought more and more difficult, less and less necessary. If we are not to make the situation of the professor into an analogy for the waning power of the priesthood—faced by unbelief on the one hand and television evangelism on the other—this requires us to be very clear about our relation to the institution, to give up being priests altogether. In other words, the ruins of the University must not be, for students and professors, the ruins of a Greco-Roman temple within which we practice our rites as if oblivious to their role in animating tourist activities and lining the pockets of the unscrupulous administrators of the site.

In attempting to sketch how one might dwell in the ruins of the University without belief but with a commitment to Thought, I want to return to what I said about the problem of evaluation. The challenge that faces those who wish to preserve the task of thinking as a question is a difficult one that does not admit of easy answers. It is not a matter of coming to terms with the market, establishing a ratio of marginal utility that will provide a sanctuary. Such a policy will only produce the persistent shrinking of that sanctuary, as in the case of old-growth timber in the United States. How many philosophers, or redwoods, are required for purposes of museification? If the grand project of research and the minimal argument of species-preservation are likely to prove unsuccessful, it is necessary that our argument for certain practices of Thought and pedagogy measure up to the situation and accept that the existing disciplinary model of the humanities is on the road to extinction.

Within this context, a certain opportunism seems prescribed. To dwell in the ruins of the University is to try to do what we can, while leaving space for what we cannot envisage to emerge. For example, the argument has to be made to administrators that resources liberated by the opening up of disciplinary space, be it under the rubric of the humanities or of Cultural Studies, should be channeled into supporting short-term collaborative projects of both teaching and research (to speak in familiar terms) which would be disbanded after a certain period, whatever their success. I say "whatever their success" because of my belief that such collaborations have a certain half-life, after which they sink back into becoming quasi-departments with budgets to protect and little empires to build. Or to put it another way, they become modes of unthinking participation in institutional-bureaucratic life.

What I am calling for, then, is not a generalized interdisciplinary space but a certain rhythm of disciplinary attachment and detachment, which is designed so as not to let the question of disciplinarity disappear, sink into routine. Rather, disciplinary structures would be forced to answer to the name of Thought, to imagine what kinds of thinking they make possible, and what kinds of thinking they exclude. It is perhaps a lesson of structuralism that, when faced with a disciplinary project, a crucial way of situating that project is by considering what it is *not*, what it excludes. Thus a concentration in European philosophy, for example, would be obliged—by the nature of the interruptive pattern that I propose—to address both non-European philosophy and European non-philosophy.

The intellectual advantages of such an organizational structure reside in the fact that it can draw on the energy of the North American tendency toward "free electives," while detaching the terms of such choice from consumerism. The system of course-choice that Charles Eliot introduced at Harvard had two problems, both consequent upon making the student the sole locus of elective choice: it presumed a student capable of informed choice as to how to become informed, and it presumed that knowledge had an organic structure through which the student could navigate. Indeed, Eliot's opponents were quick to remark upon the need for a core curriculum or a distribution requirement, in order to limit student choice and to preserve the structure of knowledge from simple market conditions.[14] The result was a compromise, so that the tension between choice and distribution requirements has continued to agitate debates on curriculum in U.S. universities.

My argument is that the market structure of the posthistorical University makes the figure of the student as consumer more and more a reality, and that the disciplinary structure is cracking under the pressure of market imperatives. The means by which the question of the structure of knowledge can be preserved as a *question* in such a situation, the means by which knowledge can be something other than marketed information, are not the reassertion of a fixed disciplinary structure by dictatorial fiat. What makes the William Bennetts of this world so angry is that such a solution is no longer competitive. Hence I suggest that we make the market in courses a matter of Thought and discussion by situating it on the side of the faculty and administration, rather than by leaving it as solely a matter for student desire—which the faculty seeks to satisfy and the bureaucracy seeks to manage.

Thus I propose an abandonment of disciplinary grounding but an abandonment that retains as structurally essential the *question of the disciplinary form that can be given to knowledges*. This is why the University should not exchange the rigid and outmoded disciplines for a simply amorphous interdisciplinary space in the humanities (as if we could still organize knowledge around the figure of "Man"). Rather, the loosening of disciplinary structures has to be made the opportunity for the installation of disciplinarity as a *permanent question*. The short-term projects I suggest are designed to keep open the question of what it means to group knowledges in certain ways, and what it has meant that they have been so grouped in the past. This keeps open the question of disciplinarity at the heart of any proposal for the grouping of knowledges in a constellation such as "Modern Art History" or "African-American Literature." Only by being constrained periodically to reinvent themselves can such groupings remain attentive to the terms of their production and reproduction. However, before we commit ourselves to loosening the disciplinary structures of the University, it would first be necessary to make some very firm deal about hiring prospects on the basis of an overall ratio of tenured faculty to students rather than, as now, on the rather specious basis of "disciplinary coverage." It is remarkable how few departments of English, for example, actually turned out to "need" so many medievalists.[15]

I have a certain diffidence about such plans as this, though, which always smack of bad utopianism, since there is no general model, no *the* University of the Future, merely a series of specific local circumstances. I supply these suggestions merely in the interest of attempting to find possibilities that work in the service of Thought in the current (and, I think, implacable) bourgeois economic revolution in the University. It is essential to understand that this is not a move of "big politics," not an attempt to divert the process toward another result, a different end. Rather, it seems to me, recognizing the University as ruined means abandoning such teleologies and attempting to make things happen within a system without claiming that such events are the true, real, meaning of the system. The system as a whole will probably remain inimical to Thought, but on the other hand, the process of dereferentialization is one that opens up new spaces and breaks down existing structures of defense against Thought, even as it seeks to submit Thought to the exclusive rule of exchange-value (like all bourgeois revolutions). Exploiting such possibilities is not a messianic task, and since such efforts are not structured by a redemptive metanarrative, they require of us the utmost vigilance, flexibility, and wit.

Given the prospect of such a generalized disciplinary regroupment, it seems to me necessary that we engage in a consideration of how the University might function as a place where a community of thinkers dwell, with the proviso that we rethink critically the notion of community, so as to detach it from both the organicist tradition and the feudal corporation. On this basis, it may become possible to provide

178

some hints as to the kinds of institutional politics that might be pursued in order to transvalue the process of dereferentialization, to make the destruction of existing cultural forms by the encroachment of the open market into an opportunity for Thought rather than an occasion for denunciation or mourning.

~ 12

The Community of Dissensus

I have already discussed the way in which the community of scholars in the University is presumed to serve as a model for rational political community at large, both for the German Idealists and for more contemporary thinkers. This model is not without its variations: Fichte's body of students and professors is not Rawls's veiled tribunal, for instance. But there consistently remains a strong tendency in modernity to imagine the University as a model of the rational, the just, or the national community, which incarnates a pure bond of sociality around the disinterested pursuit of the idea. Indeed, the only hope of an existence beyond market imperatives that Alfonso Borrero Cabal in his report for UNESCO can hold out for the University as a contemporary institution is the vague assertion that the University can "serve culture" by virtue of its "principal commitment to being" the "model and pattern" for the society that surrounds it—a direct echo of the German Idealists.[1] Never mind that such an argument has already been undermined by his calls for the University to be "internationalized" as a global institution, which means the rupture of any such link between a given University and the society that surrounds it.

Anyone who has spent any time at all in a University knows that it is not a model community, that few communities are more petty and vicious than University faculties (suburban "model communities" might be an exception). And yet the story persists. The University is supposed to be the potential model for free and rational discussion, a site where the community is founded in the sharing of a commitment to an abstraction, whether that abstraction is the object of a tradition or of a rational contract. The medieval guild was a practical community among others (glassblowers, painters, victuallers); the medieval University as a society for the study of knowledge was a corporate community, in the medieval sense like a guild. In modernity, the University becomes the model of the social bond that ties individuals in a common relation to the idea of the nation-state. Of course, this change is an uneven and variable process, and some universities are more modern than others. Like the role of trustees, the degree to which religion continues to function in University foundations is a significant variant here, one with which Newman struggles in particular.

However, what is central to the thought of community in the modern model University is the notion of *communication,* of a mutual transparency that permits the executive action of Kant's judge as much as it does the bonding of Fichte's professors and students. Nor is this understanding of community in terms of communication restricted to the University. To understand how the modern University can be a model for society, we have to look at the way modernity approaches community: in terms of the state. The notion of the state is the abstract ground that assumes the community is disinterested and autonomous. Modern community is founded upon the autonomous decision of individuals to communicate with each other as subjects of a state. Community does not come about because of a heteronomous obligation of subjects to a monarch, a tribe, or a land. The modern assumption is that the question of what it means, for instance, to be American is the object of a decision made with the free assent of Americans, rather than an essence inscribed in a race or climate, or a decision made by a monarch to whom a primordial allegiance is owed. Hence, those who are born as subjects of a modern state supposedly possess the power to alter that social contract by such processes as voting.

The effect of domination inherent in this fiction of the state is apparent once we consider how the alleged autonomy of the subject, its freedom to participate in communicational transactions such as this, is conditional upon its subjection to the idea of the state. The subject is "free" only insofar as she or he becomes, for her- or himself, primarily subject *to* the state. The state positions individuals as subjects subject to the idea of the state as an instance of community. Subjects, that is, first have an allegiance to the idea of the state. Thus, since the individual is subject to the state, his or her relation to other people is a relation to them as subjects of the state in their own turn. In short, all interactions are mediated through the abstract idea of the state. The singularity or difference of others is reduced, since community with others becomes possible only insofar as those others are, identically with oneself, civil subjects. In modernity, the abstract idea of the state thus underpins the very possibility of communication and civil society.

In this sense, the modern community is inherently universalizing, since it is based upon the assumption of a shared *human* capacity for communication. Specific nations merely compete to best incarnate their essential humanity. The United Nations is a modern institution in that it seeks to resolve the contradiction between nationalism and the ideal of human community, positioning nations analogously to the subjects of the nation-state, as subjects in a community (of nations). The horizon of consensus that guides the modern thought of community is guaranteed by the assumption that the nature of the social bond can itself become the object of free and rational discussion and agreement between subjects, so that they can each freely consent to it. Paradoxically, an agreement that founds the possibility of free and fair communication is presumed to have been made freely and fairly, despite the absence of the agreement.

Such a metalepsis can only be permitted if it is assumed that the language in which differences are sorted out is not itself prey to the action of those differences. We can only agree to disagree if we can establish agreement concerning what it is that we are disagreeing about, and we can only establish communication if we can ascertain that we are in communication without first communicating that fact. Hence all problems of communication, any differences of idiom, must be presumed to be merely secondary to, or parasitical upon, a fundamental clarity of communication—an ideal speech situation.

Culture, as I have shown, claims to be the natural birth of rational communication, mediating between brute nature and articulated reason. According to the German Idealists, a sense of communitarian be-

no! →

182

culture: true because I believe
rational: believe because true

longing, which would otherwise be the object of abstract reasoning, occurs spontaneously. Culture both teaches brute nature how to be rational and makes reason accessible to nature. To take an example, the subject says to her- or himself: "I feel a sense of attachment; I know a rational state. By understanding myself as culturally German, I can reconcile the two." Culture here serves to unify the desire to speak and the power to mean. Or to put it another way, culture unifies sentiment — *No* ⌡ and logic. Nothing in the world, however, guarantees the assumption that the force of sentiment and the clarity of logic can be harnessed, that communicative transparency is possible. Culture claims that it can provide such a guarantee in that it is both the *object* of communication (what is communicated) and the *process* of communication (something that is produced in communicative interaction). Culture, in short, is both *Wissenschaft* (what we talk about) and *Bildung* (the very act of our talking together).

The University of Culture's ideological function in modernity is, then, to pretend to be the institution that is not an institution but simply the structure you get if transparent communication is possible. The University, that is, is presumed to institutionalize the very principle that renders possible the functioning of institutions as bearers of the social bond. This allows universities to appear as pure instances of communication between subjects rather than examples of brute domination.

The majority of left-wing critics have shared in this logic, merely arguing that the egalitarian assumption at the heart of communicational transparency should be fully realized and that domination is an effect of failed communication. This is one of the reasons for which leftists have proved such excellent functionaries of the University, even in conservative regimes: they believe that they are the guardians of a true culture of which the extant regime is merely a false or ideological version. For them, all that is required to set things right is clearer (true) communication: the truth will set us free. I have already given ample account of my sense that this belief is misplaced. To say this, however, is not to say that there is no such thing as interaction, as is often claimed by those who read deconstruction or postmodernity through the lens of Matthew Arnold as restatements of the late-Victorian crisis of faith.

The work of Jacques Derrida and Jean-François Lyotard has been greeted with considerable hostility for the very reason that they raise some fundamental doubts about the assumption that communication is, in principle, transparent. Derrida's powerful readings of the Western philosophical tradition are marked by his insistence that every attempt at communication is attended by a foundational violence (the reduction of the Other to the status of addressee) and by a structurally implicit failure of representation.[2] For his part, Lyotard has insisted upon the radical heterogeneity of idioms in a way that renders the organization of phrases under a common horizon of truth impossible. His is a pragmatic consideration of speech in terms of a performative notion of "doing justice" rather than a constative attempt to speak the truth—a consideration upon which I have already drawn in Chapter 10 when discussing the scene of pedagogy.

Questioning the transparency of communication, as Derrida and Lyotard do, does not then lead to a claim as simpleminded as "we cannot speak to one another," which has been the conclusion of some. Rather, while we are constantly speaking to one another (Lyotard insists that even silence is a way of saying something, so that Pontius Pilate was not innocent), to describe what happens in terms of an ideal notion of "communication" (even in terms of degrees of successful communication) is to miss the point. Effects of communication may occur; speech contexts may be temporarily stabilized by apparent assent between interlocutors. But such occurrences are never more than acts of stabilization; they are not revelations of a fundamental stability or transparency to communication. Furthermore, such stabilizations are never total, since the very phrases that seek to establish assent to the grounding rules of communication cannot themselves be subject to the rules they establish. Indeed, the presumption of communication, as the Charge of the Light Brigade testifies, causes the most disastrous effects of misunderstanding.

If the assumption that we speak a common language lights the way to terror,[3] in what terms can we speak of community? What is the nature of the social bond, if it cannot simply be the object of free choice and rational assent in communication? And what are the implications for the University, the institution supposed to incarnate this model of communicational community? Is the only alternative to a community founded in communicational transparency a world of atomistic subjects who clash by night in absolute ignorance of one another? If community is grounded neither upon some fundamentally shared ethnic bond (the pre-modern community of blood and soil) nor upon modernity's assumption of a shared possibility of communication, how is it even possible to form? My suggestion is that in thinking about the University we must take seriously the critique of modernity's claim to communicational transparency; we must work out what it means to become what the Miami Theory Collective felicitously calls a "community at loose ends."[4] As such, the question of the community that the University harbors needs to be phrased differently than it is in the modernist model. We need to think about a community in which communication is not transparent, a community in which the possibility of communication is not grounded upon and reinforced by a common cultural identity.

The thought of community without identity has been above all the work of Jean-Luc Nancy and Maurice Blanchot, in *The Inoperative Community* and *The Unavowable Community* respectively.[5] Structured by a constitutive incompleteness (Blanchot) or by the sharing of an absence (Nancy), such a community is not made up of subjects but of *singularities.* The community is not organic in that its members do not share an immanent identity to be revealed; the community is not directed toward the production of a universal subject of history, to the cultural realization of an essential human nature. Rather, singularities (*"I's"* not *egos,* as Nancy puts it) variously occupy the positions of speaker and listener.

This seems particularly important in the context of thinking about the University because, to recall my observations in Chapter 10, it is noteworthy how often intellectuals tend to forget about the position of the listener in favor of worrying solely about the speaking position or position of enunciation. By contrast, what the "community at loose ends" remembers is that the singularity of the "I" or the "you" is caught up in a network of obligations that the individual cannot master. That is, the network of obligations in which an individual is caught up is not entirely available to the subjective consciousness of that individual, so that we can never pay all our debts. Indeed, the assumption that we can pay all our debts is fundamentally unethical, since it presumes the possibility of overcoming all responsibilities and obligations, achieving "freedom" from them. Autonomy, as freedom from obligation to others, holds out the impossible imagination of subjective self-identity: I will no longer be torn up, divided from myself by my responsibilities to others.

It is the desire for subjective autonomy that has led North Americans, for example, to want to forget their obligations to the acts of genocide on which their society is founded, to ignore debts to Native American and other peoples that contemporary individuals did not personally contract, but for which I would nonetheless argue they are *responsible* (and not only insofar as they benefit indirectly from the historical legacy of those acts). In short, the social bond is not the property of an autonomous subject, since it exceeds subjective consciousness and even individual histories of action. The nature of my obligations to the history of the place in which I live, and my exact positioning in relation to that history, are not things I can decide upon or things that can be calculated exhaustively. No tax of "x percent" on the incomes of white Americans could ever, for example, make full reparation for the history of racism in the United States (how much is a lynching "worth"?). Nor would it put an end to the guilt of racism by acknowledging it, or even solve the question of what exactly constitutes "whiteness."

Fuller discussion of these questions would require another book. However, I raise these issues in order to suggest how the nature of the social bond should be rethought. One might say that this is a "thickening" of the social bond, or that the social bond is becoming opaque to the consciousness of the modern rational subject. The sheer fact of obligation to others is something that exceeds subjective consciousness, which is why we never get free of our obligations to others, which is why nobody is a *model* citizen (the citizen who would not have any bond to anyone else in the community because he or she would stand for the community as a whole).

A useful analogy can be drawn here with Agamben's portrait of the community of singularities as a "whatever" community, where the social bond is characterized in lighter terms than I have used so far: not as obligation but as *transience,* the solidarity of those who have nothing in common but who are aggregated together by the state of things.[6] This description can help us see that to speak of obligation is to engage with an ethics in which the human subject is no longer a unique point of reference. The obligation is not to other humans but to the condition of things, *ta pragmata.* This is why, as Aristotle points out, a man can be made unhappy after his death by the social disgrace of his children. The social bond exceeds subjective consciousness.[7] What we call language is not exhausted as an instrument of communication or representation. As a structure that is incapable of self-closure, language escapes instrumentality to mark the indifference of the state of things to the subject.

A distinction must be drawn between the political horizon of consensus that aims at a self-legitimating, autonomous society and the heteronomous horizon of dissensus. In the horizon of dissensus, no consensual answer can take away the question mark that the social bond (the fact of other people, of language) raises. No universal community can embody the answer; no rational consensus can decide simply to agree on an answer. To preserve the status of the social bond as a question is to tolerate difference without recourse to an idea of identity, whether that identity is ethnic ("we are all white, we are all French"), or even rational ("we are all human"). It is to understand the obligation of community as one to which we are answerable but to which we cannot supply an answer. Such a community is heteronomous rather than autonomous. It does not pretend to have the power to name and determine itself; it insists that *the position of authority cannot be authoritatively occupied.* No consensus can legitimate the University or the State as the authoritative reflection of the consensus it represents. Thought can only do justice to heterogeneity if it does not aim at consensus. To abandon consensus says nothing about limited or provisional forms of agreement and action, rather it says that the opposition of inclusion to exclusion (even a total inclusion of all humanity over and against the space alien) should not structure our notion of community, of sharing.

To argue for the political as an instance of *community* rather than as an instance of society is to make a distinction between the political closure of a party line (society) and the uncertain experience of being-together that no authoritative instance can determine (community).[8] To be more precise here, the political as an instance of community is a sharing that does not establish an autonomous collective subject who is authorized to say "we" and to terrorize those who do not, or cannot, speak in that "we."[9] A dissensual community would thus be a development of the social bond as a necessity of sharing, of community. However—and this is a crucial restriction—necessity and community cannot themselves be made the object of a consensus. The social bond is the fact of an obligation to others that we cannot finally understand. We are obligated to them without being able to say exactly why. For if we could say why, if the social bond could be made an object of cognition, then we would not really be dealing with an obligation at all but with a ratio of exchange. If we knew what our obligations were, then we could settle them, compensate them, and be freed from them in return for a payment.

This is the point to which the logic of exchange has penetrated such questions in the United States, where children sue their parents for monetary compensation in relation to their failure to live up to parental obligation. Such action is perfectly logical in the terms of capitalism: if there exists an obligation between parents and children, then it must have a monetary value (or it is not real) and potentially be the object of an agreed settlement. That is to say, the capitalist logic of general substitutability (the cash-nexus) presumes that all obligations are finite and expressible in financial terms, capable of being turned into monetary values. This is the logic of the restricted or closed economy.

Of course, once one begins, as I have done, to speak of a non-finite obligation, people easily think of religion, since this is precisely the discursive sphere in which the awareness of the possibility of an incalculable (and hence unpayable) debt has been preserved as an anachronism in modernity. This is why it is easy to sound mystical when speaking of incalculable obligation or unknowable (and hence unpayable) debt, of non-finite responsibility toward the Other. But I am not trying to sound mystical. I am saying something rather simple: that we do not know in advance the nature of our obligations to others, obligations that have no origin except in the sheer fact of the existence of

Otherness—people, animals, things other to ourselves—that comports an incalculable obligation.

To bring this back once again to my argument about pedagogy in Chapter 10, the sense of incalculable otherness of the student affects the scene of pedagogy. To a certain extent, the students are always more aware of the otherness of the teacher, and this becomes clear when they say or respond in a way that forces the teacher to rethink her or his ideas, although almost never in the exact way suggested by the students. Similarly, while teachers may be (and I hope are) in the process of making their students rethink their own ideas, the end result remains incalculable in the final instance. The pedagogic relationship, that is, compels an obligation to the existence of otherness.

To take a slightly different kind of example, one of the reasons family relationships are so difficult, as Freud noted, is that neither children nor parents come with instruction manuals. Again, we do not know the nature of our obligations in advance, and any attempt to determine strictly the nature of mutual obligation, to regulate the reciprocal debt, merely produces psychotics instead of neurotics. I cite the problem of families in a non-normative way to make the point that we never really "grow up," never become fully autonomous and capable of cognitive determination. As a result, we can never settle our obligations to other people. There is no emancipation from our bonds to other people, since an exhaustive knowledge of the nature of those bonds is simply not available to us. It is not available because the belief that we could fully know our obligation to the Other, and hence in principle acquit that obligation, would itself be an unjust and unethical refusal to accept our responsibility.

The desire to know fully our responsibility to others is also the desire for an alibi, the desire to be irresponsible, freed of responsibility. Our responsibility to others is thus inhuman in the sense that the presumption of a shared or common humanity is an irresponsible desire to know what it is that we encounter in the other, what it is that binds us. To believe that we know in advance what it means to be human, that humanity can be an object of cognition, is the first step to terror, since it renders it possible to know what is non-human, to know what it is to which we have no responsibility, what we can freely exploit. Put simply, the obligation to others cannot be made an object of knowledge under the rubric of a common humanity.

We are left, then, with an obligation to explore our obligations without believing that we will come to the end of them. Such a community, the community of dissensus that presupposes nothing in common, would not be dedicated either to the project of a full self-understanding (autonomy) or to a communicational consensus as to the nature of its unity. Rather, it would seek to make its heteronomy, its differences, more complex. To put this another way, such a community would have to be understood on the model of *dependency* rather than emancipation. We are, bluntly speaking, addicted to others, and no amount of twelve-stepping will allow us to overcome that dependency, to make it the object of a fully autonomous subjective consciousness. The social bond is thus a name for the incalculable attention that the heteronomous instance of the Other (the fact of others) demands. There is no freeing ourselves from the sense of the social bond, precisely because we do not come to the end of it; we can never totally know, finally and exhaustively judge, the others to which we are bound.[10] Hence we cannot emancipate ourselves from our dependency on others. We remain in this sense immature, dependent—despite all of Kant's impatience.

This long and rather thorny excursus into the problems of obligation and the social bond has been necessary in order to point out a peculiar paradox. As Gianni Vattimo has argued, modern society is "the society of generalized communication."[11] Yet as Vattimo also points out, the dream of self-transparency at the heart of the modernist project has been undermined rather than fulfilled by the mass media's "intensification of social communication" (21). The utopia of self-transparency, of a society immediately present to itself in which all members communicate unrestrictedly with all of the others all of the time and without misunderstanding or delay—the German Idealist fantasy of the Greek *polis*—has not been realized. And this is not because of technical limitations but because of technical success. That is to say, the development of technologies capable of processing and transmitting information (of "informationalizing" the world) has expanded so that the speed and range of information exchange exceeds the capacities of the subject who had been destined to master such information. One effect of globalization is to undermine the possibility of a single subject's mastering the complexities of the social bond, metonymically incarnating it as a personal relation to culture. Globalization paradoxically undoes the possibility of a single world culture (or a single world history), because the single world market it proposes is no longer predicated upon the relation of subject to state as the point at which the system acquires meaning.[12]

Hence, in a global economy, the University can no longer be called upon to provide a model of community, an intellectual Levittown. And the appeal to the University as a model of community no longer serves as the *answer* to the question of the social function of the University. Rather, the University will have to become one place, among others, where the attempt is made to think the social bond without recourse to a unifying idea, whether of culture or of the state. In the University, thought goes on alongside other thoughts, we think beside each other. But do we think together? Is our thinking integrated into a unity? There is no property in thought, no proper identity, no subjective ownership. Neither Kant's *concordia discors,* nor Humboldt's organic idea, nor Habermas's consensual community can integrate or unify thinking. Working out the question of how thoughts stand beside other thoughts is, I believe, an act which can push the impulse of Cultural Studies beyond the work of mourning for a lost idea of culture that needs political renewal.

Such is the force of my suggestions concerning disciplinarity. Instead of a new interdisciplinary space that will once and for all reunify the University, I have attempted to propose a shifting disciplinary structure that holds open the question of whether and how thoughts fit together. This question is not merely worthy of study; it is the massive challenge that faces us. An order of knowledge and an institutional structure are now breaking down, and in their place comes the discourse of excellence that tells teachers and students simply not to worry about how things fit together, since that is not their problem. All they have to do is get on with doing what they always have done, and the general question of integration will be resolved by the administration with the help of grids that chart the achievement of goals and tabulate efficiency. In the University of Excellence, teachers and students can even go on believing in culture if they like, as long as their beliefs lead to excellent performance and thus help the aim of total quality.

The problem that students and teachers face is thus not so much the problem of what to believe as the problem of what kind of analysis of institutions will allow any belief to count for anything at all. What kind of belief will not simply become fodder for evaluation in terms of excellence? At the same time, the very openness to activity that the process of dereferentialization fosters in the University of Excellence allows considerable room for maneuver, provided that students and teachers are ready to abandon nostalgia and try to move in ways that keep questions open.

The thought of community that abandons either expressive identity or transactional consensus as means to unity seems to me to refer to what the posthistorical University may be. The University is where thought takes place beside thought, where thinking is a shared process without identity or unity. Thought beside itself perhaps. The University's ruins offer us an institution in which the incomplete and interminable nature of the pedagogic relation can remind us that "thinking together" is a dissensual process; it belongs to dialogism rather than dialogue.

Such a thought as I am proposing does not amount to a social mission for the University, since it begins by giving up the link between the University and national identity that has assured power, prestige, and research funds for some University intellectuals for almost three centuries. But it also does not mean the abandonment of social responsibility. Real responsibility, ethical probity, is simply not commensurate with the grand narrative of nationalism that has up to now underpinned accounts of the social action of University research and teaching. The abandonment of that legitimating metanarrative is a frightening prospect, but it seems to me that it is inevitable. Such an abandonment will occur gradually without us, if we ignore it. Hence I suggest we pay attention to the prospect of this dereferentialization that will make the preservation of the activity of thinking considerably more difficult. That a major shift in the role and function of the intellectual is occurring is clear. What it will come to have meant is an issue upon which those in the University should attempt to have an impact. An attention to this problematic is necessary. How we pay attention to it is not determined. Therein lies both the freedom and the enormous responsibility of Thought at the end of the twentieth century, which is also the end of what has been the epoch of the nation-state.

⤳ Notes

1. Introduction

1. A typical recent publication is entitled *Bankrupt Education: The Decline of Liberal Education in Canada*. The book's epigraph is from Matthew Arnold, and the authors lambaste the Canadian secondary school system for abandoning the "unique hybrid of Anglo-European influences including Hegelianism and Scottish commonsense philosophy" that had, they contend, until recently characterized Canadian educational theory and practice. Peter C. Emberley and Waller R. Newell, *Bankrupt Education: The Decline of Liberal Education in Canada* (Toronto: University of Toronto Press, 1994), p. 11.

2. Recent events at Bennington College are one example of this: where "academic restructuring" has led to the immediate sacking of some 20 faculty members out of 78. Their replacements will tend to be local part-timers, working under a stripped-down "core faculty" of full-time professors. Thus, for instance, "area musicians" will teach courses in instrumental music. Likewise, new employees will no longer be eligible for presumptive tenure: "instead, professors will work under individual contracts of different lengths." Denis K. Magner, "Bennington Dismisses 20 Professors . . ." *Chronicle of Higher Education,* June 29, 1994, p. A16. Whether we call this piecework or freelancing, the general implication is clear: full-time staff will be increasingly called upon to manage part-time teachers. At larger research universities in the United States, the number of such part-timers can be expected to rise as the collapse of the job market causes the graduate student teaching assistants of the old apprenticeship model to be increasingly replaced by part-timers (many of them with recent doctorates).

3. A good general introduction to the Soros project can be found in Masha

Gessen, "Reaching to the Critical Masses," *Lingua Franca,* 4, no. 4 (May/June 1994), pp. 38–49.

4. Alfonso Borrero Cabal, *The University as an Institution Today* (Paris and Ottawa: UNESCO and IDRC, 1993).

5. This is, of course, primarily a reference to C. P. Snow's argument against what he saw as "the intellectual life of the whole of Western society . . . increasingly being split into two polar groups," the "literary intellectuals" and the "scientists." *The Two Cultures and a Second Look* (Cambridge: Cambridge University Press, 1957), pp. 3–4. In response to this division, Snow argued forcefully that "the scientific culture is really a culture, not only in an intellectual but also in an anthropological sense" (9), and called for a dialogue between the two cultures based on mutual respect.

6. Of course, there are other disciplinary divisions within the University besides that of the humanities and the natural sciences. In what follows, I hope to show the ways in which the humanities have proved in the past to offer such powerful paradigms for the function of the University.

7. Jean-François Lyotard, *The Postmodern Condition,* trs. Geoffrey Bennington and Brian Massumi (Minneapolis: University of Minnesota Press, 1984), p. xxv.

8. Johann Gottlieb Fichte, "Deductive Plan of an Institution of Higher Learning to be Founded in Berlin" (1807, pub. 1817) in *Philosophies de l'Université: l'idéalisme allemand et la question de l'Université,* ed. Luc Ferry, J.-P. Pesron, and Alain Renaut (Paris: Payot, 1979), p. 172, my translation. The original German version, *Deduzierter Plan einer zu Berlin su errichtenden höhern Lehranstalt, die in gehöriger Verbindung mit einer Akademie de Wissenschaften stehe,* can be easily found in Engel et al., *Gelegentliche Gedanken über Universitäten,* ed. Ernst Müller (Leipzig: Reclam Verlag, 1990), pp. 59–159.

9. Jaroslav Pelikan, *The Idea of the University: A Reexamination* (New Haven: Yale University Press, 1992). This book suggests that Newman was largely correct, and that all that universities require is some updating of his suggestions to meet present circumstances. In general, Pelikan believes that: "The affirmation of the unity of the human race is, for the university and its scholars, both an ideal and a fact: a fact without which, as that kind of ultimate context, research into this or that particular and local phenomenon is fatally skewed; and an ideal that cannot be realized without just such research into this or that particular and local phenomenon" (53). Religious faith in this unity will, presumably, allow the hermeneutic circle sketched here to be overcome. One cannot but add, however, that it has done little to protect the victims of ethnocentrism.

10. Allan Bloom, *The Closing of the American Mind* (New York: Simon and Schuster, 1987), p. 336.

11. Jacques Barzun, *The American University: How It Runs, Where It Is Going,* 2nd

ed. with an Introduction by Herbert I. London (Chicago and London: University of Chicago Press, 1993), first published 1968. Further references noted by page number in the text; a similar policy will be followed for other works discussed.

12. On this particular structure, see Diane Elam, *Romancing the Postmodern* (London and New York: Routledge, 1992). She argues persuasively for the problematic status of both postscript and preface, and their tendency to become confused, as symptomatic of a general problem of textuality.

13. "Within the department, continuity is best assured by the administrative assistant, usually a woman" (103). Remember that the administrative deans are consistently referred to as "men," and one cannot but be reminded that the generic form "man" is not as inclusive as anti-feminists usually claim.

14. Jacqueline Scott, panel discussion among Canadian Woman University Presidents on "Morningside," CBC radio, March 10, 1994. I am grateful to the University of Trent for supplying the radio on which I heard this broadcast.

15. Here, as elsewhere in this book, I use the term "ideology" very precisely. Some of those to whom I have presented previous versions of this argument have wanted me to use the term "ideology" when referring to the discourse of excellence since, as they tend to claim, "everything is ideological." If everything were ideological, then it would quite simply be impossible to know ideology as such. For the term "ideology" to have a critical usefulness, we have to presume an outside to ideology, be it a Lukácsian notion of "objective truth" or an Althusserian account of "critical self-consciousness." The assumption is that, once the standpoint of objective truth or self-consciousness is reached, the discourse to which we are opposed appears as contradictory and hence powerless—which does not explain why workers continue to vote against what intellectuals perceive to be their best interest.

The great contribution of Louis Althusser's work on ideology was to insist upon its tie to the state apparatus, even while laying aside simplistic notions of "falsification." In order to preserve the term's critical utility, Althusser clearly distinguished between ideology and critical science. Even though there is no end to ideology, no pure and simple positivism, there has to be an outside to ideology, which comes for Althusser at the point when critical science, by means of an "epistemological break," achieves self-knowledge, becomes the ideology that knows itself to be an ideology. Such self-knowledge, he argues, is only possible for Marxism, which can know itself to be the ideology of the proletariat, which is to say, of the historical process itself. Positive knowledge is not possible except within the horizon of an achieved revolution, whose terms the pre-revolutionary thinker can only hope to imagine. Nonetheless, the pre-revolutionary thinkers can lift themselves above the pre-revolutionary framework within which they find themselves through the exercise of critical thought, by finding the contradictions inherent in their own system of thinking—such was Marx's achievement, for all that Marx was a late-nineteenth-century thinker. Thus, even if the "lonely hour of the last instance never comes," it is potentially available as the deduction of its inevitability through critical science. Louis Althusser, "Ideology and Ideological State Apparatuses" in *Lenin and Philosophy and Other Essays*, tr. Ben Brewster (London: New Left Books, 1971).

16. For instance, John Beverley remarks in *Against Literature* (Minneapolis: University of Minnesota Press, 1993) on "the conversion of cultural studies from a form of radical opposition to the avant-garde of bourgeois hegemony" (20): "I believe it is still worth making the struggle for (and in) cultural studies, but just at the moment when its presence in the contemporary university seems assured, cultural studies has begun to lose the radicalizing force that accompanied its emergence as a field" (21). While I agree with Beverley's account of the institutional domestication of Cultural Studies, I am less than convinced that this is a fate that has befallen Cultural Studies as a result of individual weakness or external pressure.

2. The Idea of Excellence

1. *Maclean's*, 106, no. 46 (November 15, 1993).
2. Quoted in Aruna Jagtiani, "Ford Lends Support to Ohio State," *Ohio State Lantern*, July 14, 1994, p. 1.
3. Ibid.
4. See C. P. Snow, *Two Cultures and A Second Look* (Cambridge: Cambridge University Press, 1969).
5. Phat X. Chem, "Dean of Engineering Forced Out," *New University* (University of California at Irvine), April 4, 1994, my italics.
6. Some sense of the distance we have traveled is apparent in the historical irony of the fact that this is a letter written to criticize the University on March 22, the very date recalled in the naming of the revolutionary movement in French universities in 1968 as "The Movement of March 22." *Sic transit*.
7. "Summer Faculty Fellowships: Information and Guidelines," Indiana University, Bloomington Campus, May 1994.
8. As a purely internal unit of value, excellence shares with Machiavelli's *virtù* the advantage of permitting calculation to be engaged in on a homogeneous scale. On *virtù*, see Machiavelli, *The Prince*, ed. and tr. Robert M. Adams (New York: Norton, 1977).
9. "News You Can Use," *U.S. News and World Report*, 117, no. 13 (October 3, 1994), pp. 70–91. *U.S. News and World Report* has not limited its focus simply to undergraduate education, as this particular issue might seem to suggest. Earlier in the same year, it published a special "info-magazine" issue devoted

entirely to "America's Best Graduate Schools." That the issue was sponsored by a car company—specifically, a car: the "Neon" from Plymouth and Dodge—is an irony that should not be lost here.

10. That the link between consumerism and the rhetoric of excellence appeals to a wide audience is certainly a fact that these magazines count on, not only to sell copies of individual issues but also to keep readers coming back for more information and more magazines in the future. Interestingly enough, the measures of excellence and value-for-money in universities seem to change on a yearly basis, not unlike those in the car industry. To keep up with these trends, each year the wise consumer should allegedly pick up *Maclean's* and/or *U.S. News and World Report* to have the most up to date information possible. For instance, while McGill held first place in *Maclean's* "Medical/Doctoral" category in 1993, by 1994 it had dropped to a less impressive third overall: *Maclean's,* 107, no. 46, (November 14, 1994). Likewise, the reader who would like to be fully informed about the criteria *U.S. News and World Report* used to calculate the "Most Efficient" and "Best Value" universities must also buy the previous issue of the magazine, because, as we are told in the article that accompanies the tables, "Only schools that finished in the top half of our rankings of national universities and national liberal arts colleges, *published last week,* were considered as potential best values" (October 3, 1994, p. 75, my italics). Being fully informed is presumably a two-issue affair for *U.S. News and World Report.*

11. Obviously, not all universities welcome the implication that they resemble car sales. As Edwin Below, director of financial aid at Wesleyan University, puts it: "I am much more likely to see if we overlooked something [in the financial aid offer] when families are honest about their financial concerns than if they treat the process like they were buying a used car" (quoted in *U.S. News and World Report,* October 3, 1994, p. 72). However, not all University officials seem to mind the similarities, even if they are not willing to draw the exact parallel themselves. According to the same issue of *U.S. News and World Report,* "a growing number of schools, such as Carnegie Mellon University in Pittsburgh, are letting families know that they welcome [financial aid] appeals. In letters sent this spring to all prospective students offered aid, the university's message was clear: 'Send us a copy of your other offers—we want to be competitive' " (72).

12. Publicity brochure, October 1, 1992, published by the Direction des Communications, Université de Montréal, my translation. The original reads as follows: "Créée en 1972, la Faculté des études supérieures a pour mission de maintenir et de promouvoir des standards d'excellence au niveau des études de maîtrise et de doctorat; de coordonner l'enseignement et la normalisation des programmes d'études supérieures; de stimuler le développement et la coordination de la recherche en liaison avec les unités de recherche de l'Uni-

versité; de favoriser la création de programmes interdisciplinaires ou multi-disciplinaires."

13. Michel Foucault, *Discipline and Punish*, tr. Alan Sheridan (New York: Vintage, 1979), pp. 227–228.

14. Alfonso Borrero Cabal, *The University as an Institution Today* (Paris and Ottawa: UNESCO and IDRC, 1993) p. xxiv, my italics.

15. Karl Marx, *Capital: A Critique of Political Economy*, vol. 1, tr. Ben Fowkes (Harmondsworth: Penguin, 1976), p. 169, n. 31.

16. Hence ancient texts can now be read in considerably stranger ways, ways that recognize historical discontinuity without immediately recuperating it in terms of a Fall narrative as "the glory we have lost." One of the more striking examples of this is the contemporary recognition by thinkers such as Lyotard that Aristotle's notions of the "golden mean" and of *phronesis* have nothing to do with the assumptions of democratic centrism—producing a much more politically radical account of Aristotle's call for prudent judgment on a case-by-case basis. The point Aristotle makes in the *Nichomachean Ethics* is that the mean is refractory with regard to the individual and that no rule of calculation will allow the judge to arrive at it, since what constitutes prudent behavior radically differs from case to case. I have discussed the political implications of this "revolutionary prudence" in "PseudoEthica Epidemica: How Pagans Talk to the Gods," *Philosophy Today*, 36, no. 4 (Winter 1992).

17. "1876 Address on University Education (Delivered at the opening of the Johns Hopkins University, Baltimore)," in T. H. Huxley, *Science and Education*, vol. 3 of *Collected Essays* (London: Macmillan, 1902), pp. 259–260.

18. As Giner de los Rios puts it, the Scottish University shares with the American a greater influence of the German research University: "The British type is seen in its pure form in Oxford and Cambridge, or modified more towards the Latin or German type in Scotland or Ireland, in new universities, and in the United States." *La universidad espanola: obras completas de Francisco Giner de los Rios*, vol. 2 (Madrid: University of Madrid, 1916), p. 108; quoted in Borrero Cabal, *The University as an Institution Today*, p. 30.

19. Ronald Judy, in the short history of the American University with which he prefaces his *(Dis)Forming the American Canon: African-Arabic Slave Narratives and the Vernacular* (Minneapolis: University of Minnesota Press, 1993), also situates the foundation of Johns Hopkins as a crucial turning point that defines the specificity of the American University: "These movements towards academic professionalization and instrumental knowledge reached their culmination with the incorporation of Johns Hopkins University in 1870, or more precisely with the appointment of Daniel Coit Gilman as its president in 1876. Gilman made Johns Hopkins a model research institution where the human and physical sciences *(Naturwissenschaften)* flourished as disciplined methodologies" (15). Judy's account differs slightly from mine in that he associates

with the founding of Johns Hopkins the very bureaucratic ideology of meth-
odological specificity that undermines the possibility of general culture—the
displacement of culture by bureaucratically managed knowledge that I locate
as the distinguishing trait of the contemporary University of Excellence. Hence
he argues that the disciplinary specificity of the humanities curriculum arises
in the late nineteenth century, "at precisely that moment when the humanities
were no longer required to respond to the demand for relevance," pointing
to David S. Jordan's institution of the first English degree at Indiana University
in 1885 (16). Judy calls this "the professionalization of the human sciences"
and links it to the development of an overarching "culture of bureaucracy"
that unites the human and the natural sciences under a general rubric of
professionalization (17).

Judy is thus telling a story quite comparable to my own concerning the
replacement of the general idea of culture by a generalized bureaucracy, except
that he locates it in the latter half of the nineteenth century rather than in the
latter part of the twentieth. This disagreement is, I think, less historical than
cartographical. I am concerned to introduce a transitional step into the passage
from the modern German University of national culture to the bureaucratic
University of Excellence, one which positions the American University as the
University of a national culture that is contentless.

20. For an account of the debate over "performance indicators" see Michael Pe-
    ters, "Performance and Accountability in 'Post Industrial Society': The Crisis
    of British Universities," *Studies in Higher Education,* 17, no. 2 (1992).

21. Claude Allègre, *L'Âge des savoirs: pour une renaissance de l'Université* (Paris:
    Gallimard, 1993), p. 232, my translations.

22. Ibid., p. 232, my italics.

23. This statement may sound too relativistic. Of course, if it is true that, as Julie
    Thompson Klein contends in *Interdisciplinarity* (Detroit: Wayne State Uni-
    versity Press, 1990), p. 11, "all interdisciplinary activities are rooted in the ideas
    of unity and synthesis, evoking a common epistemology of convergence," such
    an idea could be supported by the left and the right, who would merely disagree
    as to where the point of convergence should lie. In fact, the account of the
    interdisciplinary that Klein gives is a convincing argument for some suspicion
    of the implicit harmonic convergence in interdisciplinary work. One of my
    major aims in this book is to suggest that in thinking about the University we
    should lay aside the automatic privileging of unity and synthesis, without how-
    ever simply making disharmony and conflict into a negative goal.

24. Rey Chow, in "The Politics and Pedagogy of Asian Literatures in American
    Universities," *differences,* 2, no. 3 (1990), has provided some useful reminders
    of how the turn to Cultural Studies in the teaching of Asian literature can
    function as a conservative strategy: "When scholars are departmentalized sim-
    ply because they are all 'doing' 'China,' 'Japan,' or 'India' what actually hap-

pens is the predication of so-called 'interdisciplinarity' on the model of the colonial territory and the nation state" (40).

Chow makes a convincing argument that the consideration of Asian literatures in terms of general culture is a marginalizing gesture that locates the Asian "only in the universalist language of 'interdisciplinarity,' 'cross-cultural plurality,' etc., in which it becomes a localized embellishment of the general narrative" (36). Like myself, Chow is not simply dismissing interdisciplinarity or Cultural Studies; what she does is provide a strong example of how the organization of the humanities is part of a process that she calls, following Edward Said, "informationalization."

25. On the informationalization of cultural knowledge, see Edward Said, "Opponents, Audiences, Constituencies and Community" in Hal Foster, *The Anti-Aesthetic: Essays on Postmodern Culture* (Port Townsend: Bay Press, 1983), and Jean-François Lyotard, "New Technologies" in *Political Writings,* tr. Bill Readings and Kevin-Paul Geiman (Minneapolis: University of Minnesota Press, 1993).

3. The Decline of the Nation-State

1. The best survey of the philosophical determination of the idea of the nation-state is Yves Guiomar, *La Nation entre l'histoire et la raison* (Paris: La Découverte, 1990). As Guiomar points out, the nation-state is the modern form of organization of human society. A useful brief summary of the major tropes of economic globalization can be found in "Les Frontières de l'économie globale," *Le Monde diplomatique: manière de voir 18* (May 1993). On the cultural and economic tensions attendant on globalization, and its relationship to the figure of the nation-state, see Immanuel Wallerstein, *Geopolitics and Geoculture: Essays on the Changing World-System* (Cambridge: Cambridge University Press, 1991).

In their 1974 book, *Global Reach: The Power of the Multinational Corporations* (New York, Simon and Schuster) Richard J. Barnet and Ronald E. Müller began to analyze the power and scope of multinationals, arguing that the men (and indeed they usually are men not women) who run these global corporations are making "a credible try at managing the world as an integrated unit" (13). As Barnet and Müller see it, "the global corporation is the first institution in human history dedicated to centralized planning on a world scale" (14). And although they attempt to qualify their predications with the remark, "reality is less neat than college-course catalogs," Barnet and Müller nonetheless argue for the real potential for global corporations to overshadow nation-states. In particular, they claim that "the more economic issues overshadow military security, the more the global corporation is likely to take power away from the nation-state" (96). Interestingly enough, one of the main

REICH

solutions they offer for increased accountability of global corporations is that their accounting procedures be made a matter of public record. That accountability is seen as closely linked to accounting will be of importance to my argument about the condition of the contemporary University.

Global Dreams: Imperial Corporations and the New World Order (New York: Simon and Schuster, 1994), which Barnet co-wrote with John Cavanagh, shows many of the predications of the earlier book to have come true in the intervening twenty years. As these authors recount, "the emerging global order is spearheaded by a few hundred corporate giants, many of them bigger than most sovereign nations . . . The architects and managers of these space-age business enterprises understand that the balance of power in world politics has shifted in recent years from territorially bound governments to companies that can roam the world" (14). "The most disturbing aspect of this system," Barnet and Cavanagh conclude, "is that the formidable power and mobility of global corporations are undermining the effectiveness of national governments to carry out essential policies on behalf of their people" (19). As these authors well know, "no world authority exists to define global welfare, much less to promote it" (419).

2. Masao Miyoshi, "A Borderless World? From Colonialism to Transnationalism and the Decline of the Nation-State," *Critical Inquiry,* 19, no. 4 (Summer 1993), p. 732.

3. As Miyoshi puts it, "to the extent that cultural studies and multiculturalism provide students and scholars with an alibi for their complicity in the TNC version of neocolonialism, they are serving, once again, just as one more device to conceal liberal self-deception." Ibid., p. 751.

4. Wlad Godzich, "Religion, the State, and Postal Modernism," afterword to Samuel Weber, *Institution and Interpretation* (Minneapolis: University of Minnesota Press, 1987), p. 161.

5. See Jean-François Lyotard, "The State and Politics in the France of 1960" in *Political Writings,* tr. Bill Readings and Kevin Paul Geiman (Minneapolis: University of Minnesota Press, 1993). For a more detailed discussion of "depoliticization," see my foreword to that volume, entitled "The End of Politics."

6. Marco Antonio Rodrigues Dias, Preface to Alfonso Borrero Cabal, *The University as an Institution Today* (Paris and Ottawa: UNESCO and IDRC, 1993), p. xi. In the report itself, Borrero Cabal reinforces this: "Now the problem [of equivalences] has increased, because as Harrel-Bond says, 'The 20th century can be characterized as the century of the refugee, of the immigrant' " (154).

7. Quoted in Borrero Cabal, *The University as an Institution Today,* p. 138.

8. Ibid., p. 138.

9. W. E. B. DuBois, "On the Dawn of Freedom," in *The Souls of Black Folk* (New York: Fawcett World Library, 1961), p. 23.

10. Giorgio Agamben, *The Coming Community,* tr. Michael Hardt (Minneapolis:

University of Minnesota Press, 1993), p. 62. Some particular praise is due to the translator here for having captured the subtle echoes of Marx and Engels in the declamatory mode.

11. See Walter Benjamin, "The Work of Art in the Age of Mechanical Reproduction," in *Illuminations*, tr. Harry Zohn (London: Fontana Collins, 1973), where he speaks of "the absolute emphasis on its exhibition value" as the characteristic of the contemporary work of art (p. 227).

12. Gérard Granel, *De l'Université* (Mauzevin: Trans-Europ-Repress, 1982). An excellent summary of Granel's argument is found in Christopher Fynsk, "But Suppose We Were to Take the Rectorial Address Seriously . . . Gérard Granel's *De l'Université*," *Graduate Faculty Philosophy Journal*, vol. 14, no. 2–vol. 15, no. 1 (1991). Fynsk draws Granel's writing on Heidegger toward conclusions that are not unlike my own, notably as concerns the necessity of a deconstructive thought of community that renders the institutional question of the University both urgent and unanswerable. However, the oxymoronic "coherent an-archy" that he proposes, following Granel, as the deconstructive idea of a university that "would attain its goal only in *knowing and remarking* its insufficiency, articulating in this way the need for its constant renewal" (350), remains in my view too optimistic (I say this with the reservation that pessimism is not the only alternative). Fynsk and Granel, concerned as they are to redeem Heidegger, end up seeking to redeem the University by giving it a negative coherence. This is basically a stronger version of the argument of Robert Young, which I discuss later on.

4. The University within the Limits of Reason

1. A good description of Charles Eliot's place both at Harvard and in American higher education in general is provided by W. B. Carnochan, *The Battleground of the Curriculum: Liberal Education and American Experience* (Stanford: Stanford University Press, 1993), pp. 9–21.

2. "This is why it is important that a single individual, who is moreover only *primus inter pares* inside the university, but who is for the external world clothed in the dignity of the whole of the professorial body, should represent the professorial body to the ministries of State, to individuals, and above all, to young people. This is the true idea of a University Rector who, in order not to limit the democratic character of the whole, must be elected from among those he represents and chosen by them, according to a fixed procedure and for a limited period." Friedrich Schleiermacher, "Occasional Thoughts on the German Conception of Universities" (1808), in *Philosophies de l'Université*, ed. Luc Ferry, J.-P. Pesron, and Alain Renaut (Paris: Payot, 1979), p. 302, my translation. The original German text can be found in *Gelegentliche Gedanken über Universitäten*, ed. H. Müller (Leipzig: Reclam Verlag, 1990), pp. 159–237.

3. If, as Carnochan says, "there are no more Charles Eliots" (*Battleground of the Curriculum,* p. 112), this is not simply because they lack time or influence, as he claims. Rather, it is because the president's place in the system is no longer understood to be connected to the curriculum as a matter of content, but to the whole system as a matter of *administration.* Thus, it is fund raising rather than general policy-making that occupies the majority of the University president's time.

   This shift is perhaps nowhere made clearer than in William H. Honan, "At the Top of the Ivory Tower the Watchword Is Silence," *New York Times,* July 24, 1994, p. E5. We are reminded here that "once upon a time, university presidents had something to say to the outside world." Now things are very different. To paraphrase Vartan Gregorian, president of Brown University, University presidents "are so preoccupied with fund raising that they fear offending virtually any faction." The article concludes with several telling remarks from Stanley N. Katz, president of the American Council of Learned Societies, who draws out Gregorian's remarks even further by using another startling parallel between the auto industry and the University: "Mr. Katz said that current academic leaders are silent largely because they are overwhelmed with administrative burdens since universities have exploded in size, complexity and cost. 'These institutions require feeding 24 hours a day,' he said. 'It's the same in industry. Nobody even knows who the head of Chrysler is today. That's because the people who run these organizations are swamped with administrative work.' "

4. Immanuel Kant, *The Conflict of the Faculties,* tr. Mary J. Gregor (Lincoln: University of Nebraska Press, 1992). Selections are readily available in English, translated as "The Contest of Faculties" in Immanuel Kant, *Political Writings,* ed. Hans Reiss (Cambridge: Cambridge University Press, 1970).

5. Jacques Derrida, "Mochlos; or, The Conflict of the Faculties" in *Logomachia: The Conflict of the Faculties,* ed. Richard Rand (Lincoln: University of Nebraska Press, 1992).

6. Kant, *The Conflict of the Faculties,* pp. 151, 165, translation modified. For the convenience of readers, I reproduce H. R. Nisbet's translation of this passage, from Immanuel Kant, *Political Writings,* p. 187: "It is the duty of monarchs to govern in a *republican* (not a democratic) manner, even though they may *rule autocratically.* In other words, they should treat the people in accordance with principles akin in spirit to the laws of freedom which a people of mature rational powers would prescribe for itself, even if the people is not literally asked for its consent."

7. As Derrida puts it, according to Kant, the higher faculties have the responsibility to "represent the interests of State power and forces that support it." *Du droit à la philosophie* (Paris: Galilée, 1991), p. 419, my translation. They thus have responsibility for action and must speak the purely performative language

of giving orders. Philosophy, which is responsible for truth, must speak a purely constative language: "The members of the 'lower' faculty as such cannot and must not give orders *(Befehle gehen)*. In the last instance, the government has the power by contract to control and censor everything in their statements that would not be constative and, in a certain sense of this word, representational. Think of modern subtleties in the analysis of non-constative statements, of the effect that they would have on such a concept of the University, on its relationships with civil society and State power! Imagine the training which would have to be given to censors and to government experts, charged with checking the purely constative nature of university discourses. Where would these experts be trained? By what faculty—the higher faculties or the lower? And who would decide this matter?" (427).

8. Hans Ulrich Gumbrecht, "Bulky Baggage from the Past: The Study of Literature in Germany," in *Comparative Criticism II* (1990).

9. See Jean-François Lyotard, *The Postmodern Condition,* tr. Geoff Bennington and Brian Massumi (Minneapolis: University of Minnesota Press, 1979), pp. 31–34. Lyotard argues that the French focus on "humanity as the hero of liberty" directs educational policy "toward a politics of primary education, rather than of universities and high schools" (31). The German narrative of speculative knowledge, however, argues that "the only valid way for the nation-state itself to bring the people to expression is through the mediation of speculative knowledge" (34). Two excellent brief accounts of the debates surrounding French Revolutionary policy on education are supplied by Peggy Kamuf in "The University Founders: A Complete Revolution," in *Logomachia: The Conflict of the Faculties,* esp. pp. 86–90, and Christie McDonald, "Institutions of Change: Notes on Education in the Late Eighteenth Century," in the same volume, an essay that is particularly interesting on Diderot and Mirabeau.

5. The University and the Idea of Culture

1. Friedrich Wilhelm Joseph Schelling, "Leçons sur la méthode des études académiques" (1803), in *Philosophies de l'Université: L'idéalisme allemand et la question de l'Université,* ed. Luc Ferry, J.-P. Pesron, and Alain Renaut (Paris: Payot, 1979), p. 93, my translations. The German original is *Vorlesungen über die Methode des akademischen Studiums,* ed. Walter Erhardt (Philosophische Bibliothek).

2. Friedrich Schiller, *Letters on the Aesthetic Education of Man,* tr. E. M. Wilkinson and L. A. Willoughby (Oxford: Clarendon Press, 1967).

3. Friedrich Schleiermacher, "Pensées de circonstance sur les universités de conception allemande," in *Philosophies de l'Université,* my translations.

4. Mirabeau, in *Une éducation pour la démocratie: textes et projets de l'époque révolutionnaire,* ed. B. Baczko (Paris: Garnier, 1982), p. 71, my translation.

5. We enter a problem of translation here. As Samuel Weber notes, in *Institution and Interpretation, Wissenschaft* is translated in French as "science," which stands over and against *savoirs* or *connaissances,* the forms for "knowledges." In English, science names the ensemble of knowledges in the hard sciences rather than the unifying principle of all knowledge-seeking. To translate *Wissenschaft* as the substantive "learning" would be attractive, if it did not raise massive confusion with the process of learning represented by *Bildung* (which also could be translated by the participle "learning").

6. Schelling, "Leçons sur la methode," p. 64.

7. Johann Gottlieb Fichte, "Plan déductif d'un établissement d'enseignement supérieur à fonder à Berlin," in *Philosophies de l'Université,* p. 176, my translations.

8. Wilhelm von Humboldt, "Sur l'organisation interne et externe des établissements scientifiques supérieurs à Berlin" (1809), in *Philosophies de l'Université,* pp. 321–322, my translations. The German original, "Über die innere und äußere Organisation der höheren wissenschaftlichen Anstalten in Berlin," is reprinted in *Gelegentliche Gedanken über Universitäten,* ed. E. Müller (Leipzig: Reclam Verlag, 1990), pp. 273–284.

9. Schelling, "Leçons sur la methode," p. 73.

10. See Schleiermacher, "Pensées de circonstance," pp. 259, 288, 275–276, 293–295.

11. Fichte, "Plan déductif," p. 168.

12. These are the notions that guide John Henry Cardinal Newman's reflection on the production of cultivated gentlemen in *The Idea of a University* and whose underlying concept of temporality owes more to the nineteenth century than to the Enlightenment—as we shall see in the next chapter.

13. Schleiermacher, "Pensées de circonstance," p. 271.

14. Fichte, "Plan déductif," p. 176.

15. Ibid., p. 251.

16. Humboldt, "Sur l'organisation interne et externe," p. 324.

17. Ibid., p. 325.

18. Jean-François Lyotard makes a similar observation in *The Postmodern Condition,* tr. Geoff Bennington and Brian Massumi (Minneapolis: University of Minnesota Press, 1979) when he remarks that the "more liberal" proposal of Humboldt was chosen over that of Fichte for the plan of the University of Berlin (32).

6. Literary Culture

1. Friedrich Schlegel, *Lectures on the History of Literature, Ancient and Modern* (New York: Smith and Wright, 1841), p. 9.

2. For detailed discussions of the development of German literature see especially Rainer Rosenberg's three excellent works, *Literaturwissenschaftliche German-istik* (Berlin: Akademie-Verlag, 1989); *Zehn Kapitel zur Geschichte der Germanistik* (Berlin: Akademie-Verlag, 1981); *Literatur—verhältnisse im deutschen Vormärz* (München: Kürbiskern und Tendenzen, 1975); and Jurgen Fohrmann's *Das Projekt Der Deutschen Literaturgeschichte* (Stuttgart: J. B. Metzlersche Verlagsbuchhandlung, 1989).

3. See *Conversations de Goethe avec Eckermann,* ed. Claude Roëls, tr. Jean Chuzeville (Paris: Gallimard, 1988).

4. Sir Philip Sidney, *A Defence of Poetry,* ed. J. A. Van Dorsten (Oxford: Oxford University Press, 1973), p. 25. A rhetorical exemplum is an example given to the collective memory (itself one of the five branches of rhetoric) rather than to subjective consciousness. An orator possesses a stock of such examples, some of which are utterly contradictory, and applies them as it seems appropriate in the circumstances rather than according to a unified logic. In this respect, they are not unlike proverbs. Hence it is perhaps more accurate to think of these "speaking pictures" as emblems than as examples in the modern sense. They exist as objects, jumbled together in the memorial space of a *wunderkabinett* or treasure house.

5. Peter Uwe Hohendahl, *Building a National Literature: The Case of Germany, 1830–1870* (Ithaca: Cornell University Press, 1989); Chris Baldick, *The Social Mission of English Criticism: 1848–1932* (Oxford: Clarendon Press, 1983); Franklin E. Court, *Institutionalizing English Literature: The Culture and Politics of Literary Study: 1750–1900* (Stanford: Stanford University Press, 1992); Gerald Graff, *Professing Literature* (Chicago: University of Chicago Press, 1987); *The Institutionalization of Literature in Spain,* Hispanic Issues I, ed. Wlad Godzich and Nicholas Spadaccini (Minneapolis: Prisma Institute, 1987). Gauri Viswanathan's *Masks of Conquest: Literary Study and British Rule in India* (New York: Columbia University Press, 1989) takes the effects of national literature beyond, strictly speaking, national borders, exploring the "uses to which literary works were put in the service of British imperialism" (169).

6. Philippe Lacoue-Labarthe, *La Fiction du politique* (Paris: Christian Bourgois, 1987).

7. John Henry Cardinal Newman, *The Idea of a University: Defined and Illustrated* (London: Longmans, Green and Co., 1925), p. 106. This text combines the "Nine Discourses" (1852) and a set of essays on "University Subjects" (1858) that were later delivered at University College, Dublin.

8. T. H. Huxley, "Science and Culture," in *Science and Education,* p. 141. Huxley became Rector of the University of Aberdeen in 1874.

9. In Newman's words: "whatever name we bestow on it, it is, I believe, as a matter of history, the business of a University to make this intellectual culture its direct scope" (125).

10. W. B. Carnochan, *The Battleground of the Curriculum: Liberal Education and American Experience* (Stanford: Stanford University Press, 1993), pp. 43–46.

11. Here are the full terms of the choice that Newman proposes: "I protest to you, Gentlemen, that if I had to choose between a so-called University, which dispensed with residence and tutorial superintendance, and gave its degrees to any person who passed an examination in a wide range of subjects, and a University which had no professors or examinations at all, but merely brought a number of young men together for three or four years, and then sent them away as the University of Oxford is said to have done some sixty years since . . . I have no hesitation in giving the preference to that University which did nothing, over that which exacted of its members an acquaintance with every science under the sun" (145).

12. Matthew Arnold, *Culture and Anarchy (1868),* ed. J. Dover Wilson (Cambridge: Cambridge University Press, 1932).

13. Matthew Arnold, "The Function of Criticism at the Present Time," (1864) in *Selected Criticism of Matthew Arnold,* ed. Christopher Ricks (New York: New American Library, 1972), p. 97.

14. Graff, *Professing Literature.*

15. "In addition to the reasons which I have already assigned for beginning my account of literature in general, with a description of that of the Greeks, I may notice, that they are the only people who can be said to have, in almost every respect, created their own literature; and the excellence of whose attainments stand almost entirely unconnected with the previous cultivation of any other nations." Schlegel, *Lectures on the History of Literature,* p. 14.

16. John Dryden, *Works,* vol. 17, ed. Swedenberg, Miner, Dearing, and Guffey (Berkeley: University of California Press), p. 55.

17. See my entry on Dryden in *The Johns Hopkins Guide to Literary Theory and Literary Criticism,* ed. Michael Groden and Martin Kreiswirth (Baltimore: Johns Hopkins University Press, 1993), and also "Why Is Theory Foreign?" in *Theory Between the Disciplines,* ed. Mark Cheetham and Martin Kreiswirth (Ann Arbor: University of Michigan Press, 1990).

18. F. R. Leavis, "The Idea of a University" in *Education and the University* (1943) (Cambridge: Cambridge University Press, 1979).

19. A detailed institutional history of the *Scrutiny* group, for which the writings of Leavis serve metonymically in this argument, is provided by Francis Mulhearn in *The Moment of Scrutiny* (London: Verso New Left Books, 1979).

20. F. R. Leavis, "Mass Civilization and Minority Culture," in *Education and the University;* F. R. Leavis, *Nor Shall My Sword* (New York: Barnes and Noble, 1972).

21. See L. C. Knights, "How Many Children Had Lady Macbeth?" in *Selected Essays in Criticism* (Cambridge: Cambridge University Press, 1981).

22. Lacoue-Labarthe, *La Fiction du politique*.
23. Wolf Lepenies, "The Direction of the Disciplines," in *Comparative Criticism II* (1990).
24. Wolf Lepenies, *Between Science and Literature* (Cambridge: Cambridge University Press, 1988).
25. Jürgen Habermas, "The Idea of the University," in *The New Conservatism*, ed. and tr. Shierry Weber Nicholsen (Cambridge, Mass.: MIT Press, 1989).
26. Ibid., p. 24.
27. See John Guillory, *Cultural Capital: The Problem of Literary Canon Formation* (Chicago: University of Chicago Press, 1993).
28. E. D. Hirsch, *Cultural Literacy: What Every American Should Know* (Boston: Houghton Mifflin, 1987). The political assumptions behind such tests in cultural literacy seem dubious at best. They are tainted with the historical application of "literacy tests" in the United States as a means of preserving Jim Crow laws and disenfranchising the African-American population.
29. Edgar Eugene Robinson, "Citizenship in a Democratic World," reprinted in Carnochan, *The Battleground of the Curriculum*, p. 132.
30. This loosening is not a "death of literature" as the product of extraneous political agendas, in the sense proposed by Alvin Kernan in *The Death of Literature* (New Haven: Yale University Press, 1990). Kernan is not subtle about making this point and states precisely that "the result has been the radical politicalization of literature . . . Texts have becomes primarily political documents" (85–86). He then provides a confused picture of how this happens: deconstruction is accused of both "intellectual Maoism" and "anarchic freedom" on the same page (85). Maoists and anarchists, however, do not usually get along very well; a point Kernan does not seem to register.

    I would also say that while Kernan is right to argue that the place of literature as a disciplinary structure is in question, his rather confused explanation is phrased in the very terms of the romantic view of literature that he recognizes is no longer functional. On the one hand, the internal treason of left-wing clerks has robbed literature of its spiritual content, while on the other hand the external force of media technology is assaulting the sacred form of language. Hence moments of lucidity (when Kernan seems to recognize the historically relative function of the category "literature") alternate throughout the book with rants against what various "theys" have done to the literary song that Kernan liked to sing. Here is one of Kernan's passages on the decline of the sacred form of language, which once apparently was the repository of moral truth, logic, and decency: "Most educated people wince with good reason at the jargon of blight and bloat that floods the media, for it is not just a matter of the old rules of grammar being broken, anarchy overtaking spelling, comma fault and dangling modifiers becoming brazen, and the jargons of a pompous dullness being amplified and broadcast with high-wattage sound equipment and even more powerful self-satisfaction throughout the land. The most inventive and powerful words heard in modern America are used in an openly immoral fashion, without, that is, any real concern for truth or logic or decency" (169).

7. Culture Wars and Cultural Studies

1. For a detailed discussion of the decline of the figure of the intellectual, see the essays from *Tombeau de l'intellectuel* in Jean-François Lyotard, *Political Writings,* tr. Bill Readings and Kevin Paul Geiman (Minneapolis: University of Minnesota Press, 1993), together with my synthesis of Lyotard's argument in the introduction to the volume.

2. Two further fine explorations of this topic appear in the electronic journal *Surfaces,* vol. 2 (1992): Bruce Robbins, *Mission impossible: l'intellectuel sans la culture,* and Paul Bové, *The Intellectual as a Contemporary Cultural Phenomenon,* available via gopher from the Université de Montréal gopher site.

3. See Antony Easthope, *Literary into Cultural Studies* (London and New York: Routledge, 1991), and Cary Nelson, "Always Already Cultural Studies: Two Conferences and a Manifesto" *Journal of the Midwestern Modern Language Association,* 24, no. 1 (Spring 1991).

4. This is a large and rather cruel assertion. I say cruel, since the appeal to "queerness" is usually made in the name of increased political radicalism, rather than as a claim for higher academic standards. And it is also cruel in that some of the work done—such as the essays collected in *Inside/Out,* ed. Diana Fuss (New York and London: Routledge, 1991), and *Fear of a Queer Planet,* ed. Michael Warner (Minneapolis: University of Minnesota Press, 1993)—makes an important case for thinking sexuality as a radically unstable field of difference. It recognizes the need to think about the notions of subjectivity and representation in discussing sexuality. Michael Warner, for instance, explicitly recognizes the difference between queer culture and the cultural model of multiculturalism (*Fear of a Queer Planet,* pp. xvii–xx). If I may be provocative, however, I would argue that the radicalism of queer theory risks being an academic one, designed to render queer theory susceptible to introduction across the curriculum, by analogy with Cultural Studies. To put this another way, insofar as queer theory risks ending up acknowledging that everyone is queer in their own way, it is much easier to evaluate the "excellence" of a Queer Studies program than that of a Gay and Lesbian Studies program. A queer theory that canonizes a generalized idea of sexuality as an object of academic study is nothing more than the opening of sexuality to academic administration. I am all for Queer Studies, if they mean a Gay and Lesbian Studies capable of distinguishing among the concepts of identity, experience,

and object-choice. But I fear that some of the energy behind the renaming of a discipline comes from elsewhere.

5. *Relocating Cultural Studies: Developments in Theory and Research,* ed. Valda Blundell, John Shepherd, and Ian Taylor (London and New York: Routledge, 1993).

6. See Raymond Williams, "Culture Is Ordinary" and "The Idea of a Common Culture," in *Resources of Hope: Culture, Democracy, Socialism,* ed. Robin Gable (London and New York: Verso, 1989). E. P. Thompson's *The Making of the English Working Class* (Harmondsworth: Penguin, 1968) discusses the concept of class in "culturalist" terms, defining class in terms of groups defining their own interests among themselves and in opposition to other groups, while his *The Poverty of Theory* (London: Merlin Press, 1978) more overtly attacks the European Marxist tradition of theorizing the notion of class and thus approaching the history of class struggle from a primarily theoretical standpoint.

7. Of course, at times in Williams's work this appeared to mean a sentimentalization of the working class as bearer of a tradition of an educated and participating democracy.

8. Raymond Williams, *Politics and Letters: Interviews with the New Left Review,* (London: New Left Books, 1981), p. 115.

9. Williams, *Resources of Hope,* p. 7.

10. Ibid., p. 108.

11. See Williams, *Politics and Letters.*

12. It would, I think, be fair to cite William Empson's *Some Versions of Pastoral* (London: Chatto and Windus, 1935) as a parallel questioning of the exclusive perspective of the ruling class upon the question of social wholeness, one which clearly influences Williams's own study in *The Country and the City* (London: Chatto and Windus, 1973).

13. Williams, *Resources of Hope,* p. 18.

14. That this is not the only sense in which literature may be topographical is made clear in a brilliant study of Derrida's account of the literary by J. Hillis Miller: "Derrida's Topographies," *South Atlantic Review,* 59, no. 1 (January 1994). Miller unpacks Derrida's account of the literary as marked by the topography of the secret in a way that disbars the kind of easy referentiality that the romantic literary landscape seems to offer. One might even go so far as to say that tourism is the desire to suspend the question of the literary opened up by this topography of the secret, to allay the anxiety opened up by literature's performative suspension of reference. One would, of course, have to make it clear that this is a notion of literature radically at odds with that with which we are familiar from the history of university teaching of national literatures.

15. Larry Grossberg, *It's a Sin: Essays in Postmodernism, Politics and Culture* (Sydney: Power Publication, 1988), p. 14. The question of the personal in Cultural

Studies has recently been addressed at length by Elspeth Probyn in *Sexing the Self: Gendered Positions in Cultural Studies* (London and New York: Routledge, 1993).

16. Patrick Brantlinger, *Crusoe's Footprints: Cultural Studies in Britain and America* (New York and London: Routledge, 1990); Easthope, *Literary into Cultural Studies* (1991); *Cultural Studies,* ed. Larry Grossberg, Carey Nelson, and Paula Treichler (New York and London: Routledge, 1992); Graeme Turner, *British Cultural Studies: An Introduction* (London: Unwin and Allen, 1990).

17. Easthope, *Literary into Cultural Studies,* p. 174.

18. Hence it is now "impossible to sustain a study founded on the privileging of literary over popular culture," since " 'literature' and 'popular culture' are now to be thought together within a single frame of reference as signifying practice" (71, 107). As for the question of fact and fiction, we are reminded that "all texts are historical texts" while at the same time "history is real but only accessible to us discursively, in the form of historical narratives, as a construction of the historical" (157).

19. Dick Hebdige, *Subculture: The Meaning of Style* (London: Methuen, 1979).

20. *Cultural Studies,* p. 3.

21. *Relocating Cultural Studies,* pp. 4, 6.

22. *Reading into Cultural Studies* (London and New York: Routledge, 1992), ed. Martin Barker and Anne Beezer, p. 18.

23. Ronald Judy, *(Dis)Forming the American Canon* (Minneapolis: University of Minnesota Press, 1993), p. 17. Judy's point has interesting parallels with Diane Elam's argument concerning the institutionalization of feminism in her *Feminism and Deconstruction: Ms. en Abyme* (London and New York: Routledge, 1994). Judy's own book is a powerful argument for African-American writing as articulating "a defiance of signification itself," which leads him to propose "emergent studies" as radically at odds with the project of building or studying African American "culture." For the notion of "African-American culture," as he points out, reinserts the African within the "production of cultural value" by the University that is the legitimating discourse for the emergence of the European State (287).

24. For an especially revealing visualization of this point, see Pierre Bourdieu's chart of the French University system in *Homo Academicus,* tr. Peter Collier (Stanford: Stanford University Press, 1988), p. 276.

25. John Guillory, *Cultural Capital: The Problem of Literary Canon Formation* (Chicago: University of Chicago Press, 1993), p. 325.

26. Similar symptoms appear in Guillory's treatment of "theory," as in one particularly interesting lapsus: "The Continental (mostly French) provenance of theory in the several discourses of anthropology, philosophy, linguistics, criticism, or political analysis restricts the practice of theory to no single discipline, and that circumstance has made the signifier 'theory' perhaps less institution-

ally significant in the country of theory's origin than in the United States" (*Cultural Capital,* p. 177). The passage from Continental to "French" appears in the first part of this sentence to be a simple statement of fact, but by the end of the sentence we are told that theory has a "country of origin." And so it may seem, from within the American perspective; however, that does not make it true. Yet in order for "theory" to be analyzed as a discourse of cultural capital in the United States, Guillory must reduce his own perspective to the most narrowly nationalistic. It is as if Barthes were describing the connotations of "italicity" in a French pasta advertisement as the basis for an account of Italy rather than as a statement about French advertising.

27. Bourdieu, *Distinction: A Social Critique of the Judgement of Taste,* tr. R. Nice (Cambridge, Mass.: Harvard University Press, 1984).

28. See Guillory, *Cultural Capital,* pp. 326–327.

29. This problem with the international currency of culture extends to Cultural Studies as a whole. Hence both Andrew Ross and Graeme Turner have questioned the political stakes in the exportation of radical critical methodologies from the metropole to the ex-colonies (the United States and Australia respectively). Yet their remarks on the need to attend to the specificity of national cultures miss the central point: the taking of the nation-state as the primary unit of cultural analysis, as the name of the *langue* in reference to which the signification of each cultural *parole* is determined. Thus Cultural Studies becomes exportable *along with the nation-state* (which is why writers in Cultural Studies tend to flavor their appeals to popular culture with a certain nationalist tinge, wherever the content of national ideology might take on a leftist bent). See Andrew Ross, *No Respect: Intellectuals and Popular Culture* (London and New York: Routledge, 1989), and Graeme Turner, " 'It Works for Me': British Cultural Studies, Australian Cultural Studies, Australian Film," in *Cultural Studies.*

30. These problems leave their mark upon Guillory's book. The preface organizes the chapters as case studies around the general problem of literary canon formation that is discussed in the first chapter. But each chapter ends with a general observation and an exhortation to new directions upon which the book never really delivers. Chapter 1 calls for an analysis of the "systematic constitution and distribution of cultural capital" (82) as part of a "project of political integration." Chapters 2 and 3 perform such analyses, yet leave us none the wiser as to what should happen on the other side, how an understanding of "literature" as "cultural capital" will lead to a reconception of the literary curriculum, let alone to political integration. In this sense they seem curiously parasitical on the system they expose and denounce. Chapter 4, on the canonization of "literary theory," ends by demanding a reconceptualization of the object of literary study (265), without, however, suggesting what direction this might take. The same goes for the attack on institutional pedagogy, where

Guillory, having denounced charismatic teaching and the role of affect, having detected in de Man and Lacan's interest in rigor "the desire that the disciples form a church" (202), offers no account of an alternative pedagogy or institutional practice.

That is to say, there is much talk of the need to reconceive the literary curriculum but little evidence of what kind of work that might involve, other than that provided by the example of the book itself. So the reader is finally left with the impression of a curious circularity: the literary curriculum will be replaced by courses and books providing an analysis of its sociological formation and exhorting a move beyond it. This kind of circularity is nothing absolutely new. In fact, it conforms to the kind of problem that Guillory acutely analyzes in the case of Leavis: adversarial culture is devoted to its own effacement, since success would mean failure (loss of adversarial status).

31. Gerald Graff, *Beyond the Culture Wars: How Teaching the Conflicts Can Revitalize American Education* (New York: Norton, 1992).

32. Guillory's *Cultural Capital* devotes its first chapter to a detailed and reasoned rebuttal of the notion that the literary canon is primarily to be understood as *reflecting* the society for which it is canonical.

33. *Beyond a Dream Deferred: Multicultural Education and the Politics of Excellence*, ed. Becky W. Thompson and Sangeeta Tyagi (Minneapolis: University of Minnesota Press, 1993), p. xxxi.

34. Here are two examples from the contributors' notes of *Beyond a Dream Deferred*, p. 258: "Evelynn M. Hammonds, assistant professor in the Program in Science, Technology, and Society at the Massachusetts Institute of Technology, is the author of the ground-breaking 1986 article "Race, Sex, AIDS: The Construction of Other." As an African-American feminist, she was deeply troubled by the Senate hearings on the nomination of Clarence Thomas to the U.S. Supreme Court and by the treatment of Professor Anita Hill, which she wrote about in "Who Speaks for Black Women?" (*Sojourner,* October 1991)." "Ian Fidencio Haney Lopez, assistant professor of law at the University of Wisconsin, is researching police-Chicano relations in East Los Angeles, as well as the idea of race in American law. Haney Lopez was born and raised in Hawaii, the son of a Salvadorean mother and an ethnic Irish-American father." The qualitative homogenization of difference is nowhere more apparent than in the tautological qualification of "Irish-American" by "ethnic"—presumably it implies that some Irish-Americans are more ethnic than others, which means that a homogeneous standard of true difference (that is, of identity or sameness) is being invoked.

35. This is a process of which Bruce Robbins is painfully aware in his discussion of contemporary modes of what he calls "legitimation talk" in *Secular Vocations: Intellectuals, Professionalism, Culture* (London and New York: Verso, 1993).

36. *Beyond a Dream Deferred,* p. xxx.
37. The damaging assumption that thinking and describing are one and the same activity is, of course, endemic in the canon debate.
38. As Michael Peters remarks: "To say that the university in Western society is in a state of crisis is simply to echo the thoughts and sentiments of a generation of post-war commentators. The word *'crisis,'* accordingly, has lost almost any conceptual purchase." "Performance and Accountability in 'Post-Industrial Society': The Crisis of British Universities," *Studies in Higher Education,* 17, no. 2 (1992).
39. Dinesh D'Souza, *Illiberal Education* (New York: Free Press, 1991); Robert Hughes, *The Culture of Complaint: The Fraying of America* (New York and Oxford: New York Public Library and Oxford University Press, 1993); Sande Cohen, *Academia and the Luster of Capital* (Minneapolis: University of Minnesota Press, 1993).
40. See Gilles Deleuze and Félix Guattari, *A Thousand Plateaus,* tr. Brian Massumi (Minneapolis: University of Minnesota Press, 1987).
41. This questioning has been carried out in the form of critiques of the notion of self-presence (the pretension that one is at one with oneself in hearing oneself speak when, in fact, self-consciousness is mediated by linguistic representation, which comes from elsewhere) and by refusals of the pretended neutrality and "unmarked" status of the subject of reason, who is actually male, white, heterosexual, etc. The collection *Who Comes After the Subject?* ed. Eduardo Cadava, Peter Connor, and Jean-Luc Nancy (New York and London: Routledge, 1991), and Judith Butler's *Bodies That Matter* (New York and London: Routledge, 1993), are good examples of these critiques.

8. The Posthistorical University

1. Theodor W. Adorno, "Cultural Criticism and Society," in *Prisms,* tr. Samuel and Shierry Weber (Cambridge, Mass.: MIT Press, 1990).
2. See Cary Nelson, "Always Already Cultural Studies: Two Conferences and a Manifesto," *Journal of the Midwestern Modern Languages Association,* 24, no. 1 (Spring 1991).
3. Wilhelm von Humboldt, "Sur l'organisation interne et externe des etablissements scientifiques superieurs a Berlin" (1809), in *Philosophies de l'Université: L'idealisme allemand et la question de l'Université,* ed. Luc Ferry, J.-P. Pesron, and Alain Renaut (Paris: Payot, 1979), p. 323, my translation.
4. Johann Gottlieb Fichte, "Deductive Plan for an Institution of Higher Learning to be Founded in Berlin," in *Philosophies de l'Université,* pp. 180–181, my translation.
5. Friedrich Schleiermacher, "Pensées de circonstance sur les universités de conception allemande" in *Philosophies de l'Université,* p. 283, my translation.

pragmatism." Observing that "the concept of youth is now almost totally divorced from the idea of radicalism," the article goes on to explain that working for Labour rather than the Conservatives is viewed in terms of career opportunities, while student politics is "issue-based rather than ideological," as if there were a clear difference. Sean Langan, "The Quiet Revolutionaries," *Sunday Times,* October 23, 1994, pp. 10.4–10.5.

5. Pierre Bourdieu, *Homo Academicus,* tr. Peter Collier (Stanford: Stanford University Press, 1988), p. 188.

6. See ibid., pp. 190, 168. To show the extent to which Bourdieu is willing to go to make this kind of argument, it is worth quoting one of his remarks at length: "We cannot account for the crisis, or at least for the structural conditions of its appearance and its generalization, without mentioning the principal effects of the increase in the number of pupils, that is, a devaluation of academic diplomas which causes a generalized downclassing ... creating a structural hiatus between the statutory expectations—inherent in the positions and the diplomas which in the previous state of the system really did offer corresponding opportunities—and the opportunities actually provided by these diplomas and positions at the moment we are considering" (162–163).

7. John Guillory, *Cultural Capital: The Problem of Literary Canon Formation* (Chicago: University of Chicago Press, 1993), pp. 248–255.

8. Julien Benda, *The Treason of the Intellectuals,* tr. Richard Aldington (New York: Norton, 1969).

9. See, for example, Jacques Derrida, *Du Droit à la philosophie* (Paris: Gallimard, 1990); Paul de Man, *The Resistance to Theory* (Minneapolis: University of Minnesota Press, 1986); Samuel Weber, *Institution and Interpretation* (Minneapolis: University of Minnesota Press, 1987); Barbara Johnson, *A World of Difference* (Baltimore: Johns Hopkins University Press, 1987).

10. *The Phantom Public Sphere,* ed. Bruce Robbins (Minneapolis: University of Minnesota Press, 1993).

11. Arjun Appadurai, "Disjuncture and Difference in the Global Cultural Economy," and Michael Warner, "The Mass Public and the Mass Subject," in *The Phantom Public Sphere.*

12. *Humanus sum, nihil humanum me alienum puto.*

13. Immanuel Kant, "Answering the Question: What Is Enlightenment?" in *Foundations of the Metaphysics of Morals,* tr. Lewis White Beck (Indianapolis: Bobbs-Merrill, 1959), p. 87.

14. Jürgen Habermas, *The Structural Transformation of the Public Sphere,* tr. Thomas Burger (Cambridge, Mass.: MIT Press, 1989).

15. Warner, "The Mass Public and the Mass Subject," p. 243.

16. Here I perhaps slip slightly away from Warner, who goes on to rephrase identity politics as something other than essentialism, as a refusal of the pretended neutrality of the liberal subject of the public sphere. While his corrective is an

important one, the work it invokes is not, to my mind, merely an acceptance of the possibilities of identity politics. Rather, a general analysis of the terms within which meaning can be produced has to recognize the relative decline of the political as the instance in terms of which individuals seek to give their lives meaning. For a more extended treatment of this problematic, see my "The End of the Political," foreword to Jean-François Lyotard, *Political Writings*, tr. Bill Readings and Kevin Paul Geiman (Minneapolis: University of Minnesota Press, 1993), esp. pp. xviii–xxi and xxiii–xxvi. I argue that the disappearance of "the political," which Lyotard calls "depoliticization," does not mean an end of politics, far from it, but an end to "big politics," to the positioning of the political sphere as the site where the question of being-together is to be solely raised and exhaustively answered.

17. David Caute, *The Year of the Barricades: A Journey through 1968* (New York: Harper and Row, 1988), p. 214.

18. Christopher Fynsk, "Legacies of May: On the Work of *Le Doctrinal de Sapience*," *Modern Language Notes*, 93 (1978), pp. 963–967.

19. In a sense, I draw the lesson that it is necessary to think the institution from deconstruction. As Derrida reminds us: "Thus, if it is to have any effect, what we sloppily call deconstruction is never a set of technical discursive procedures, still less a new hermeneutical method working on archives or statements under the protection of a given and stable institution. Deconstruction is also, at least, the act of taking a position, in the very work it does, with regard to the politico-institutional structures that constitute and regulate our practices, our competencies and our performances. Precisely because it has never simply been concerned with signified content, deconstruction should be inseparable from this politico-institutional problematic and should require a new interrogation of responsibility, an interrogation which should not necessarily trust inherited codes of politics or ethics" (*Du Droit à la Philosophie*, p. 424, my translation). We see here an insistence on the part of Derrida that deconstruction is not blind, must not be blind, to the institutional problematic that frames the work of analysis and critique, lest deconstruction become merely a fancy mode of analysis.

20. This is as much as to say that deconstruction is not simply an operation that one might perform on institutions *from the outside*. Hence the inappropriateness of thinking of deconstruction's relation to institutions either as a bomb-attack or as a facelift.

21. Daniel and Gabriel Cohn-Bendit, *Obsolete Communism: The Left-Wing Alternative*, tr. Arnold Pomerans (New York: McGraw-Hill, 1968), p. 256.

22. An inability to recognize that the uncertainty expressed by Cohn-Bendit is not simply confusion and indecision is what renders David Caute, for example, utterly unable to see the challenge to History as such that 1968 poses. Thus his *The Year of the Barricades* can do little more than ceaselessly reiterate the

pointlessness of the student actions (and a fortiori of his bothering to write a history of them). While they were perhaps pointless from the perspective of historical continuity, the events of May work outside and against the modernist conception of History as the grand narrative of the realization of a subject, as Lyotard hints in his unfinished introduction to an unpublished "anti-history" of the movement of March 22: "The only way to excuse having written a history book on the March 22 movement is for it not to be a book of history, for it not to dissolve the delirium, the unjustifiability, and the passion into a simple phenomenon to be understood. Rather, such a book must in its turn be an *event*" ("March 23," *Political Writings*, p. 60).

10. The Scene of Teaching

1. Jean-François Lyotard's *The Postmodern Condition*, tr. Geoff Bennington and Brian Massumi (Minneapolis: University of Minnesota Press, 1984), is important in reminding us of this. The relevance of Lyotard's work to the question of pedagogy has not necessarily been acknowledged: the renown gained by *The Postmodern Condition* has tended to obscure its status as a report written for the Conseil des Universités of the government of Québec. As Lyotard remarks in his introduction, that book is an "occasional" text, a report on the contemporary nature of knowledge in Western societies that is addressed to university administrators, a text that "situates" the analysis of the epistemological legitimation (xxv). One significant gesture is the book's initial refusal of the role of expert in favor of the uncertainty of the philosopher, who is not sure what it is that he does and does not know (xxv). This is not just a matter of epistemological modesty; it is also a refusal to situate the writer of *The Postmodern Condition* in a position of transcendence, outside the institution he analyzes. Neither outside the institution nor completely at home in it, Lyotard foregrounds the institutional question, unable to take the institution as either merely an object of knowledge or a way of life. One of the ironies of Jameson's widely accepted critique of *The Postmodern Condition* is the way in which his imputations of insufficient political seriousness ignore this highly "practical" discursive location (Foreword to *The Postmodern Condition*, p. xx). One has to be very careful what one says to governments, after all.

   Lyotard's militant position in the events of 1968 in Paris is now perhaps more widely acknowledged, however much it may surprise those accustomed, like Peter Dews, to associate his writings with the undermining of the possibility of political action. Peter Dews, *Logic of Disintegration: Post-Structuralist Thought and the Claims of Critical Theory* (London: Verso, 1987). I shall not examine the problems of Dews's argument here. Instead, I would urge readers to consult Richard Beardsworth's excellent essay "Lyotard's Agitated Judgement," in *Judging Lyotard,* ed. Andrew Benjamin (London and New York: Routledge, 1992), which persuasively rebuts Dews's accusations.

Lyotard's essays emerging from the events of 1968 insist upon the concrete fact of militant action, as in "Nanterre, Here, Now," which situates student accounts of battles with the police alongside the text of an analysis of the situation which Lyotard had prepared for a meeting of teachers' union groups. Lyotard begins by noting the fact that he failed to deliver this address owing to the intervention of security marshals—underlining the point that one of the primary effects of the student revolt was to provide the proof that no institutional space of enunciation or of reflection is completely independent of the violence and disruption of political conflict, the fact that "in this society, knowledge is constantly compromised with power."

Hence Lyotard's analysis of 1968 refuses the choice proposed by the Fouchet plan, which offered to bring the French University "up to date." Fouchet's choice was between a quasi-feudal institution that produces erudite scholarly knowledge and a modernized, practical institution that will produce the technical know-how required in advanced capitalist society. As he argues in "Preamble to a Charter," the traditional and modern images of the University are in fact more complicit than they might seem: the humanities stress the separation of the University from society, and thus defuse critical energies in producing scholars, while the social sciences technologize social reality to produce experts. Lyotard's description of the role of the philosopher in the introduction to *The Postmodern Condition* is precisely a refusal to be either an expert or a scholar. The production of scholars in the humanities and the production of experts in the social sciences combine to prevent social critique, whether by defusing critical energies or by recuperating them so as to refine the functioning of the existing social order.

2. This is a warning that Samuel Weber has theorized in exemplary fashion in his *Institution and Interpretation* (Minneapolis: University of Minnesota Press, 1987).

3. Here I am thinking in particular of the dialogue form in the penultimate section of *Ulysses,* in which a question-and-answer session leads to a synthesis of Bloom and Stephen Dedalus, of the Hebraic and Hellenic traditions.

4. V. N. Volosinov (M. Bakhtin), *Marxism and the Philosophy of Language,* tr. L. Matejka and I. R. Titunik (Cambridge, Mass.: Harvard University Press, 1986), p. 118.

5. As Wlad Godzich puts it, "those who hold state power first co-opt individuals, thereby making them other with respect to the rest of society, and then let the state as an apparatus of power determine the configuration of the social. Thus neither the production of the other nor that of the social is collective." "Afterword: Religion, the State, and Post(al) Modernism," in Weber, *Institution and Interpretation,* p. 161.

6. As Johann Gottlieb Fichte phrases it in "Plan déductif d'un établissement

d'enseignement supérieur à fonder à Berlin," in *Philosophies de l'Université* (Paris: Payot, 1979), pp. 180–181, my translation: "A common spiritual existence . . . where they have learnt early on to know each other deeply, and to respect each other, where all their reflections begin from a base which is known to all identically and which gives no grounds for dispute."

7. Lyotard discusses these four poles at length in *The Differend,* tr. Georges Van Den Abbeele (Minneapolis: University of Minnesota Press, 1988).

8. See Saul Kripke, *Naming and Necessity* (Oxford: Blackwell, 1980).

9. As Lyotard puts it in "A Podium without a Podium," in *Political Writings,* tr. Bill Readings and Kevin Paul Geiman (Minneapolis: University of Minnesota Press, 1993), p. 94: "To admit that competence in scientific and technical matters is not illusory and that scientists, engineers and technicians really are learned, although at times there is evidence to the contrary, does not prove that the same thing goes for all questions. One can, for example, provide a rigorous demonstration that the just is not an object of knowledge and there is no science of justice. One can show the same thing for what is beautiful, or what is agreeable. Hence there is no true and certain competence in these domains, domains that, however, have a great significance in everyday life. In these domains there are only opinions. And all these opinions have to be discussed."

10. My allusion to Heidegger here is not coincidental. I follow Granel in seeing the Rectorial Address as the last serious theoretical attempt to position the University as mediating institution between Volk and technology. However, this is not an excuse to ignore Heidegger on the grounds of his Nazism. The critique of instrumental reason that Heidegger mounts is neither wholly determined by nor wholly determinant of Nazism. Understanding this point would have spared us many column inches in the *New York Times.* Heidegger's *What Is Called Thinking?* tr. F. Wieck and J. Gray (New York: Harper and Row, 1968), situates Thought as a gift (something that is caught up in a network of extended, receiving, welcoming and welcomed hands) and as a call (in the sense of something that links our essential being to thought). In both cases, what is crucial is that Thought appropriates the subject, not vice-versa: the gift Thought gives is nothing less than itself, to be called to think is both to receive a vocation and to think about what to call Thought, to attempt to furnish a name to Thought—to enter thinking without knowing in advance what it is that is to be Thought. Thus, to be concerned with the name of Thought is to preserve Thought in its status as questioning in the most extended sense.

11. Maurice Blanchot, *The Unavowable Community,* tr. Pierre Joris (Barrytown, N.Y.: Station Hill Press, 1988). The nature of this attention is up for grabs. It can be the attention of the Lacanian analytic scene, which, to paraphrase Mikkel Borch-Jacobsen, can be characterized as "absolute mastery." *Lacan: The*

Absolute Master, tr. Douglas Brick (Stanford: Stanford University Press, 1991). The difference between a pedagogy attentive to the various poles of address and Lacan's analysis is that the "other" to whom Lacan pays attention is not the analysand but the Unconscious. The pragmatics of Lacanian analytic discourse thus remain modernist in that the pole of the addressee is suppressed, becoming the empty relay that marks the place of castration, of absence, the black hole around which the privileged encounter of the analytic master and the unconscious instance of the signifier occurs. Of course, the action of this signifier is purely indexical. Pointing to its own slippage along the signifying chain, it has no signification other than the absence of the signified. Hence analytic mastery is not a matter of simple interpretation, of decoding; rather, as the case of Dupin reminds us, it is a privileged capacity for following the defiles of the signifier without being entrapped into the illusion of hermeneutic mastery, the lure of the search for a contentual meaning by which the Prefect of Police is transfixed. "Séminaire sur *La Lettre volée*," in Lacan, *Ecrits* (Paris: Seuil, 1966). Yet this abnegation of one kind of mastery is compensated by another: the privileged knowledge that there is no such meaning, armed with which the analyst can fix the analysand in the place of blindness or castration, pretext for and inert support of an encounter with the unconscious signifier.

While I applaud the exemplary anti-humanism of Lacan's gesture, I find it somewhat unjust to the analysand, who (as the rich tradition of feminist readings of Lacan has pointed out) may hesitate before the absolute identification of castration with lack and absence. In this respect, Jane Gallop's *The Daughter's Seduction* (Ithaca: Cornell University Press, 1982) seems to me an exemplary reassertion of the analysand/addressee within the framework of the Lacanian refusal of depth psychology, which is perhaps what makes it such a successful text for classroom use. However, the limitation of Gallop's Lacanian analysis is that the emergence of the addressee is contained within the dialectic of transference and counter-transference, which tends to produce an account of pedagogic affect that fits too easily into an instrumental rhetoric of manipulative seduction—a rhetoric that can be invoked as easily by the student painting her- or himself as victim as by the "lecherous professor." Desire remains a transaction between subjects, and as such can be too easily complicit with power, its flow channeled within the hierarchical distribution of places.

12. My remarks closely parallel the work of Emmanuel Levinas, which has played a major role in formulating the contemporary account of the ethical in France—a notion of ethics that diverges significantly from that found in Anglo-American philosophy. Lyotard perhaps best summarizes what has made Levinas's work so important: "it shows that the relation with the other, what he calls 'the Other' of 'the absolutely Other' is such that the request that is made of me by the other, by the simple fact that he speaks to me, is a request that can never be justified." Jean-François Lyotard and Jean-Loup Thébaud,

Just Gaming, tr. Wlad Godzich (Minneapolis: University of Minnesota Press, 1985), p. 22.

13. This should be clearly distinguished from Althusser's account of ideological interpellation, in that the other here is the sheer blank fact of otherness, not the institutional apparatus of the state (which the enlightened critic can identify). This hailing does not position the subject in an illusory autonomy (like the driver's licence), does not "suture" the subject but wounds the subject, disbarring the illusion of autonomy.

14. Clearly, I take a considerable distance here from those like Bruce Wilshire who want to think of education as a cure for alienation and as the means of return to pure self-presence. Bruce Wilshire, *The Moral Collapse of the University: Professionalism, Purity, and Alienation* (Albany: SUNY Press, 1990). Wilshire's grounding metaphysical assumption of originary self-presence (the assumption that there was a time when we were not alienated, a time to which education can return us) is not one that I can share, as my remarks in the previous chapter—where I argue that the student is born too soon and too late—may suggest. Hence Wilshire ends up with a call for an organic human community as the center of the University: "there is no substitute for human relationship and presence, for listening, for sharing silence and wonderment, and for caring" (282). In his case, the human community is going to be a little more touchy-feely and embodied than Humboldt's, with the promise of redemptive religiosity proportionally intensified.

15. This seems to me to be the risk in the "critical pedagogy" of Paulo Freire's *Pedagogy of the Oppressed* (New York: Seabury Press, 1973), the risk of a certain kind of Maoist third-worldism, in which the oppressed become the bearers of a bourgeois idealist hope for historical meaning in place of the exhausted industrial proletariat.

16. "The university belongs to the system insofar as the system is capitalist and bureaucratic," Lyotard, "Nanterre, Here, Now," p. 56.

17. See Pierre Bourdieu, *Homo Academicus,* tr. Peter Collier (Stanford: Stanford University Press, 1988); John Guillory, *Cultural Capital: The Problem of Literary Canon Formation* (Chicago: University of Chicago Press, 1993).

11. Dwelling in the Ruins

1. Gerald Graff, *Beyond the Culture Wars: How Teaching the Conflicts Can Revitalize American Education* (New York and London: Norton, 1992).

2. Stanley Fish, *There's No Such Thing as Free Speech: And It's a Good Thing Too* (Oxford: Oxford University Press, 1994). I think in particular of Fish's essay on the Milton Society of America, in which he argues that "institutional life is more durable than the vocabulary of either dissolution or revolution suggests" (271). Thus, all novelty and difference are accommodated by the self-

adjusting tradition, which rests on nothing other than its own history of self-adjustments.

3. One simple example: for a consideration of the way in which the internet threatens to delegitimize the structure of scholarly publishing, see my "Caught in the Net: Notes from the Electronic Underground," *Surfaces,* 4, no. 104 (1994), available via gopher from the Université de Montréal gopher site.

4. The University of California also has some piled ruins, which are known locally as "Stonehenge," an equally incongruous cultural reference.

5. See my "When Did the Renaissance Begin?" in *Rethinking the Henrician Era,* ed. Peter Herman (Chicago: University of Illinois Press, 1993) for a more developed account of the invention of the Renaissance and the question of the visibility of history.

6. Freud tells us in *The Interpretation of Dreams,* ed. and tr. James Strachey (New York: Avon Books, 1965), p. 530: "If we examine the . . . structure [of dreams and daytime phantasies], we shall perceive the way in which the wishful purpose that is at work in their production has mixed up the material of which they are built, has re-arranged it and has formed it into a new whole. They stand in much the same relation to the childhood memories from which they are derived as do some of the Baroque palaces of Rome to the ancient ruins whose pavements and columns have provided the material for the more recent structures."

7. Sigmund Freud, *Civilization and its Discontents,* tr. James Strachey (New York and London: Norton, 1961), pp. 16–17.

8. It implies an institutional pragmatism, what Samuel Weber calls "deconstructive pragmatics." See *Institution and Interpretation* (Minneapolis: University of Minnesota Press, 1989), esp. ch. 2, "The Limits of Professionalism." Where Stanley Fish and Richard Rorty tend to celebrate the historical fact of institutional existence in their insistence on the status of actual practices, Weber sketches the contours of an argument against disciplinary autonomy and the concomitant ideology of professional mastery. He does so by recourse to Peirce's notion of "conditional possibility" in order to refuse the fixity of disciplinary boundaries. Such a transgression of disciplinary limits exposes the phobic exclusions upon which professional authority and competence are based. As Weber points out, "the modern university was the institutional means by which the professional claim to a monopoly of competence could be established and maintained" (32). Against this he proposes not a holistic refusal of abstraction and limit but a "deconstructive pragmatics" that "would work from the 'inside' of the various disciplines, in order to demonstrate concretely, in each case, how the exclusion of limits from the field organizes the practice it makes possible" (32). This seems to me an exemplary instance of the critique of institutions without recourse to alibis: neither the alibi of the perfect institution nor the alibi of the potential absence of all institutions.

9. Leonard Cohen, "First We Take Manhattan," from *I'm Your Man* (CBS Records, 1988).

10. This is the sort of point that Andrew Ross makes in *Strange Weather* (London: Verso, 1991), although he rather exaggerates its delegitimating effect on scientific practices and norms.

11. See Gerald Graff, *Professing Literature* (Chicago: University of Chicago Press, 1987), pp. 19–36.

12. As Graff reminds us, "in literary studies, as everyone knows, the advance guard of professionalization was a German-trained cadre of scholarly 'investigators,' who promoted the idea of scientific research and the philological study of modern languages" (*Professing Literature*, p. 55).

13. See Georges Bataille, "La notion de dépense" in *La part maudite* (Paris: Minuit, 1949), for the origins of this distinction.

14. See W. B. Carnochan, *The Battleground of the Curriculum: Liberal Education and American Experience* (Stanford: Stanford University Press, 1993), for a brief and illuminating account of this debate.

15. My remarks about coverage are no slur to medievalists in particular. I think that the twilight of modernity makes the pre-modern a crucial site for understanding what a non-Enlightenment structure of thought might look like. My point is rather that the relative weakness of arguments for disciplinary coverage proceeds from the fact that such arguments presume the University to be primarily an ideological institution, when actually this is not the case. I will go further and say that my suggestion is a crucial means for preserving classical and medieval texts from the extinction that currently threatens them. I also do not have space here to get into an argument about tenure, so I merely presume its continuation in the short term. However, I think that the increasing proletarianization of the professoriat suggests that tenure may not *necessarily*—I italicize, to remind readers that I only wish to consider a possibility— be the most effective defense of faculty interests in the future. Finally, note that the notion of faculty-student ratio is an economic rationale that I believe can be sold to administrators with potentially interesting results.

12. The Community of Dissensus

1. Alfonso Borrero Cabal, *The University as an Institution Today* (Paris and Ottawa: UNESCO and IDRC, 1993), p. 130.

2. This is because the possibility of reference can only be thought as the failure of linguistic transparency, as the internal opacity or thickening of language, which permits the flawed subsumption of worldly reference under linguistic meaning.

3. Jean-François Lyotard's *The Differend*, tr. Georges Van Den Abbeele (Minneapolis: University of Minnesota Press, 1988), amply demonstrates this point.

4. This community might also be called headless, to echo Bataille, in that this community marks the necessary wound of subjectivity, while not offering to heal that wound in producing a greater subject.

5. Jean-Luc Nancy, *The Inoperative Community,* ed. Peter Connor, tr. Peter Connor, Lisa Garbus, Michael Holland, and Simona Sawhney (Minneapolis: University of Minnesota Press, 1990); Maurice Blanchot, *The Unavowable Community,* tr. Pierre Joris (Barrytown, N.Y.: Station Hill Press, 1988). Blanchot and Nancy draw on Bataille and the surrealists in an attempt to think a community without identity, without a commonly shared core that would ground the social bond.

6. Giorgio Agamben, *The Coming Community,* tr. Michael Hardt (Minneapolis: University of Minnesota Press, 1993).

7. Aristotle, *Nichomachean Ethics,* tr. Terence Irwin (Cambridge: Hackett, 1985), 1100a30.

8. Nancy draws a distinction between two versions of the political: on the one hand, the sociotechnical organization of society; on the other, the community that orders "itself to the unworking of its communication" (*The Inoperative Community,* pp. 40–41). As such, Nancy's inorganic community is distinct from the collective identity of republican democracies in which, as Lyotard remarks, "the pronoun of the first person plural is in effect the linchpin of/ for the discourse of authorization" (*The Differend,* p. 98).

9. For further discussion of Lyotard's account of the totalitarian force of the apparently democratic "we," see my "Pagans, Perverts, or Primitives," in *Judging Lyotard,* ed. Andrew Benjamin (London and New York: Routledge, 1992), pp. 174–176.

10. For a more detailed discussion of the impossibility of subsuming the relation to the Other under a cognitive synthesis, see Emmanuel Levinas, *Totalité et infini* (Paris: Livre de Poche, 1992), p. 71.

11. Gianni Vattimo, *The Transparent Society* (Baltimore: Johns Hopkins University Press, 1992), p. 14.

12. This is the process to which Lyotard has pointed in describing a loss of belief in grand narratives and the turn to a non-finite series of little narratives, in *The Postmodern Condition,* tr. Geoff Bennington and Brian Massumi (Minneapolis: University of Minnesota Press, 1984).

～ Index